I0764057

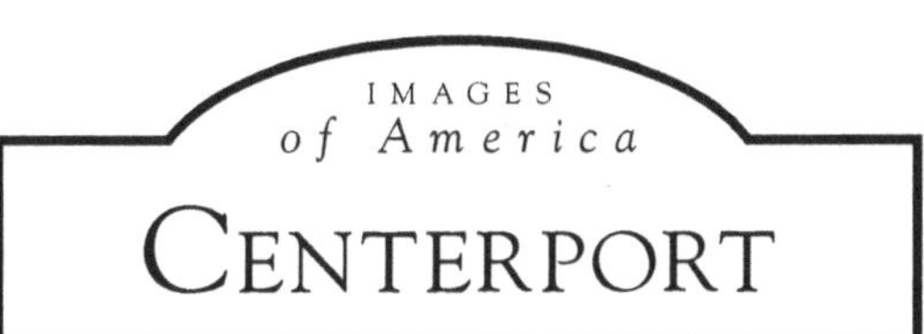
IMAGES
of America
CENTERPORT

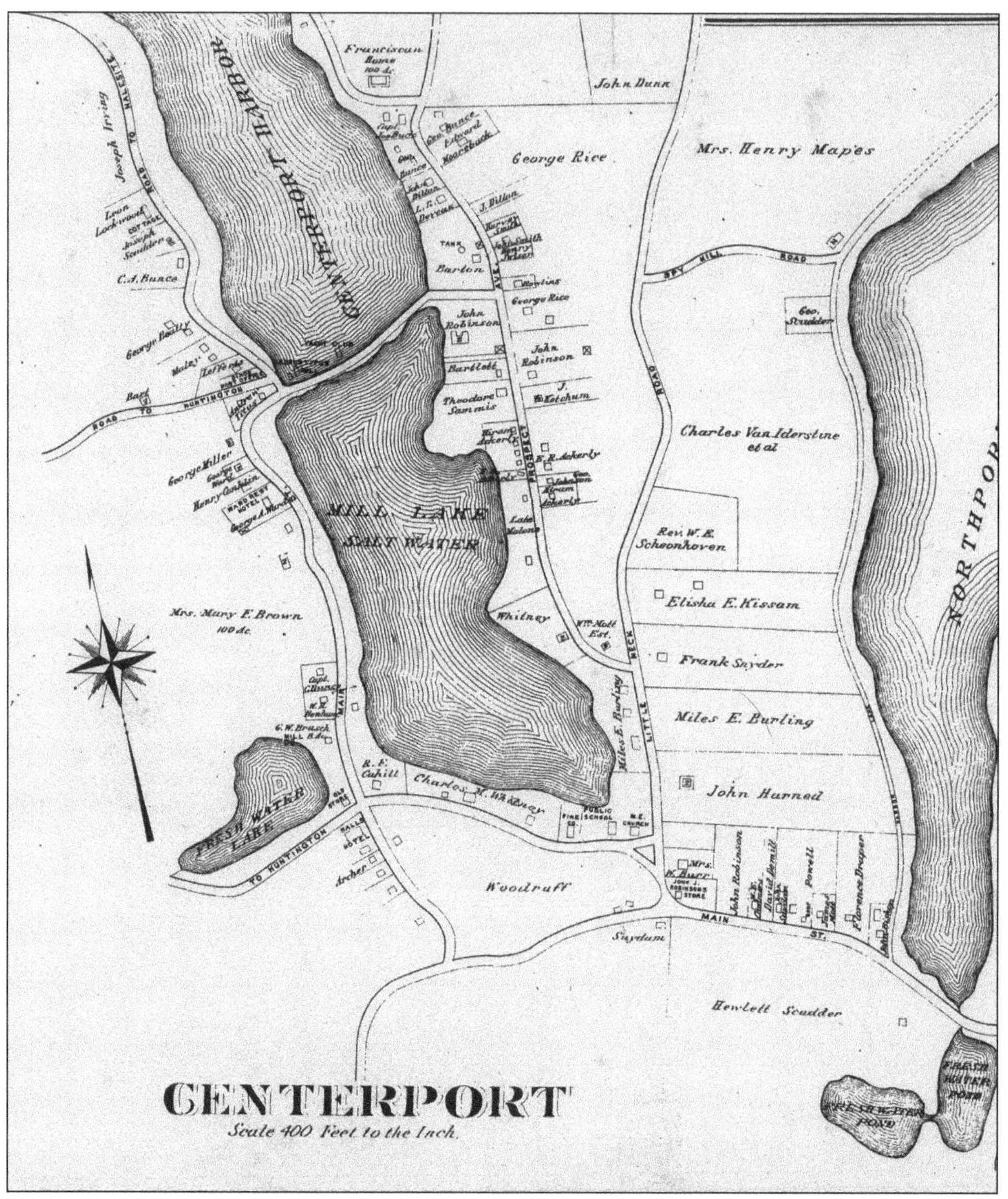

The heyday of Centerport is vividly depicted on this map, published by the Belcher Hyde Company in 1909, which shows the locations of the homes of prominent citizens such as Charles Whitney, Miles Burling, Charles Van Iderstine, and the Swope brothers. Also included are popular boardinghouses and restaurants, the Franciscan Home, the Townsend/Titus Mill, the original Centerport Yacht Club, the school, and fire department. William K. Vanderbilt II would join the community soon. (David Chalmers Clemens.)

On the Cover: Summer guests are enjoying Centerport Harbor on a pier in front of the Lockwood Irish Catholic Boarding House. In the background are the waterfront buildings of the Franciscan Brothers' Camp Alvernia. (Greenlawn-Centerport Historical Association.)

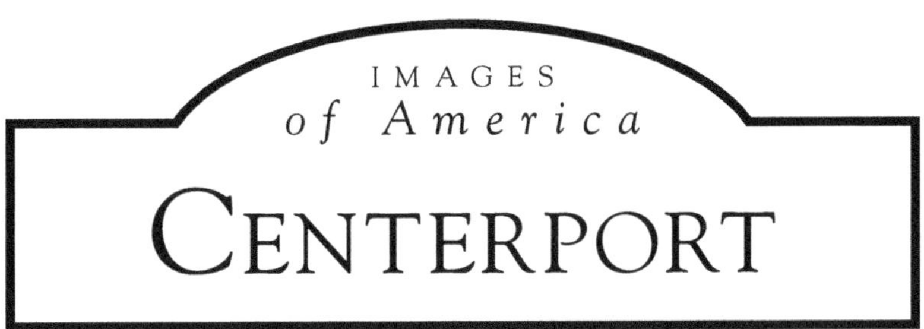

David C. Clemens and Suzanne Johnson

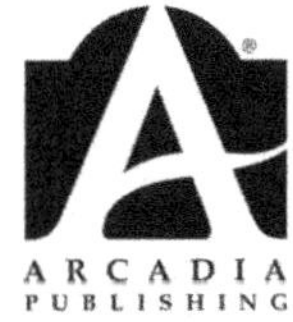

Copyright © 2019 by David C. Clemens and Suzanne Johnson
ISBN 978-1-4671-0391-6

Published by Arcadia Publishing
Charleston, South Carolina

Library of Congress Control Number: 2019933572

For all general information, please contact Arcadia Publishing:
Telephone 843-853-2070
Fax 843-853-0044
E-mail sales@arcadiapublishing.com
For customer service and orders:
Toll-Free 1-888-313-2665

Visit us on the Internet at www.arcadiapublishing.com

To Joan, James, and Janet, whose help and support were vital in the creation of this book.

Contents

ACKNOWLEDGMENTS

The inspiration for this book came from the photographs and postcards collected by the Chalmers and Bunce families over generations of living in Centerport, now in the collection of the author David Chalmers Clemens. All uncredited images are from his collection.

This book would not have been possible without the assistance of two wonderful local historians: Deanne Rathke and Karen Martin. Rathke, director of the Greenlawn-Centerport Historical Association, generously shared her knowledge and the resources of the Association. Martin, archivist of the Huntington Historical Society, provided the many wonderful photographs from the collections of the society including the work of Huntington photographer Robert Stone.

Harvey Weber (1917–1991), an award-winning *Newsday* photographer, made his home in Centerport. He published a pictorial history of the town in 1990, which included vintage scenes as well as his own photographs. He also contributed to *Long Island: People and Places, Past and Present*, published by *Newsday* in 1983. The Greenlawn-Centerport Historical Association retains his negatives. All author proceeds from the sale of this publication will go to the Greenlawn-Centerport Historical Association.

In addition, the authors are grateful to William Townsend Perks for sharing photographs and postcards from his collection, Jeff Robinson of the Huntington Beach Civic Association and the Parish of Our Lady Queen of Martyrs Church for providing information and photographs, and Tony Guarnaschelli of the Greenlawn Centerport Historical Association for sharing his knowledge of antique automobiles.

Important images of Arthur Dove and Helen Torr were obtained from the Heckscher Museum of Art (with thanks to Diane Rehm) and the McNay Art Museum in San Antonio, Texas. Harry Newman of the Old Print Shop and Preservation on Long Island provided several little-known Edward Lange views. Erik Huber of the Long Island Division of the Queens Library assisted with access to the William H. Deming photographs.

INTRODUCTION

The name Centerport appears on Long Island maps after 1895; in earlier days, it was known as Stony Harbor, Stony Brook, Little Cow Harbor (from the 1700s to 1844), Little Neck on some maps, and Centreport for many years. During its heyday in the late 19th century, Suffolk County historian Richard M. Bayles described the small town in his 1885 *Bayles' Long Island Handbook*:

> A village of 425 inhabitants, on the north side of Huntington town, 35 miles from New York city. The village lies in a valley at the head of Centreport Harbor, formerly called Little Cow Harbor, and is surrounded by hills. It contains two churches—Methodist Protestant and Methodist Episcopal—a few stores and two grist mills. The Long Island railroad station at Greenlawn is about one and a half miles south of this village, on the elevated plain. The scenery of hills, valleys, nooks and coves, is invitingly picturesque. Vessels of large size can come to a dock near the village.

Today's Centerport was included in what is referred to as "The First Purchase," an arrangement between three original white settlers in Huntington and the sachem of the Matinecock Indians, Raseokan. The deed was witnessed by Thomas Richards, Moses Johnson, and Matthias Nichols in November 1667. The property included what is now Cold Spring Harbor on the west to Centerport on the east. The price paid for this purchase was six coats, six kettles, six hatchets, six howes, six shirts, ten knives, six fathom of wampum, thirty muxes, and thirty needles, as recorded in the Huntington Town Records. Early farmers such as Thomas Fleet, Abraham Jarvis, and Thomas Bunce settled in Centerport, and were followed a century later by Miles Burling, David Chalmers, and Peter Van Iderstine.

Philip Udale operated a paper mill along a stream known as Stony Brook in the early 1600s. Shipbuilding was also an early industry. A total of 14 vessels were built in Centerport during the first part of the 19th century.

In 1774, the Townsend mill was built on the west shore of the harbor. It was a tide mill powered by a dam that created a large mill pond in the original upper harbor. The mill passed through several owners and was rehabilitated by William Titus in 1849. It operated until its demolition in 1915. Another early industry was the Northport Fire, Sand, and Clay Company, owned by the Sills family out on the end of Little Neck peninsula. The first church was built in 1812, and the first post office was established in 1831. The first schoolhouse in Centerport was built in 1836, and the first firehouse was built in 1898.

An account in the May 29, 1885, issue of *The Long-Islander* newspaper noted changes were coming to Centerport and summed up its transition from its early beginnings to the boardinghouse days of the late 19th century:

> A few years has effected a great change in the character of this quiet little village surrounding the shores of as pretty a land-locked harbor as is to be found anywhere. Formerly the few dwellers along the shore were engaged in fishing or farming, and in this quiet sequestered spot they made but little acquaintance with the march of the outside world. But with the march of the past few years the advent of the enterprising boarding home proprietors, who are fully awake to the advantages of the place as a summer resort, has completely changed the aspect of affairs. The lovely groves, the gravely beach, and calm, crystal waters are now popularized by hundreds of summer boarders that come with each successive season, anxious to escape from the heat, dust, and turmoil of city life.

These summer boarders included actress Mary Pickford, and later film star Marlene Dietrich. Summerhouses were built by the vaudeville stars Rice & Barton. Estates were built by William K. Vanderbilt II, Marius DeBrabant, Henry Gucker, Charles Whitney, Austin Corbin, Daniel Morse, and Joseph Morrell. Later, artists Arthur Dove, Helen Torr, and more recently, Roberto Bessin, would make Centerport their home. Music was made when Sergei Rachmaninoff spent two summers here. Even football legend Vince Lombardi spent time in Centerport, as a camper at Camp Alvernia.

A Centerport Improvement Association was formed in 1905. Members consisted of a combination of descendants of the original settlers and the relative newcomer summer home, estate, and restaurant owners. The membership list included Frank and William Suydam, Joseph Scudder, Percy Jarvis, James and John Bunce, Theodore Sammis, Charles Burling, F.P. Burt, Daniel Morse, J.B. Morrell, and Archie Hall. The willingness of members to give time and money for public improvements resulted in paved roads around the millpond north up Little Neck and south to the Greenlawn railroad station, a public lighting district, and improvements to public places. These projects improved the quality of life in the community and resulted in an increase in local property values.

The incorporation of Centerport as a separate village was a subject of periodic discussion by local residents in the early 20th century. The possibility became a real option in 1931 when the incorporation of Centerport and Little Neck as the Village of Center Neck was proposed by a group of local landowners. The signers of the petition included William K. Vanderbilt II, Charles and William Van Iderstine, Henry Gucker, Mary Clark DeBrabant, Charles Burling, Richard Townsend, Hiram Ackerly, George Scudder, and Mary, Lulu, and Arthur Bunce. The proposition was defeated by a vote of 49 to 40.

The popularity of guesthouses waned during the early decades of the 20th century, while large restaurants that catered to the increasing automobile tourist trade grew in popularity. After World War II, the demand for housing was satisfied by the subdivision of former farms, estates, and vacant land into residential developments as well as the conversion of Huntington Beach summer bungalows into year-round homes.

In 1892, the population of Centerport was 300. By 1925, it had reached 400. Nearly 100 years later it stands at 5,500, a tenfold increase in the same 2.3 square miles.

Today, new development pressures are felt as summer bungalows and 1950s ranches are expanded or torn down and replaced to accommodate today's tastes. Historic preservation efforts, which began with saving the Suydam house in 1989, have demonstrated the desire of our community to retain some of Centerport's past. We hope that our pictures will show modern readers a portion of the history and scenic beauty of Centerport, a hidden jewel of Long Island's north shore.

One

Little Cow Harbor

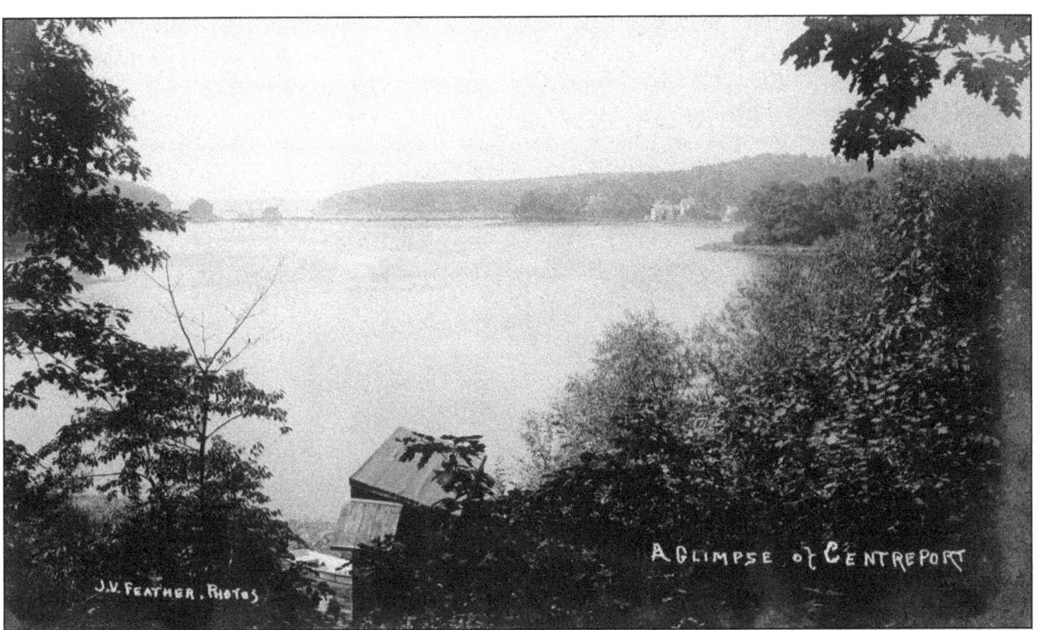

The harbor has always been the focal point of Centerport, a scenic magnet for both residents and visitors. The Centerport Mill Pond is seen here from the hill to the south. Beyond the pond and the dam is Centerport Harbor, and beyond it is Huntington Bay. The unsurpassed natural resources attracted the first settlers and provided raw materials, transportation, and waterpower for Centerport's first industries. (Huntington Historical Society.)

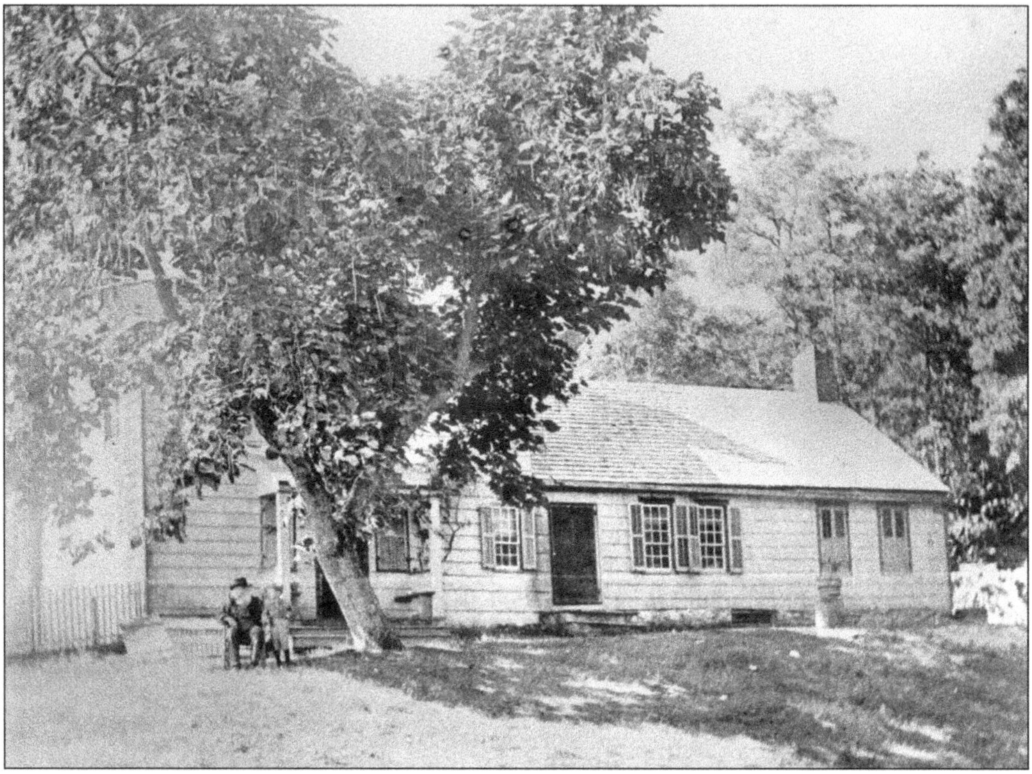

The Fleet house is probably the earliest surviving structure in Centerport. It was built prior to 1700, and a small part of it was built as early as 1660. The original owner is said to be Capt. Thomas Fleet, a Quaker who settled the west shore of Centerport Harbor in the small cove that still bears his name. His son Mortimer married into the Jarvis family of Huntington, and ownership of the house passed between the two families on at least one occasion. (Huntington Historical Society.)

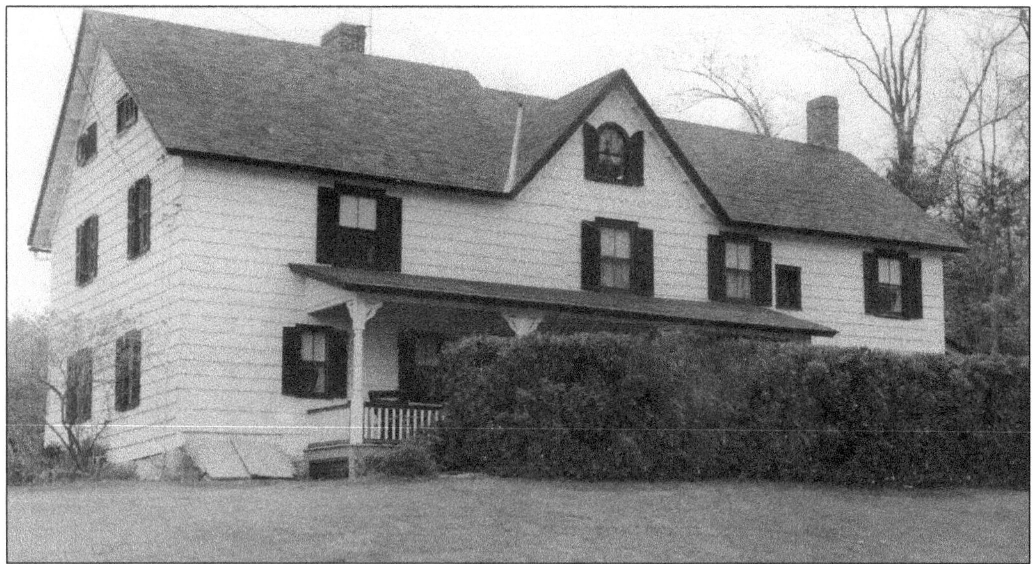

This photograph of the Fleet house from the late 19th century shows a major expansion and renovation. The original two-story house is on the left side. (Huntington Historical Society.)

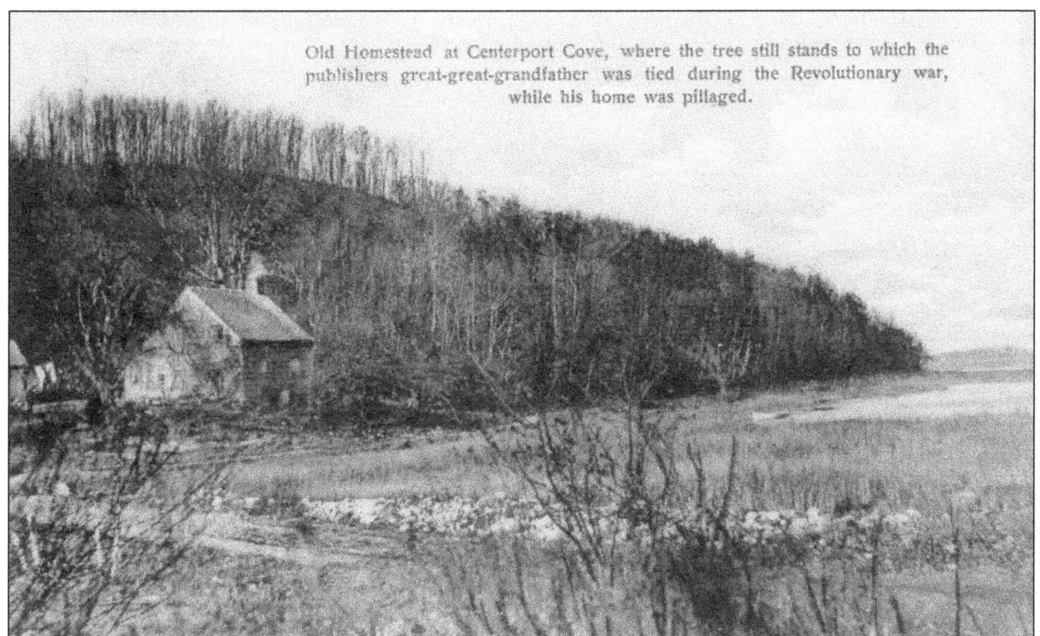

The area shown on this postcard is now known as Fleet's Cove and Knollwood Beach. The card is from a series published by James Jarvis Bunce between 1910 and 1920. Many of Bunce's ancestors lived in the area during the Revolutionary War, so it is unclear which of his great-great-grandfathers he is referring to on the card. This kind of persecution was common during the British occupation of Long Island from 1776 through 1783.

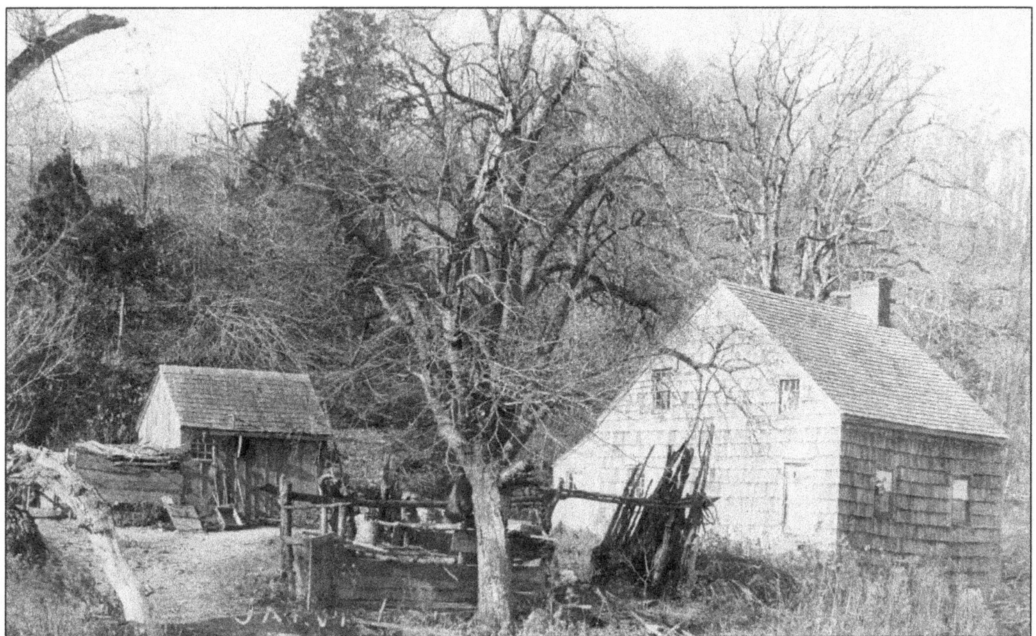

The Fleet-Jarvis house is located on the shorefront in Fleet's Cove. It is described as a Colonial shingled residence built around 1700 and enlarged in 1750. It is said that a Joe Scudder watched over the valuable oyster beds from this house in the early 1900s. It was listed in the National Register of Historic Places in 1985. (Greenlawn-Centerport Historical Association.)

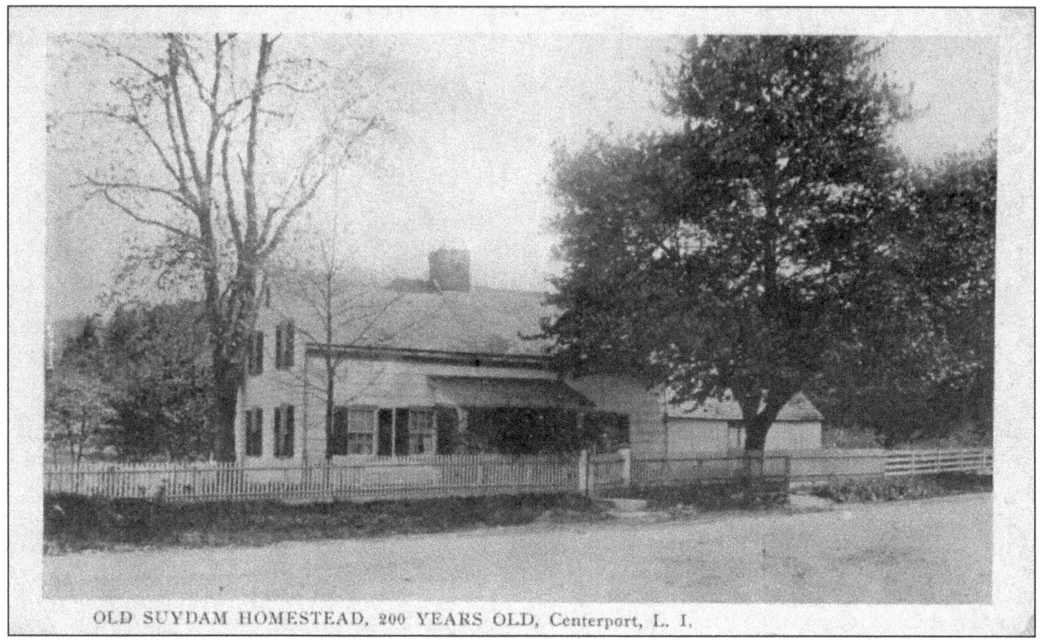

One of the oldest houses in Centerport is the Suydam Homestead, built before 1720 and occupied by descendants of the Abigail Kelsey and John C. Suydam family until 1960. It is unknown who built it. It is of post and beam construction and was expanded to the east in 1790. A separate 18th-century structure was moved to the property about 1830 and attached to the house as a west wing.

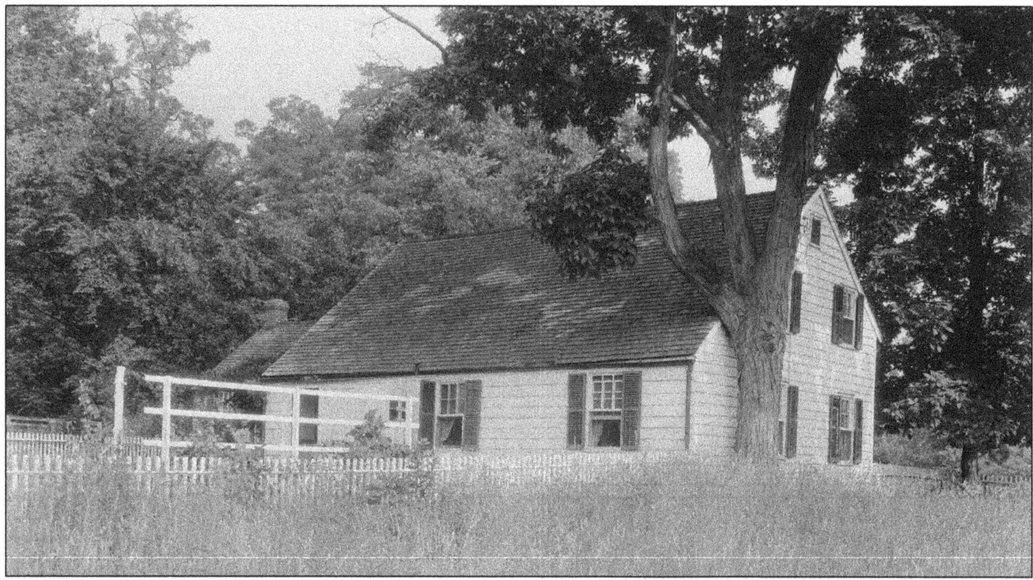

This is a rear view of the Suydam house. Suydam means "south of the dam," and the house may have been built by descendants of Hendrick Rycken of the Netherlands. The house combines Dutch and English architectural elements. Behind it were orchards, fields, a grape arbor, a garden, beehives, barns, and other outbuildings. Mary Emma Suydam Chalmers (1853–1947), who grew up in the house, said, "The windows were quite narrow with very small panes of glass," and "We only had small oil lamps using candles to go upstairs and through the rooms." (Library of Congress.)

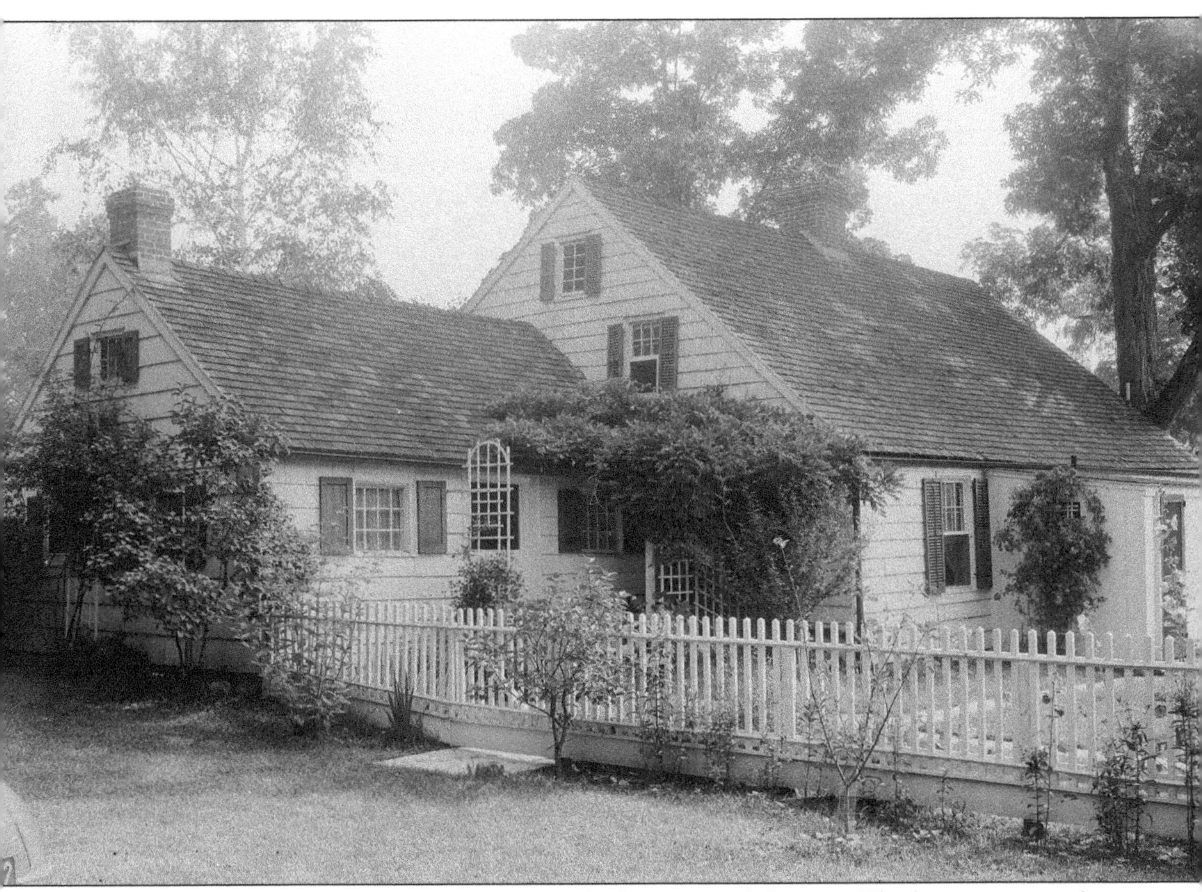

This is another rear view of the Suydam house, looking toward the east. The house was saved from demolition by the Greenlawn-Centerport Historical Association in 1989. It was listed in the National Register of Historic Places in 1988. It remains in its original location, at what is now a very busy intersection along New York State Route 25A. The Greenlawn-Centerport Historical Association built a replica of the original 18th-century barn on the site in 1990. (Library of Congress.)

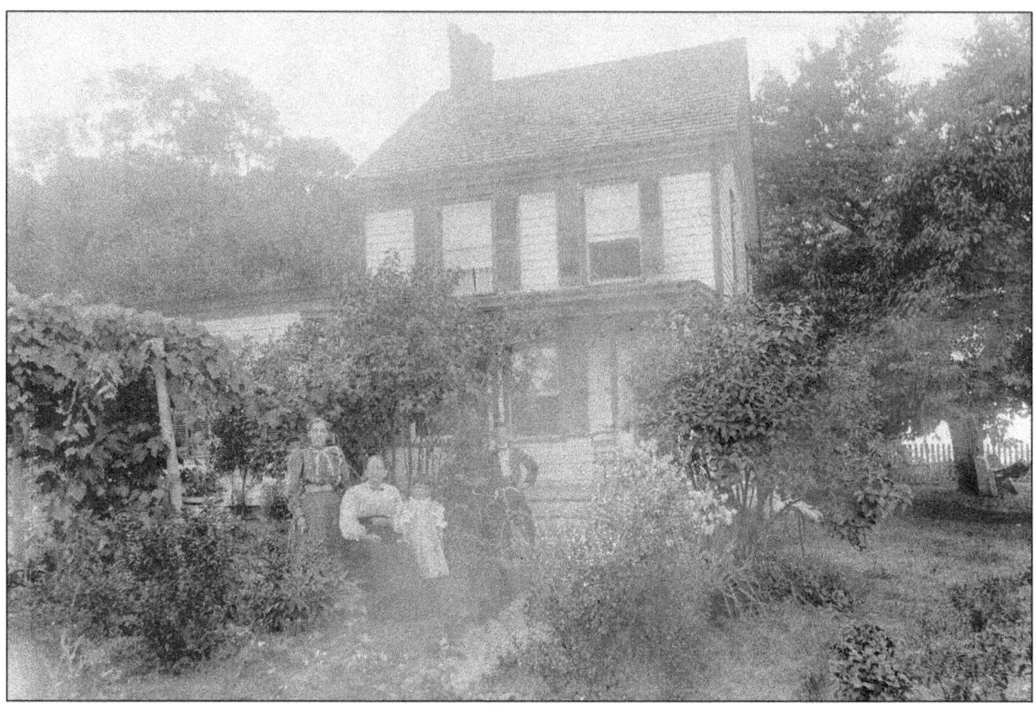

This is the Bunce-Mrazek house, built in 1793 on the west shore of Centerport Harbor by Elkanah Bunce after his marriage to Lavinia Jarvis on January 25, 1792. On the far left is Phoebe Zoeller, a relative of Nellie Bunce Zoeller's husband. Second from left is Hannah Grace Bunce, wife of Capt. Charles Bunce, holding baby Bessie Zoeller, who grew up to be postmistress in Centerport. Frank Bunce is standing beside his bicycle at far right. This picture was taken around 1880.

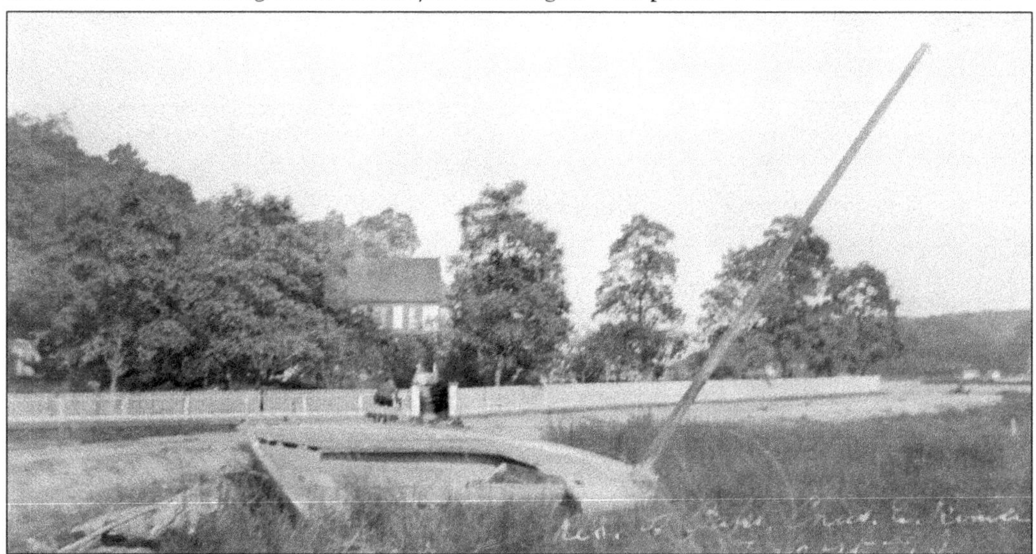

The Bunce-Mrazek house is seen in this view looking north from the dock near the mill. Ownership of the house passed to Abraham Jarvis Bunce, who married Cynthia Rogers in 1830, and then to his son Capt. Charles Bunce, who married Hanna Mann in 1862. Nellie Bunce married Thomas Zoeller, and their daughter Elizabeth "Bessie" subsequently sold it to Congressman Robert Mrazek in 1979. (William Townsend Perks.)

The original part of this house was erected around 1782 and was one of the first farmhouses on the Little Neck Peninsula. Farmland and pasture fields, including the present Vanderbilt property, surrounded the farmhouse. In the 1880s, it was owned by Phineas Sills, who owned the Northport Fire, Sand, and Brick Company. He enlarged it, called it "Glen House," and used it as a summer boardinghouse. The three men shown here around 1900 are, from left to right, the caretaker Nathaniel Scudder Sammis, his son-in-law Joseph Ellsworth Bunce, and grandson Arthur Chalmers Bunce.

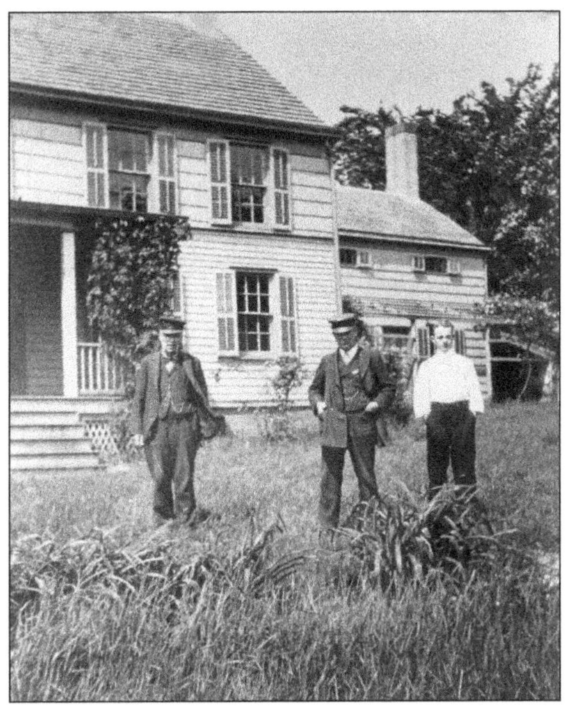

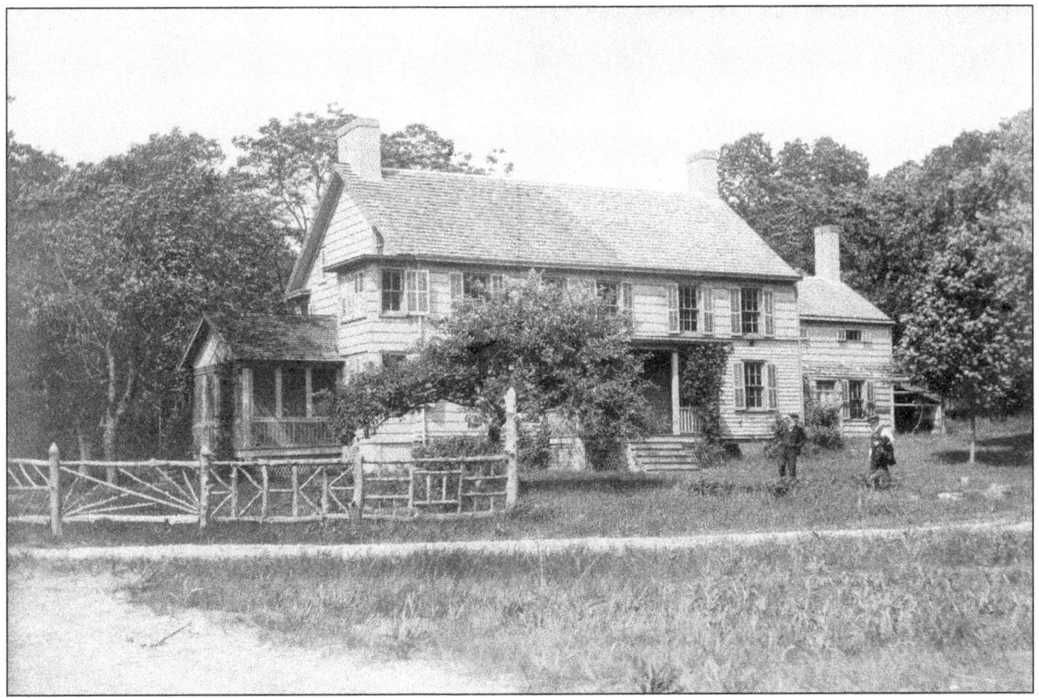

Here is a full view of the Sills house. In 1885, the house was bought by Samuel T. Carter and remained in his family until 1920. The last family member to own it was Rev. Samuel T. Carter Jr., pastor of the Old First Church of Huntington. He had 11 children and many grandchildren who used the house extensively as a summer residence until it was sold to Robert and Lilian Kessler. In 1963, they sold it to the Town of Huntington, and it is now used as the Senior Beach House.

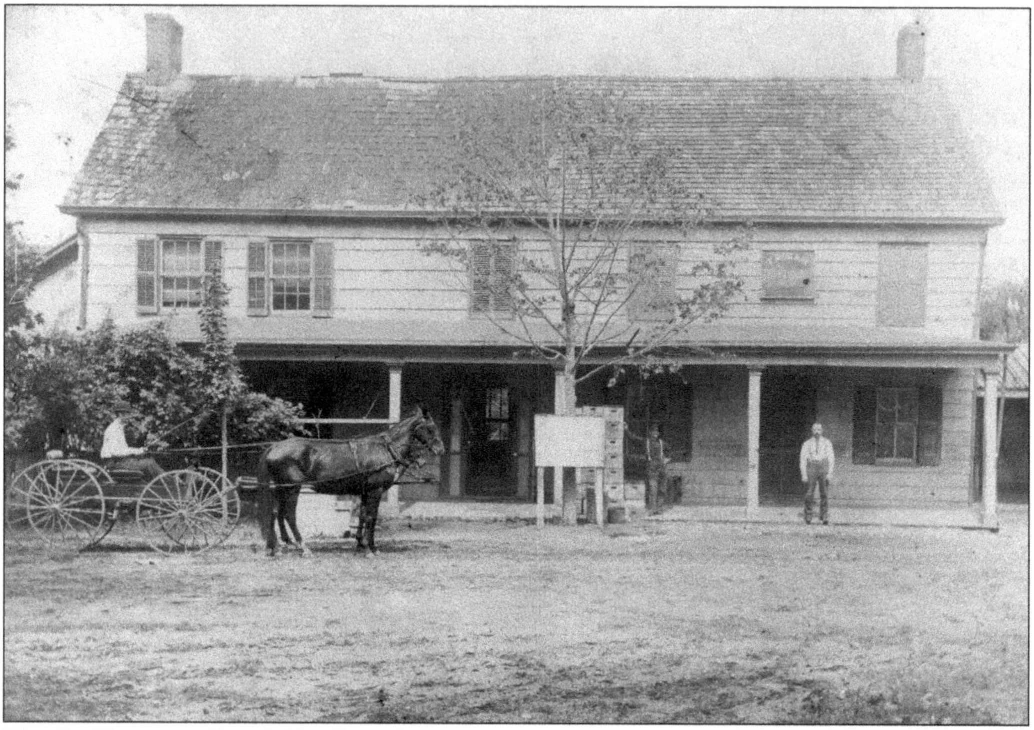

This building was Doty's Hotel, with George E. Doty as the proprietor, on the road between Huntington and Northport, now Route 25A. The hotel, formerly known as Bishop's, was established in the early 1800s and served as a tavern, general store, and post office. The hotel was the polling place for one of Huntington's six election districts for many years and had the first telephone in Centerport. The sign on the building reads, "Jacob Rupert's Extra Lager." Rupert had a brewery farm in Lloyd Neck. The men are, from left to right, George Doty, Dan Donevan, and Frank Eastwood. (Greenlawn-Centerport Historical Association.)

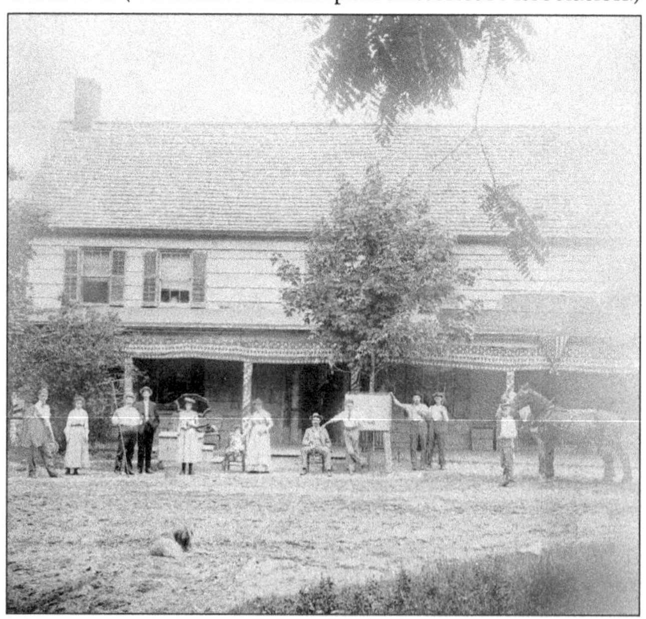

Doty's Hotel was also known as the Centerport Hotel and the Fabian House. This photograph was taken during a celebration, probably the Fourth of July. For many years, it was the meeting place of the Bicycle Club of New York. George Doty sold the hotel to John Wolfert, who leased it to Jacob Rupert in 1902, and Rupert moved his operation to Centerport, where he bottled beer and mineral water. A few of his bottles survive. The Fabian Hotel was torn down by Roscoe Bishop in 1913, and the land remains an empty lot on the north side of Route 25A opposite the current post office. (Greenlawn-Centerport Historical Association.)

Still standing on Stony Hollow Road is this one-and-a-half story, five-bay, gable-roofed house with two interior end chimneys and eyebrow windows. Built around 1760, ownership on early maps is shown as Kelsey, but by the turn of the 20th century, it was owned by Hewlett Scudder; tenants probably lived there. (Greenlawn-Centerport Historical Association.)

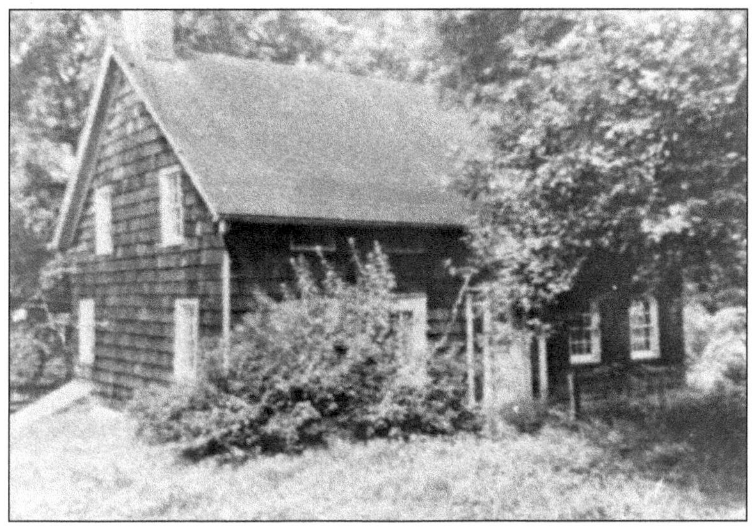

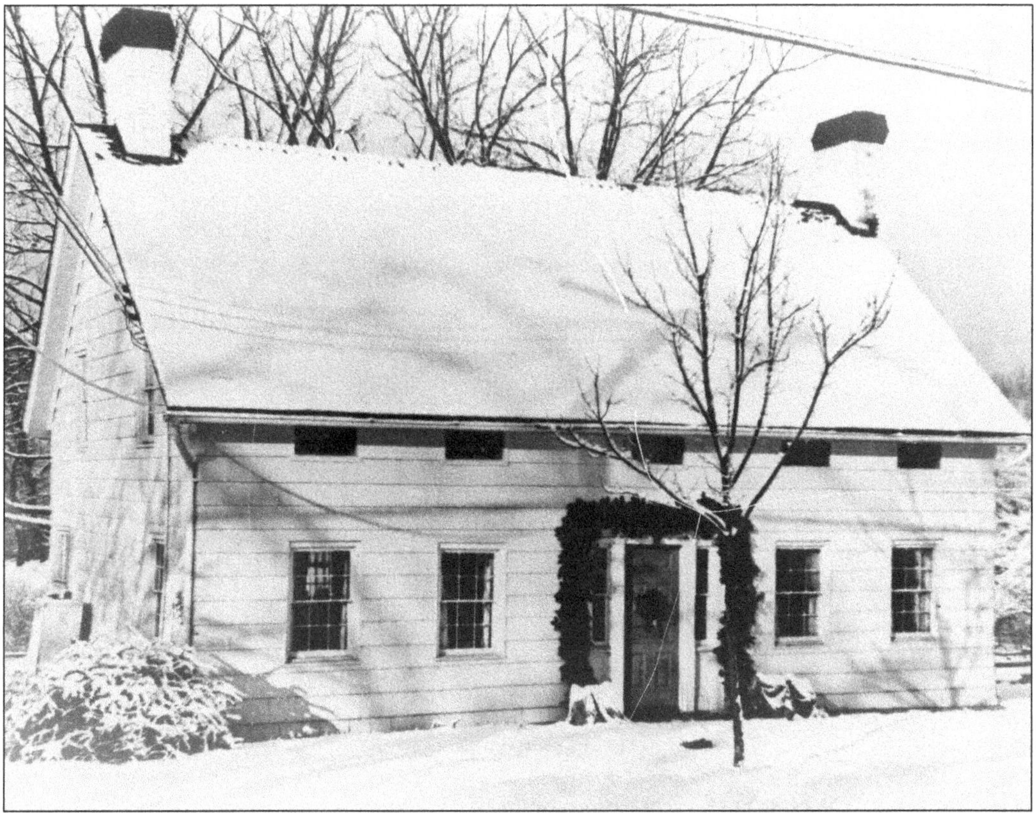

In 1941, Alfred Schultz purchased the house and 30 acres, and in 1945 restored the house to be as consistent as possible with the period in which it was originally built. Much of the land was sold for development, and the first house on what is now Overbrook Drive was built in 1952. (Greenlawn-Centerport Historical Association.)

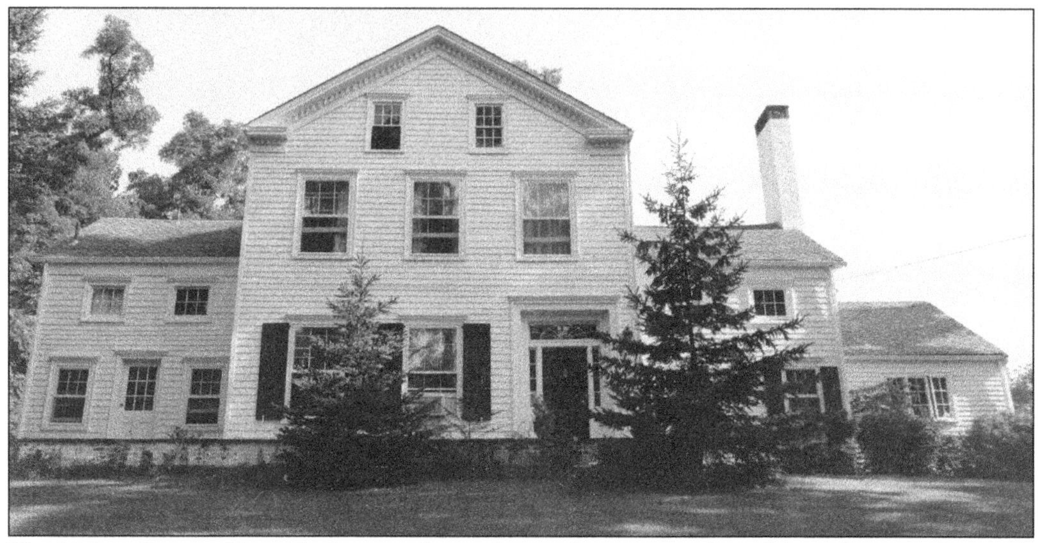

The Velsor–Draper–Van Alst house is located near the eastern edge of the village on the north side of Route 25A. It was built between 1820 and 1850, probably by a member of the Velsor family, and Velsor descendants lived in the house for more than 100 years. The house is unique in that it was built in Greek Revival style, very different from other local houses built at this time. Its first recorded owner was John Velsor, who owned the building to the east, a store that was built in the 18th century. The last family members to live in the house were local architect James Van Alst and his wife, Edith. In 1981, luxury condominiums were constructed on the east end of the property facing the head of Northport Harbor. It was listed in the National Register of Historic Places in 1985. (Greenlawn-Centerport Historical Association.)

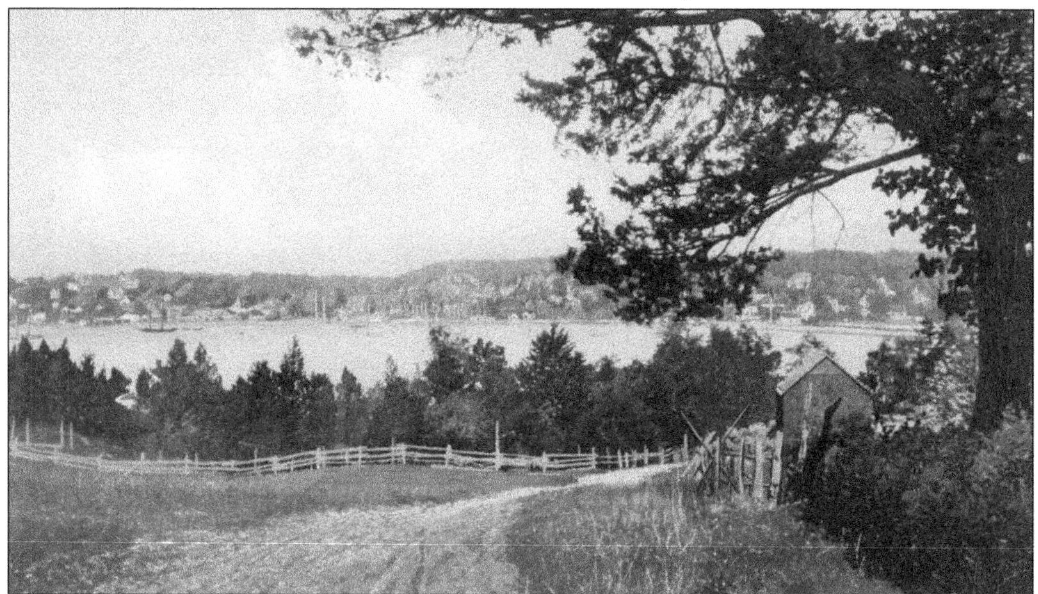

This view is from a hill on the Van Iderstine farm on Little Neck known as Spy Hill looking toward the village of Northport. Today, people do not think about Centerport being a farming community, but the business directories before 1900 list a dozen or so farmers. The Federal Census of Agriculture taken in 1880 listed six farms owned by Charles Higbie, Augustus Ackerly, Jacob Sammis, Elkanah Bunce, David Chalmers, and Peter Van Iderstine.

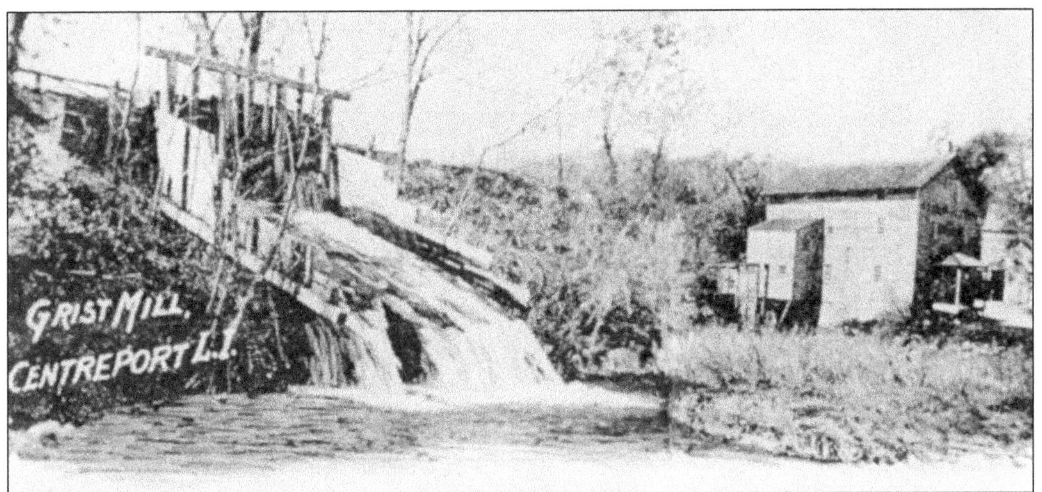

One of the earliest mills in Centerport was powered by water from a manmade pond called Spring Lake on the south side of Route 25A. Originally a paper mill run by the Lewis family, it was converted to grind grain. It operated into the early 20th century.

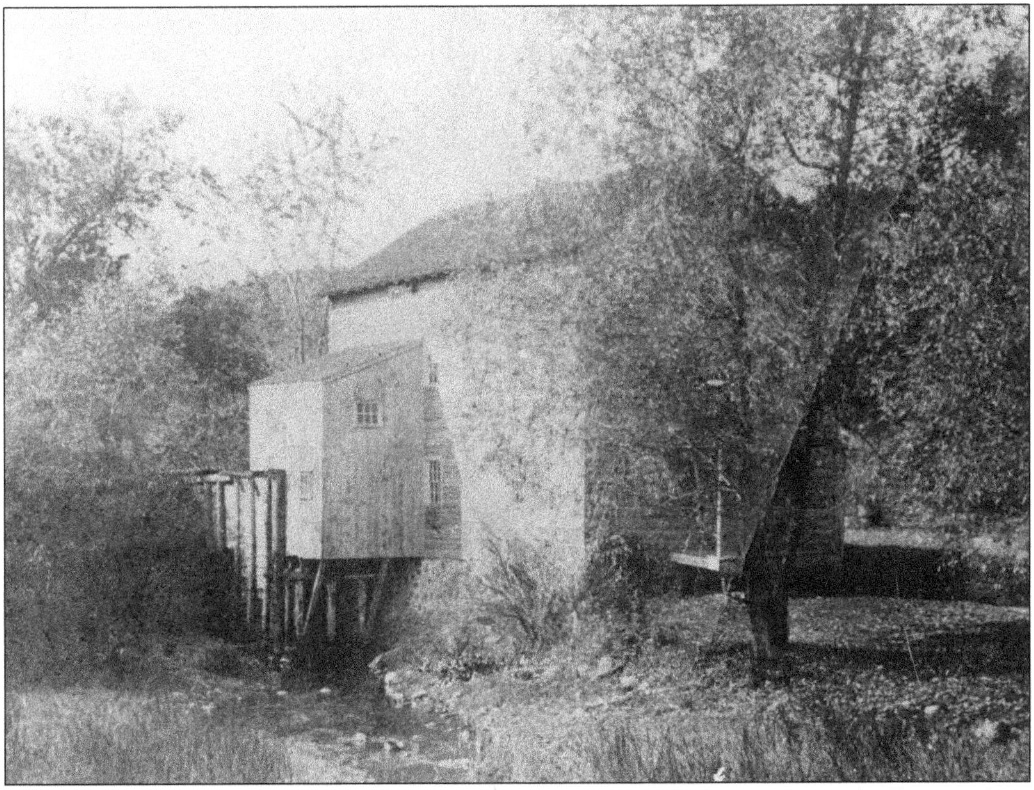

The last miller was David DeMilt, who diversified his business by harvesting and selling ice from Spring Lake. The 1897 *Brooklyn Eagle* directory for Centerport lists DeMilt as being in the ice business. When the manmade dam broke in 1885, workers were hired to repair it and raise the height in order to harvest more ice. (Greenlawn-Centerport Historical Association.)

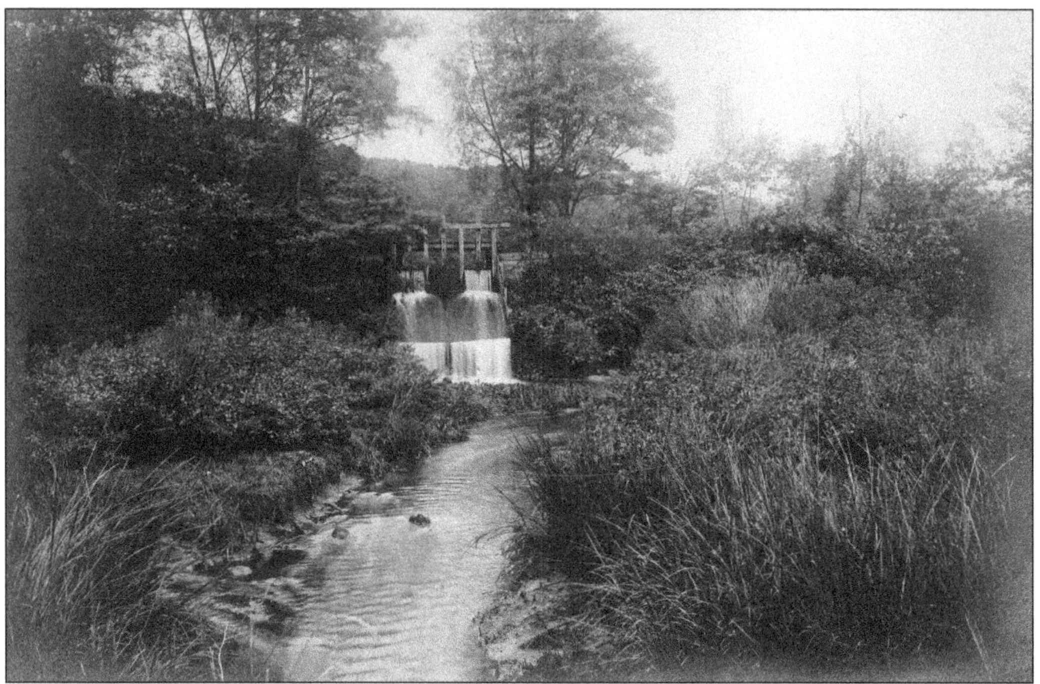

Spring Lake's water came from a stream called Stony Brook in the 18th century, as well as from a number of underground springs. Overflow from the lake fed this beautiful waterfall and the wetlands below it before running into the millpond. Today, this stream is piped under Centershore Road, and this whole area is buried under the Chalet Motor Inn's parking lot. (Huntington Historical Society.)

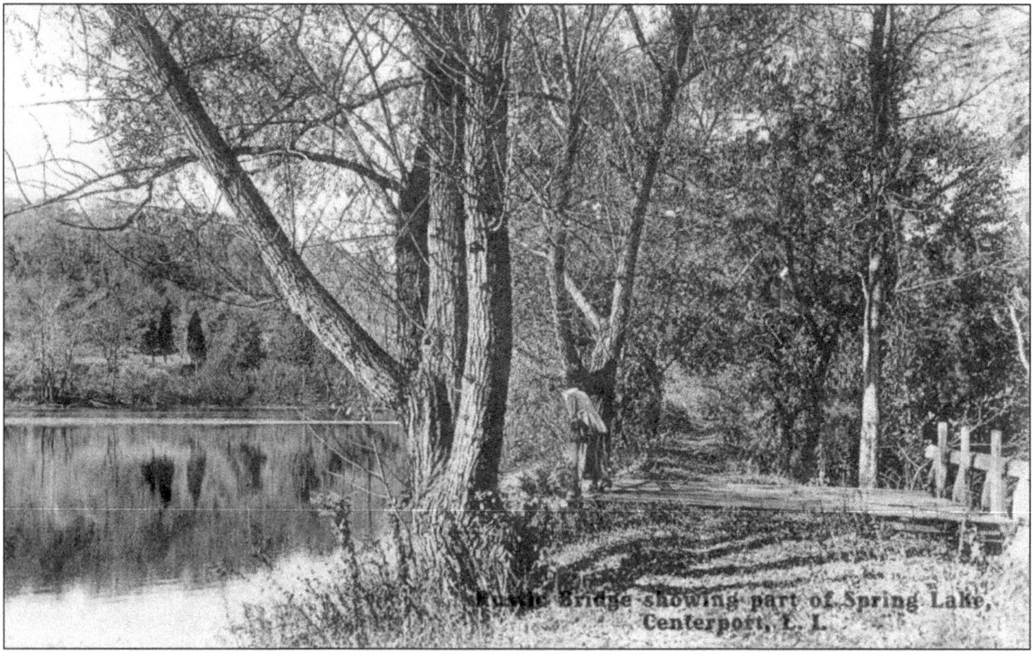

James Bunce published this postcard of the path along Spring Lake's dam and the bridge over the spillway that fed the waterfall. The young woman on the rustic bridge is his niece Velma Hontz.

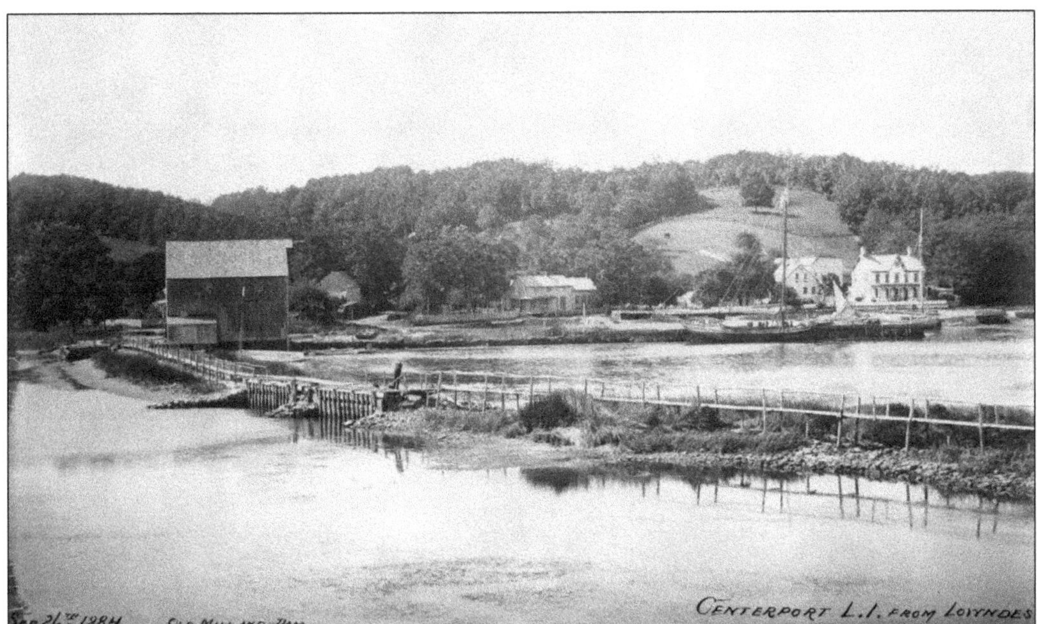

This wonderful photograph of the Centerport mill dam was taken by William H. Deming in 1884. The footbridge above the dam crosses the spillways and leads to the 1774 Townsend tide mill. A sloop is tied to the pier, and the Jarvis-Beatty-Rzehack-Coyle house and store with pastures behind complete this beautiful scene. (Queens Borough Public Library, Archives, Illustrations Collection–Centerport.)

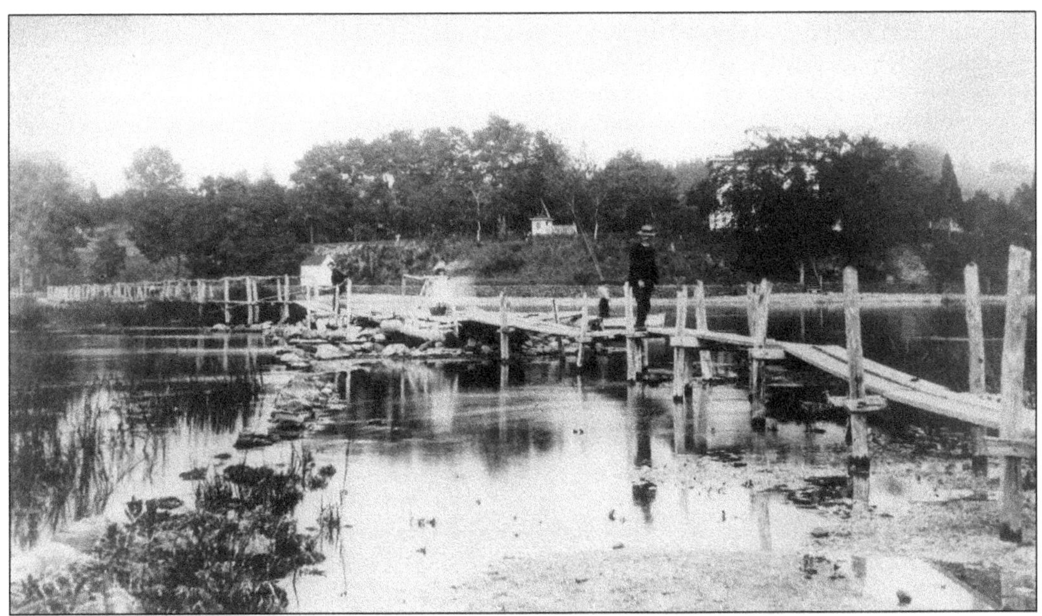

This iconic photograph of several people crossing the old plank footbridge over the mill dam was taken by Ben Conklin, a well-known photographer from Huntington. The young girl in the center is Clara Scudder Stilwell, and the man in the straw hat she is following is her father, Capt. Joseph Henry Scudder. (Huntington Historical Society.)

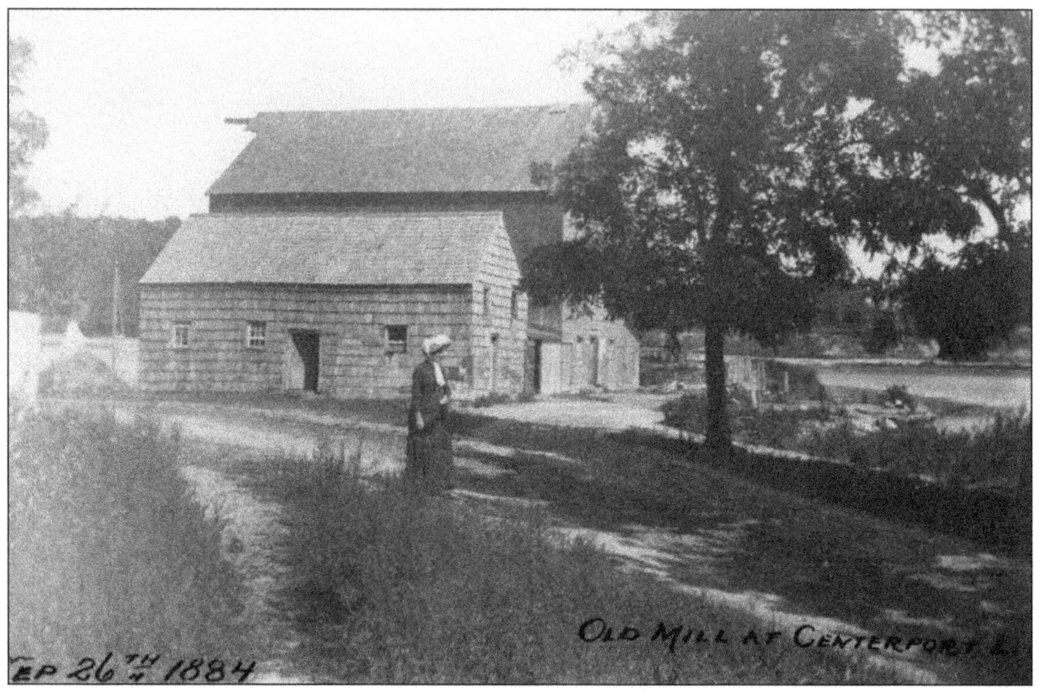

This photograph taken by William Deming in 1884 shows a woman standing in what is now Centershore Road. The mill in Centreport was established following an agreement made in January 1774 between the trustees of the Town of Huntington and Silvanus Townsend (1747–1817) of Oyster Bay, who gave him the right of "Building, Making, and running A Dam, to erect or Build A Mill or Mills on the said Dam, also make a good Grist Mill, and allways keep a good Miller and Grind all the Grain the Country People shall Bring and Grind it well." Townsend also agreed that "I will Not Hinder any Person whatsoever from fishing oystering claming or Guning anywhere in the mill pond nor Hinder any Person whatsoever from passing and repassing a Long on the Dam, and that it shall be A Publick high way forever." Townsend agreed to pay a bond of £1,000 if he forfeited on the agreement.

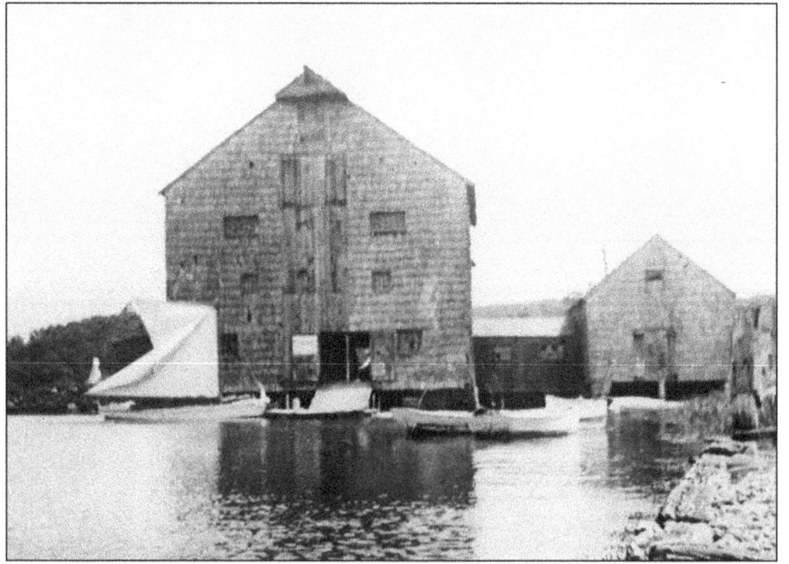

The mill was later run by William Titus and operated for more than 140 years. This print from a glass negative shows several skiffs in front, one with its sail partially hoisted. The main harbor-side door is open, and the loading ramp is visible.

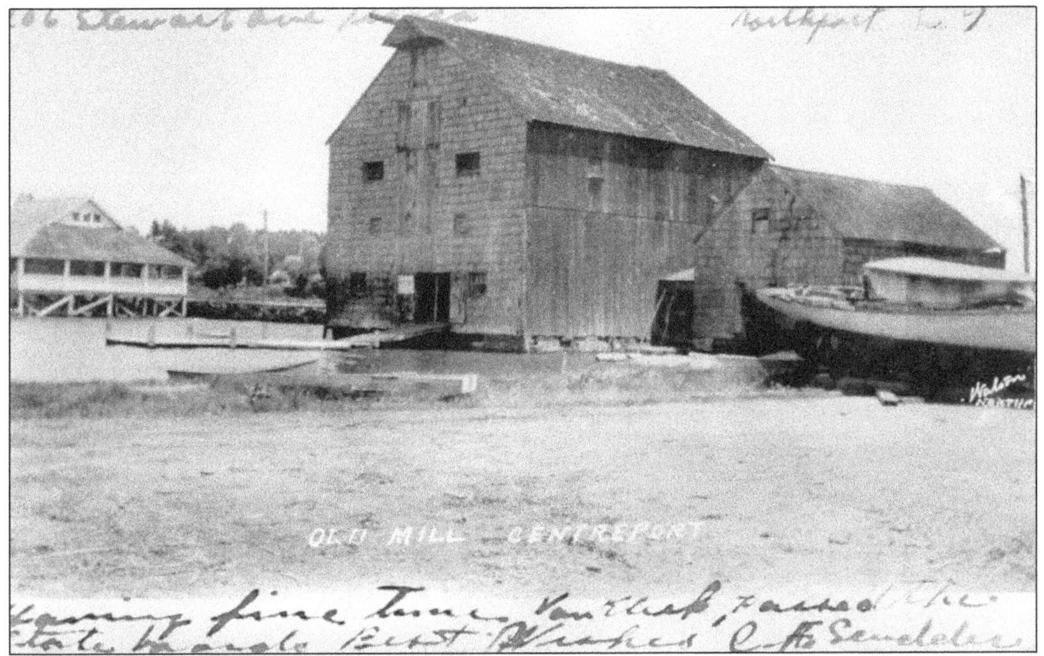

Once the most important mill in the area, the old Townsend/Titus tide mill is shown with the Centerport Yacht Club to the left and a laid-up motor launch to the right. This photograph was taken by J.E. Watson, a photographer in Northport around 1905.

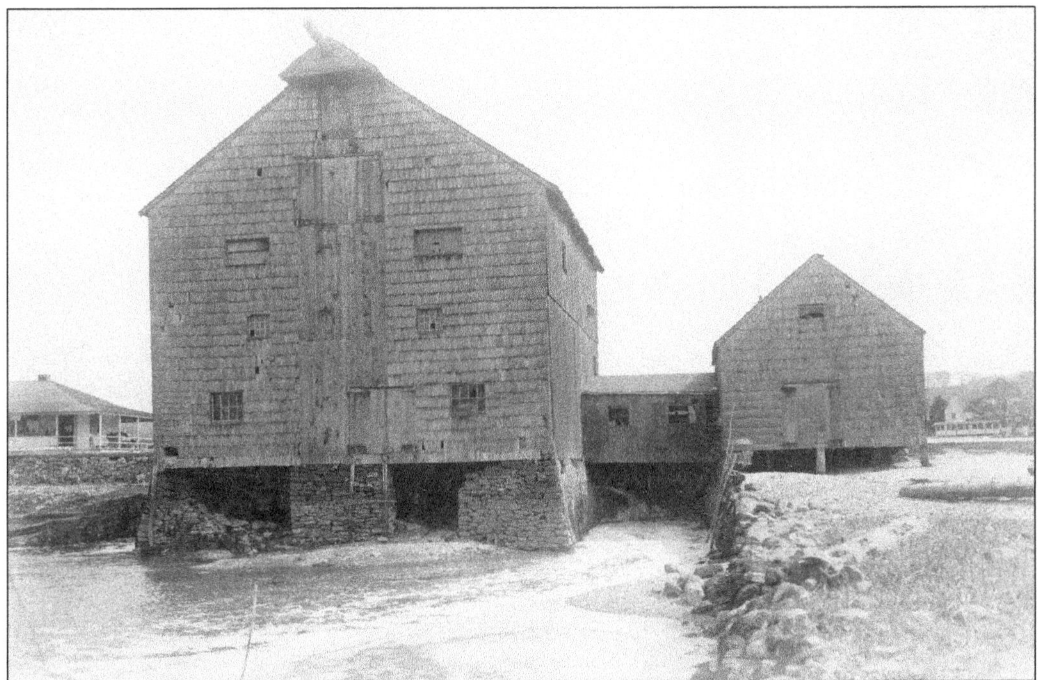

The Townsend Mill operated on power derived from the daily changes in the tide. The rising tide filled the millpond, and gates in the dam were closed. As the tide went out, the water in the pond was directed through the mill channel, where it turned a large water wheel as it rushed into the harbor. This photograph shows the mill in operation, with water flowing into the harbor.

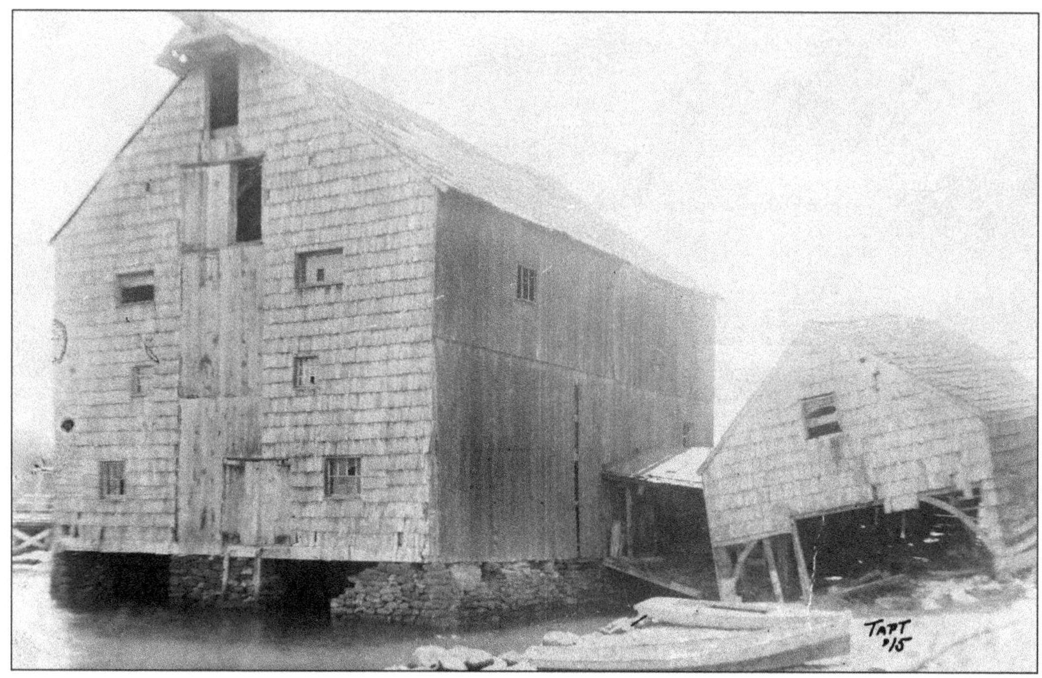

By 1915, the old mill was in a dilapidated and unsafe condition and had to be torn down. The work began in May of that year. A month later, it was announced that William K. Vanderbilt II had purchased some of the old beams, which he considered valuable because of the history of the mill building. He then shipped them to Italy to be carved for use at his estate. Several millstones survive. (Huntington Historical Society.)

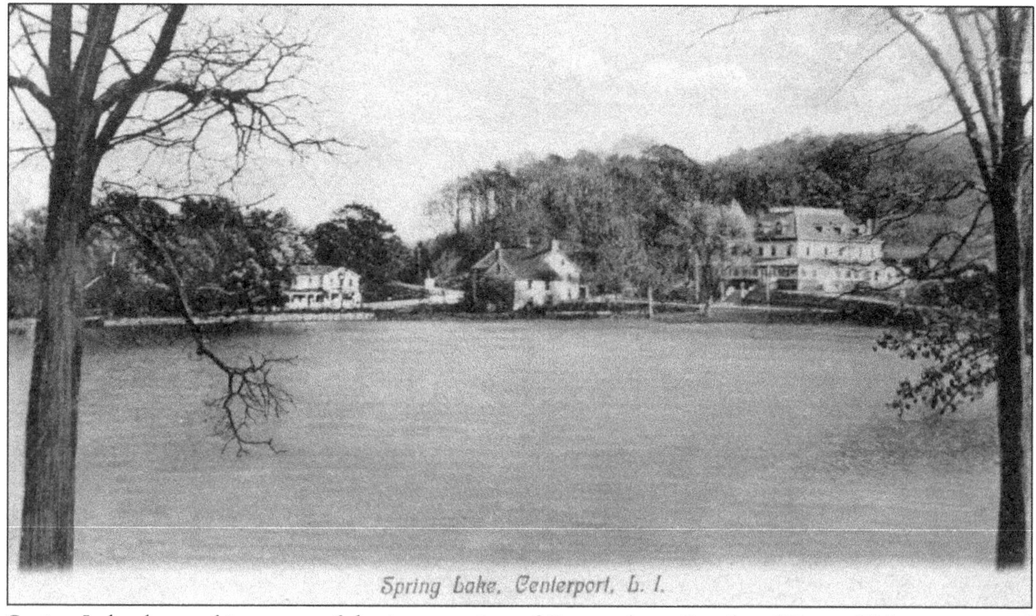

Spring Lake, located just west of the intersection of Centershore Road and Route 25A, was created by the construction of a manmade dam used to supply water to the DeMilt Mill. It remains a beautiful feature of the local landscape. This image shows the principal buildings on its shores around 1910. From left to right are the R.F. Cahill house, Doty's Hotel, and Hall's Restaurant.

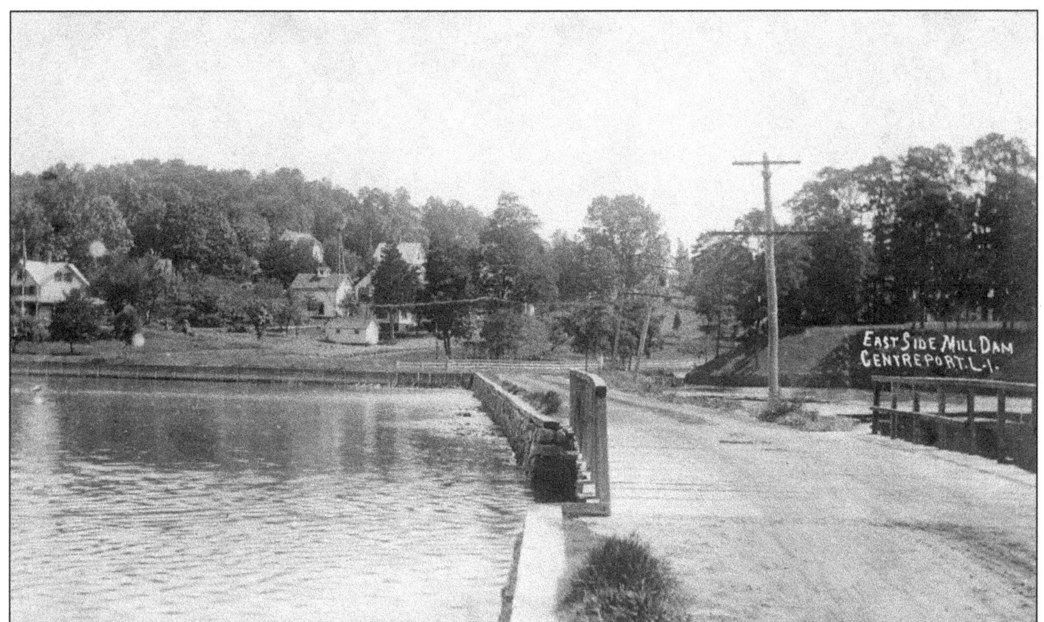

The Centerport mill dam causeway had gained stone bulkheads, an improved road, and utility poles by the 1920s. The rails on the bridge prevent people from falling into the rapidly flowing water when the mill pond gates are open. Note the old spelling of Centerport on the photograph.

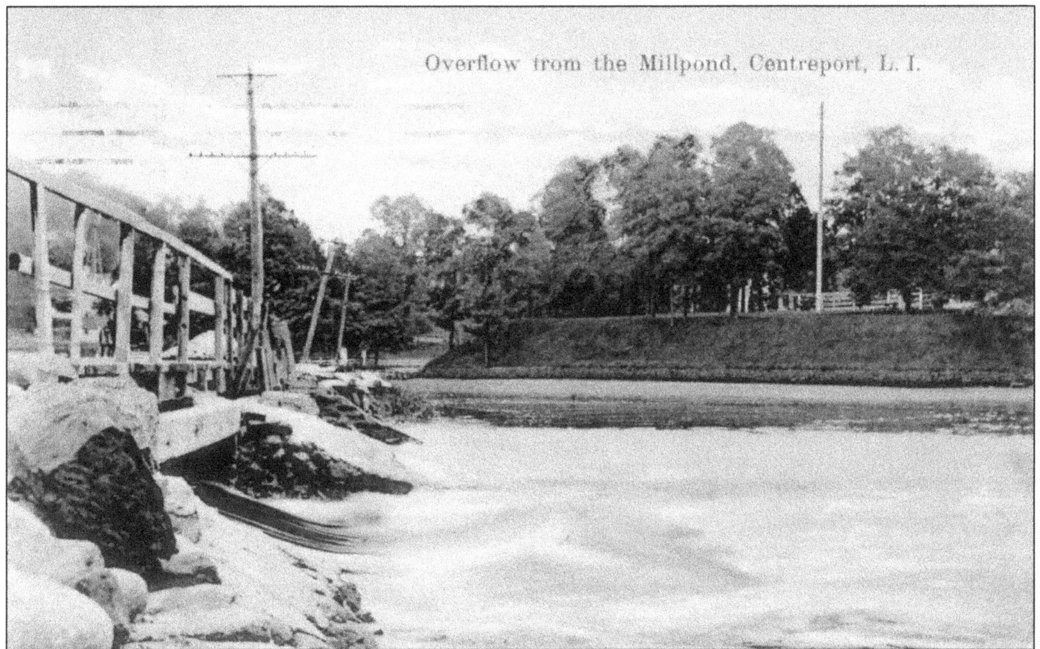

This unusual image shows the outflow from the millpond. This occurs when the tide is falling and the gates are open. When the mill was operating, the gates would be closed, forcing the water into a channel so that it turned the mill wheel on its way to the harbor. In modern times, the gates are opened periodically to allow the mill pond to flush stale water as the tide goes out and bring in new water when the tide rises.

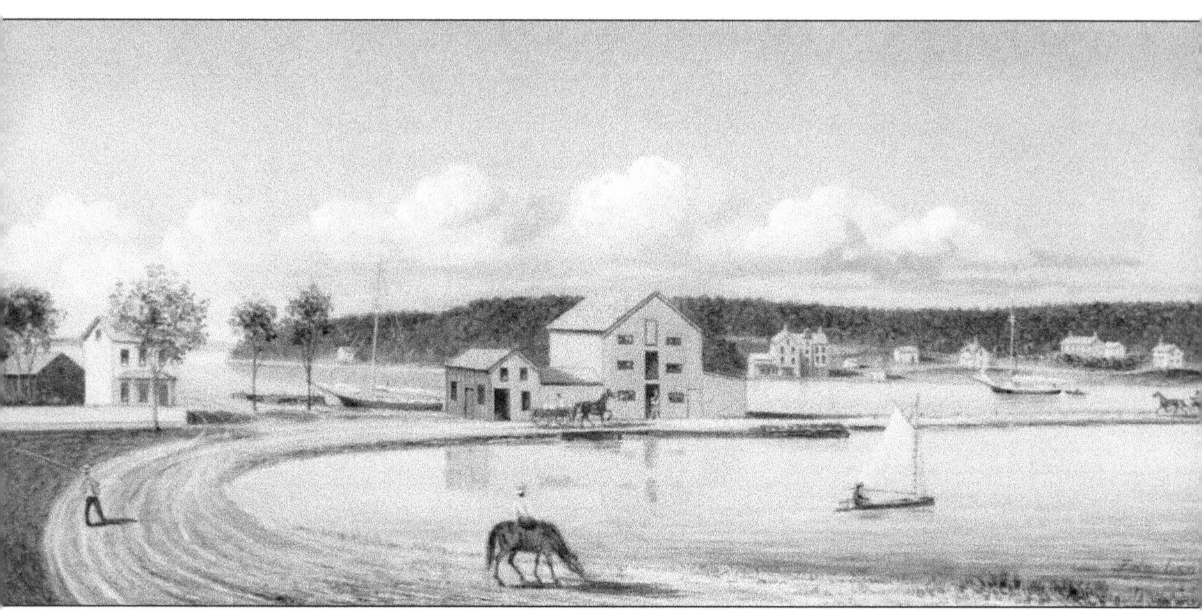

This painting by Edward Lange is titled *The Mill*. Lange (1846–1912) was born in Germany and later lived in Elwood and Commack, where he failed at farming but became a popular landscape painter of the 19th century. Local residents would commission Lange to paint their homes and farms. In addition, he painted local businesses and street scenes of the surrounding villages. His carefully executed details provide an important record for historians. In this painting done in 1880, he highlighted the Titus house on the left, the Townsend Mill in the center, and the Chalmers Place boardinghouse in the background. (Courtesy of Harry Newman, the Old Print Shop.)

Two

A Harbor at Its Heart

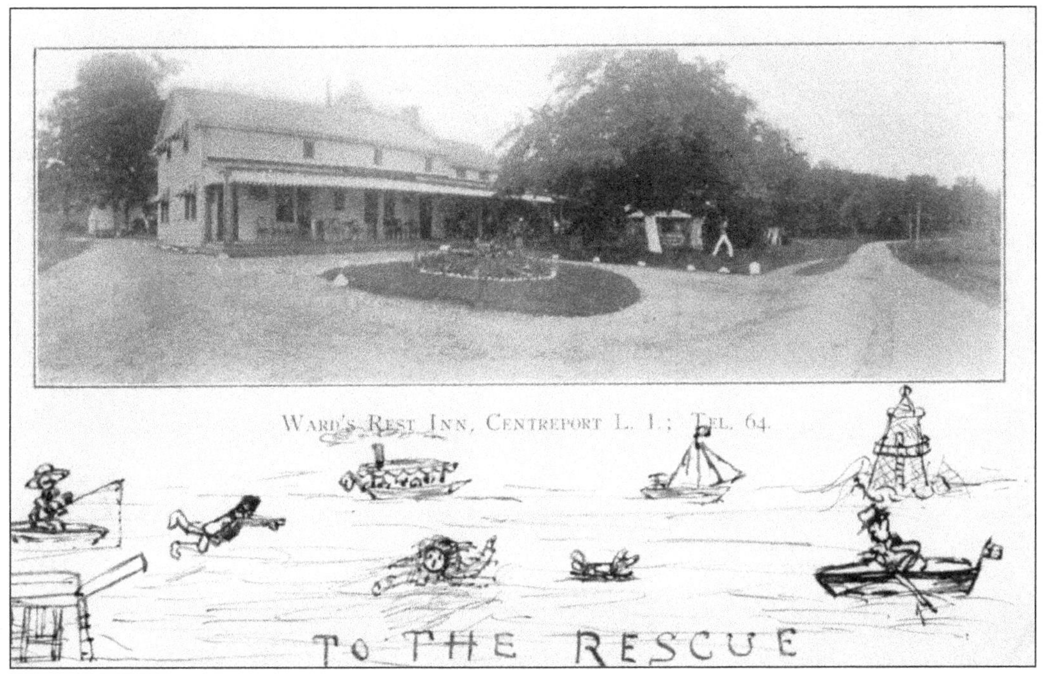

A guest at Wards Rest Inn documented the attractions of Centerport on this postcard in 1908. The natural harbor and its resources were an economic engine for many years. They have continued to be a source of recreation and enjoyment for everyone who lives here.

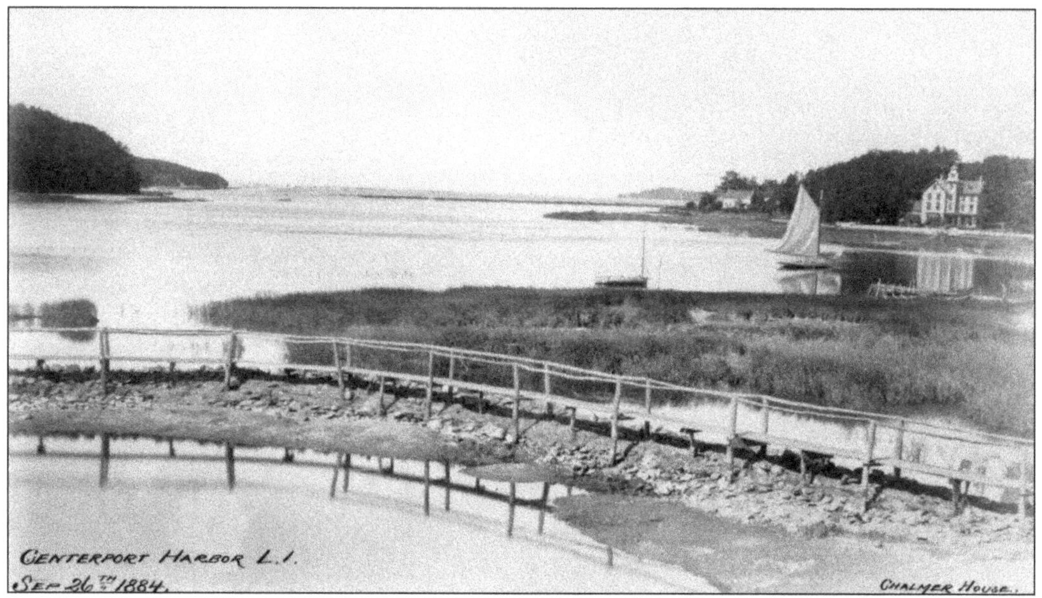

One of the earliest photographs of Centerport, this image was taken by William Deming in 1884. It shows the plank walkway over the mill dam, and in the distance are the Klinker house, a small sloop, and the Chalmers Place boardinghouse. (Queens Borough Public Library.)

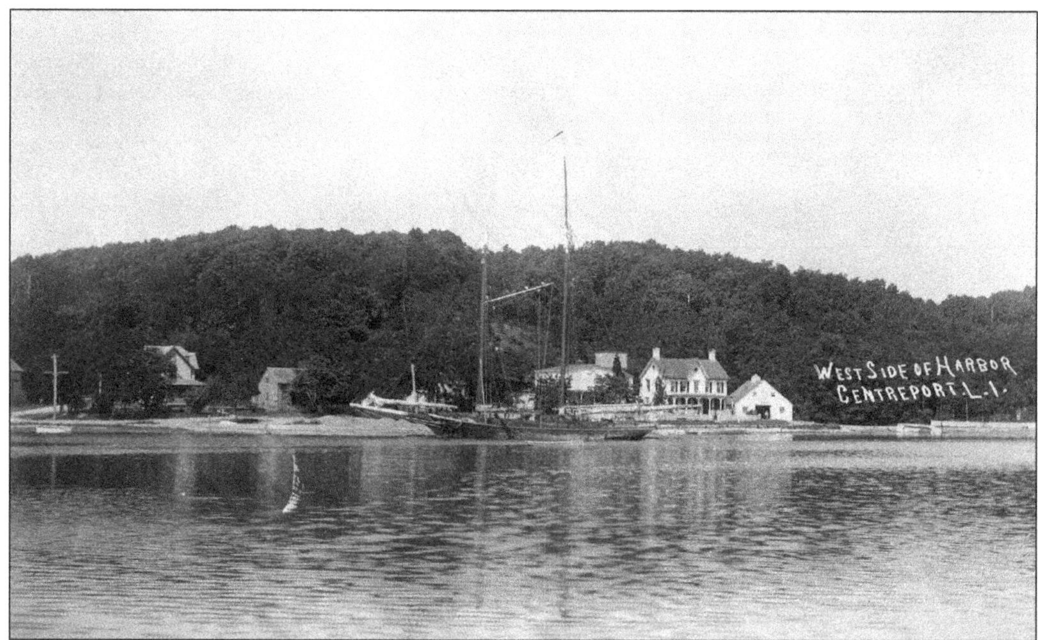

In the early years, the plentiful timber and the deep water made an ideal combination for shipbuilding. The 1885 *History of Suffolk County* lists 14 vessels built in Centerport: ten sloops, three schooners, and a brig. While major shipbuilding activities shifted to Northport, Centerport remained a deep water port. Schooners carrying grain and flour from the mill, oysters from the harbor, and sand, bricks, and cordwood were an everyday sight. Seen here is the schooner *George S. Page* at the public dock in Centerport. Note the earlier spelling of the town's name printed on this card. (Huntington Historical Society.)

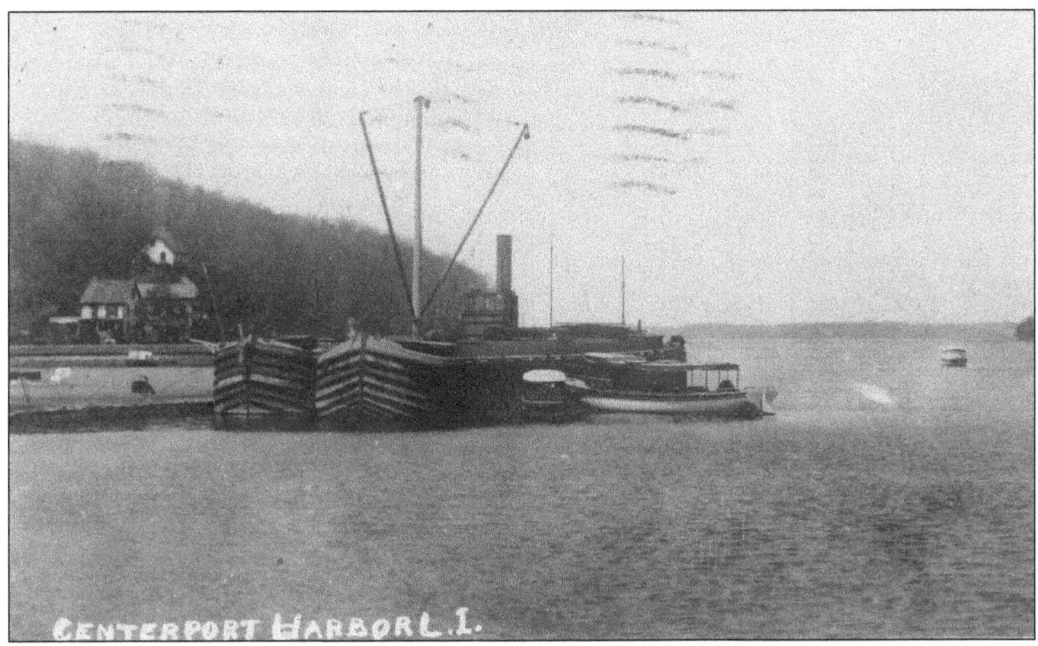

Two grain barges and a tugboat are shown here at the dock in the inner harbor around 1905. Most of the shipping of grain and flour to and from the mill was done by water.

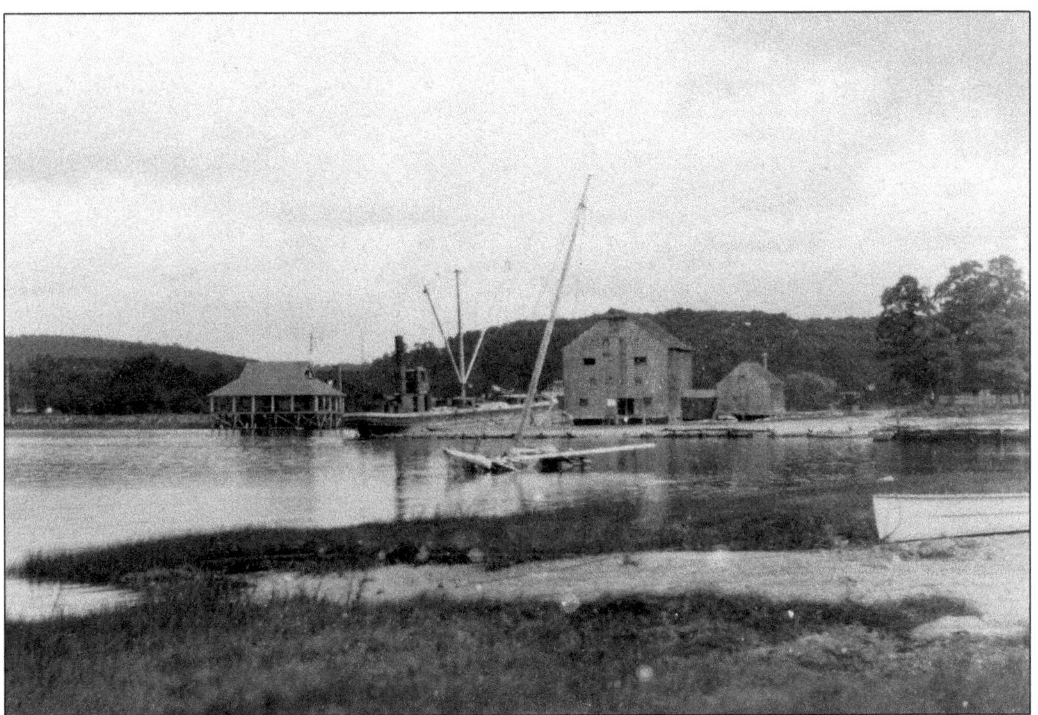

This scenic view of the western shore of the harbor from the Elkanah Bunce house shows the wreck of a sloop in the foreground. In the distance, a barge and tugboat moored by the mill can be seen.

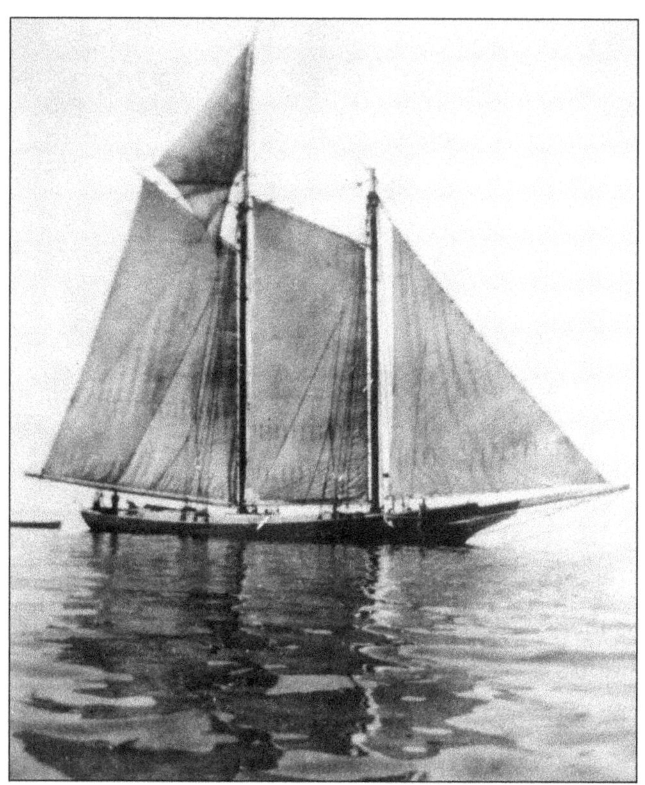

The schooner *Mary Isabel* carried sand from the Port Eaton sand works on nearby Eaton's Neck to New York City for use in construction including for building the Cathedral of St. John the Divine. Her owner and master was Charles E. Bunce of Centerport. Bunce's granddaughter Mary Emma (1890–1982) recorded this memory of the *Mary Isabel*: "One of the pleasantest recollections of my childhood is the trip my mother and I made in her to New York, where I could play on top of the load of soft white sand, as the sails filled with the breeze and the waves rippled along the schooner's sides. We were two days, I think, reaching the New York pier, but it seemed no time at all." The *Mary Isabel* often took the Methodist Sunday school children, their parents, and friends on an annual Labor Day picnic.

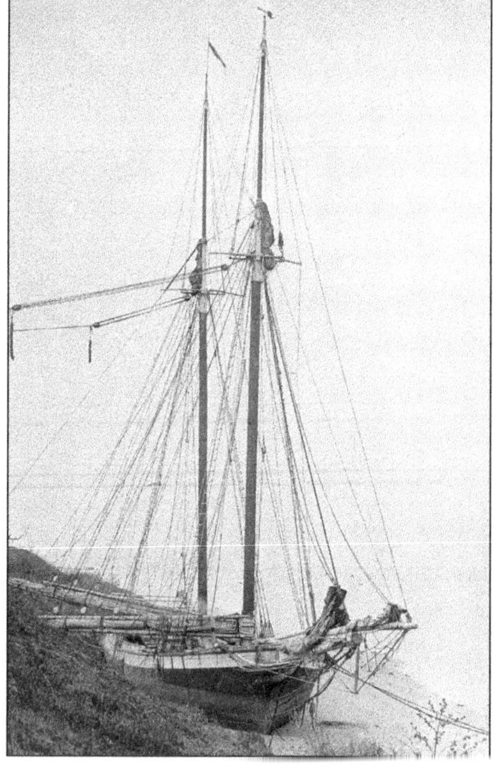

The schooner *Lizzy Godfrey*, built by Jesse Carll in Northport in 1890, is shown here. She measured 81.5 by 26 feet with a draft of 5.8 feet and weighed about 75 tons fully loaded. She was another of the vessels that carried sand from the sand and gravel works at Port Eaton. She was named for the daughter of Nicholas Godfrey, the manager of Port Eaton and the inventor of a steam-driven machine called a gravel excavator separator and sorter. Godfrey and landowner Dr. Oliver Jones were partners in the Port Eaton operation.

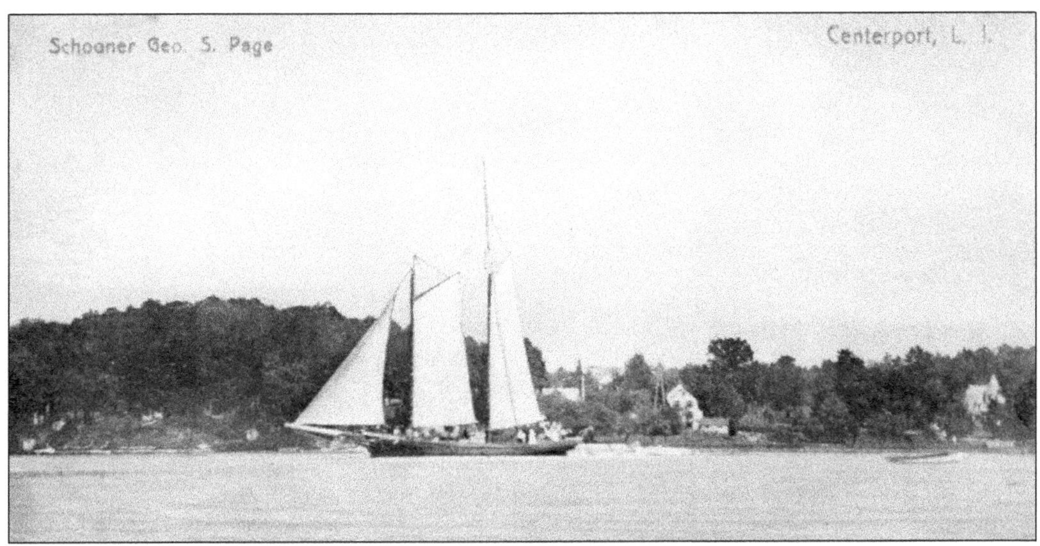

The schooner *George S. Page* was a familiar sight on Centerport harbor. She belonged to Capt. Joel Bunce. This picture shows the *Page* on an excursion with women and children aboard. Mary Emma Bunce recalled, "Captain Joe's schooner was anchored in front of our house. My family's goods and chattels were transferred to it, piano and all, and the Captain sailed them safely to New York, and then up to Newark Bay to dock in the Jersey town of our new residence." After the move to Bayonne, New Jersey, Mary and her siblings spent every summer in Centerport with their grandparents.

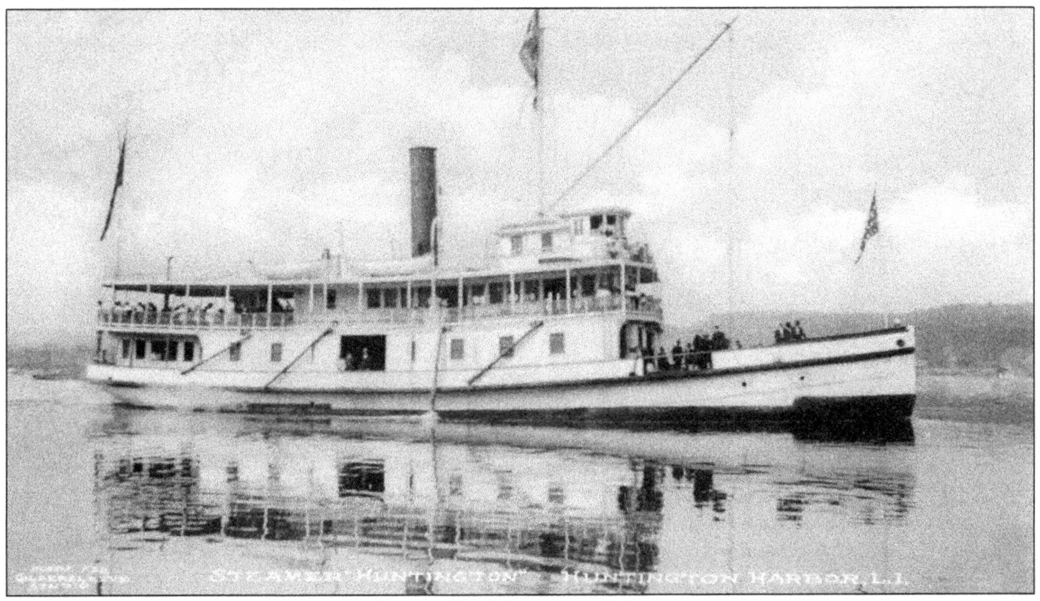

The steamer *Huntington* is shown here. The villages of Huntington and Northport had regular passenger and freight service provided by the steamers *Huntington* and *Northport*. Centerport had no service, so residents of Centerport who needed transportation to the city were forced to travel by land to Huntington. The steamer made regularly scheduled trips, at 50¢ per trip. On their return, Centerport-bound passengers usually walked from the dock at the head of Huntington harbor over the hills to the west shore of Centerport. Mary Emma Bunce recalled, "My grandfather [Nathaniel Scudder Sammis] would be on the watch, and would row over to get us. A most pleasant introduction to a summer in Centerport!"

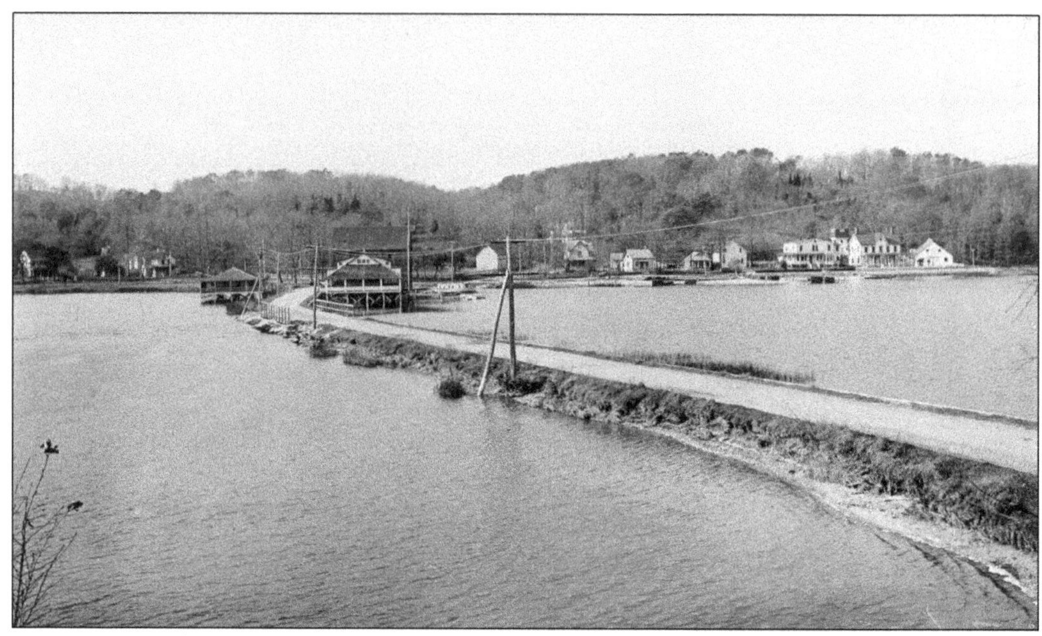

Centerport residents petitioned the town for highway access between the east and west sides of the harbor in the late 1890s. A court battle between miller Titus and the Town of Huntington over the ownership of the mill dam was still in progress when the town contracted with G.W. Brush of Northport to build a road over the dam. Work began in April 1900 and involved the construction of a seawall and a bridge across the floodgates. The work was completed by mid-August. This photograph shows the highway about 1910.

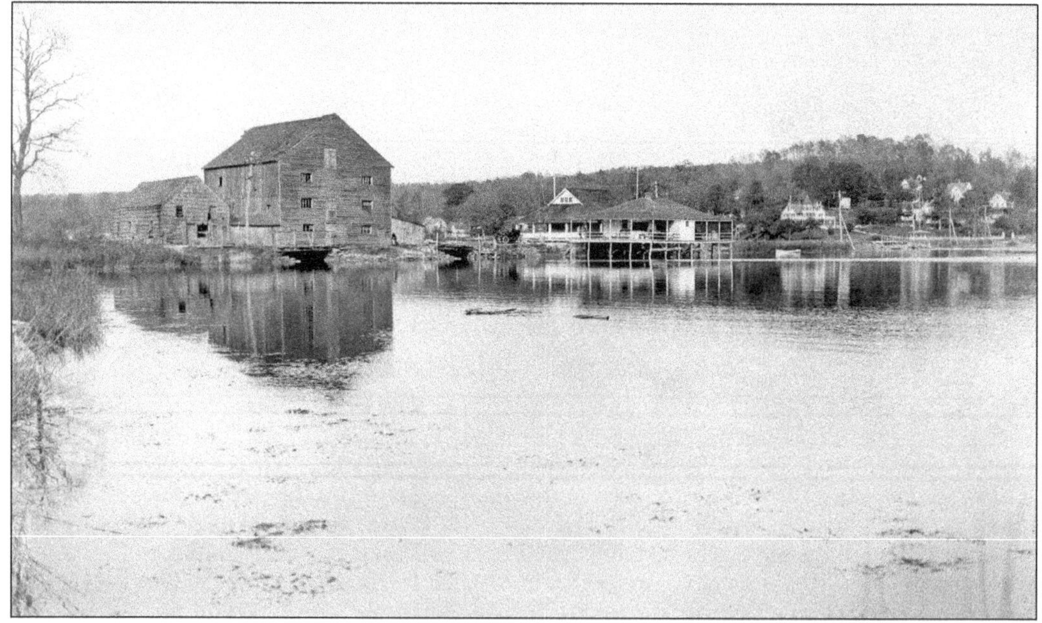

This photograph of the mill dam looking north over the pond was taken during a dead calm. No breeze disturbs the surface of the water, and a perfect mirror image of the Townsend-Titus mill is visible, along with the post office and yacht club on opposite sides of the mill dam road and the house and outbuildings of the Barton estate at far right.

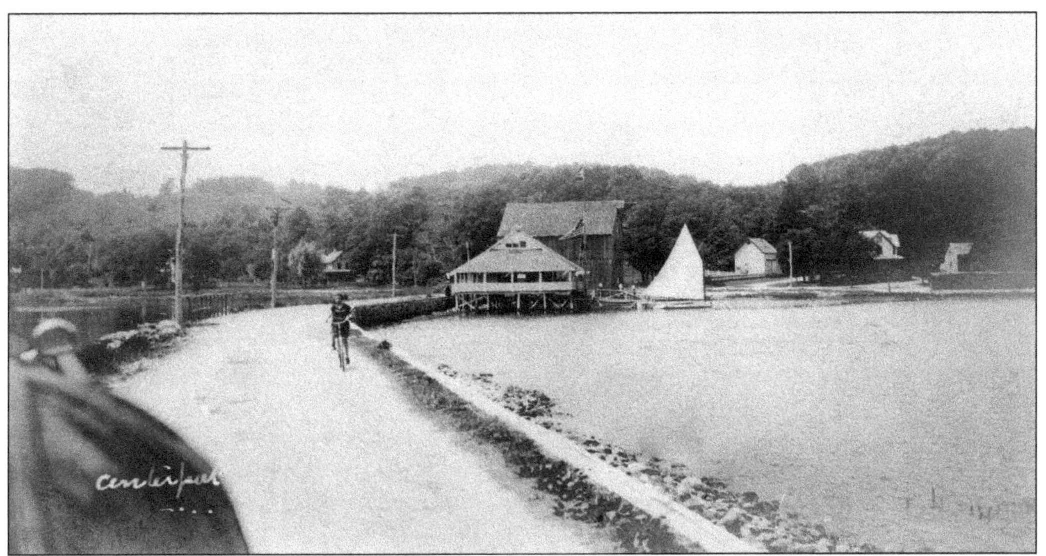

A young girl on a bicycle rides east over the mill dam. Note the absence of the post office on the south side of the causeway. The old yacht club building was built in 1906 and James J. Bunce built the post office over the mill pond in 1911, so this photograph was taken between those two dates. (Huntington Historical Society.)

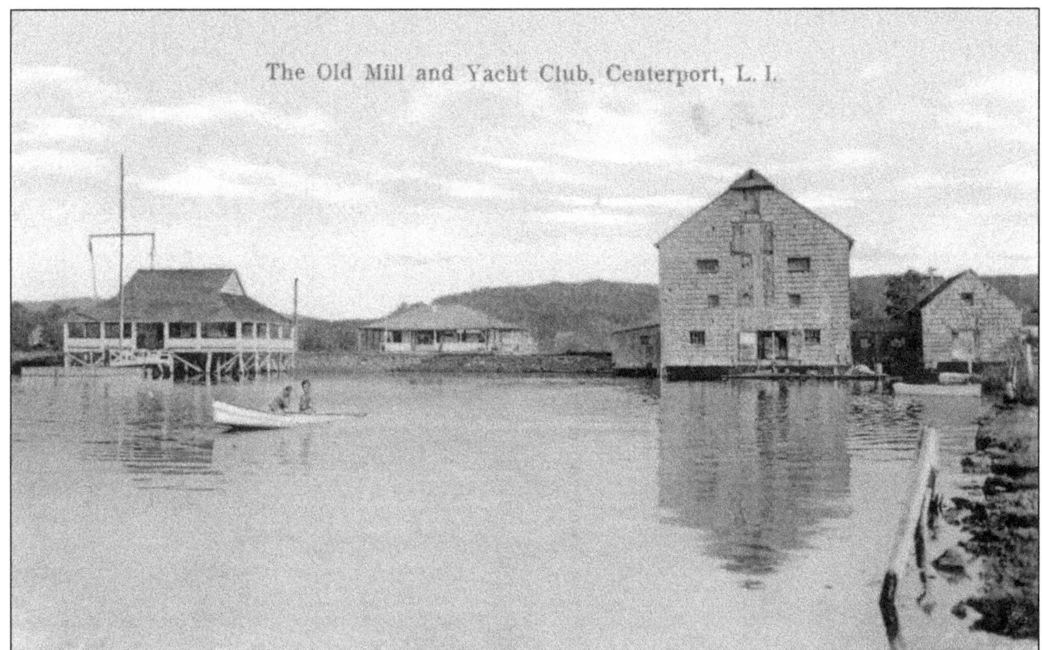

This postcard, published around 1910 by James Bunce, provides a closeup view of the three principal buildings in Centerport's commercial center. From left to right are the Centerport Yacht Club, James Bunce's store and post office, and the 18th-century mill.

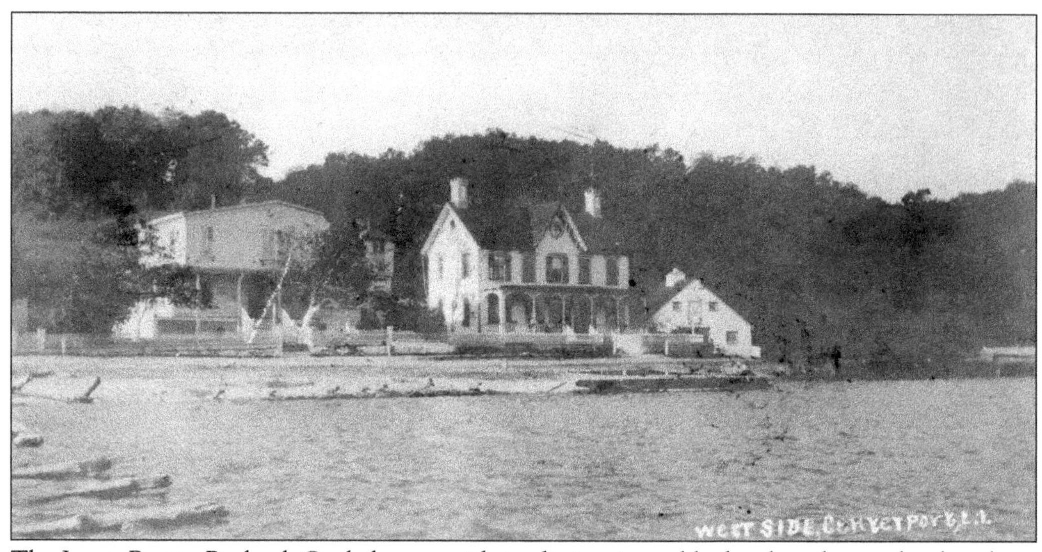

The Jarvis-Beatty-Rzehack-Coyle house, with its distinctive gable, has long been a landmark on the west side of the harbor. It is pictured with its barns and outbuildings around 1909. (William Townsend Perks.)

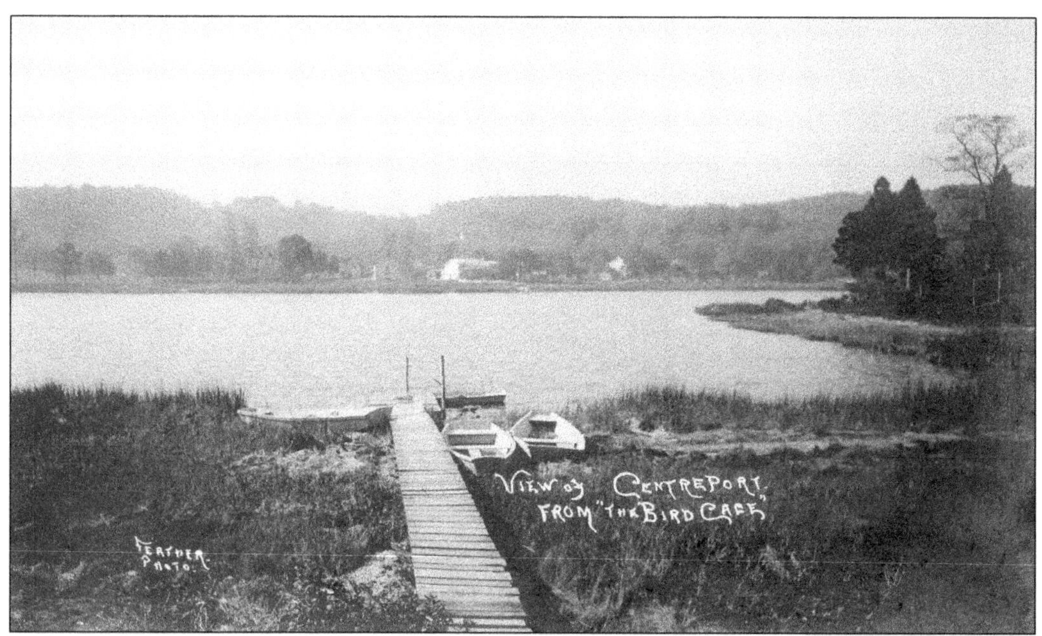

"View of Centerport from 'the Bird Cage' " is the title of this photograph by local photographer R.S. Feather. Taken from the pond shore of a house on Prospect Road, it shows a walkway over the marsh to the dock. Four small boats are in the foreground, and the Methodist Episcopal church is visible across the millpond.

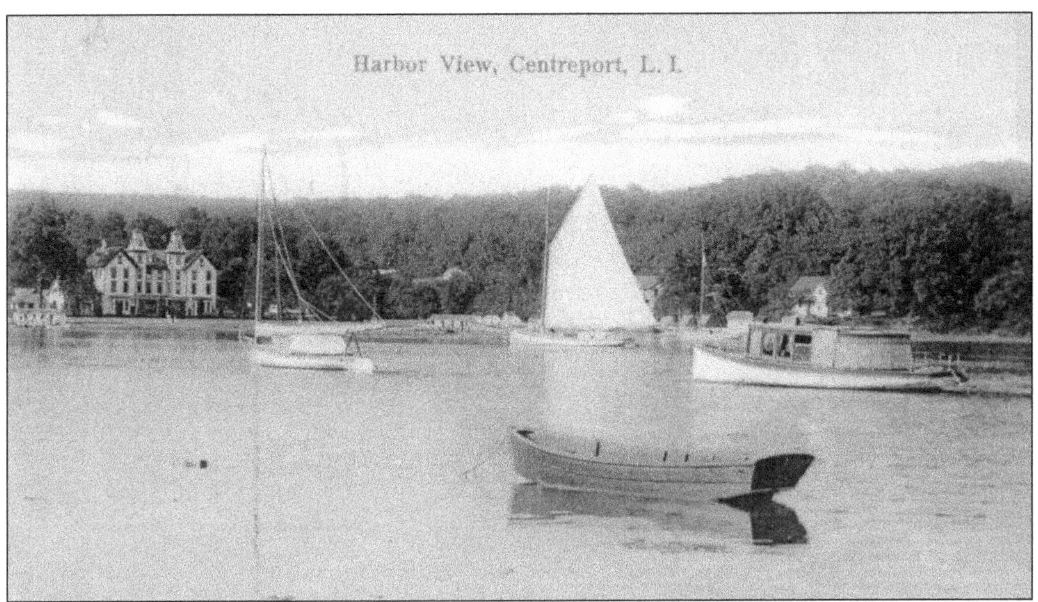

This postcard was published by James Bunce around 1915. At that time, small sailboats and rowing boats crowded the upper harbor.

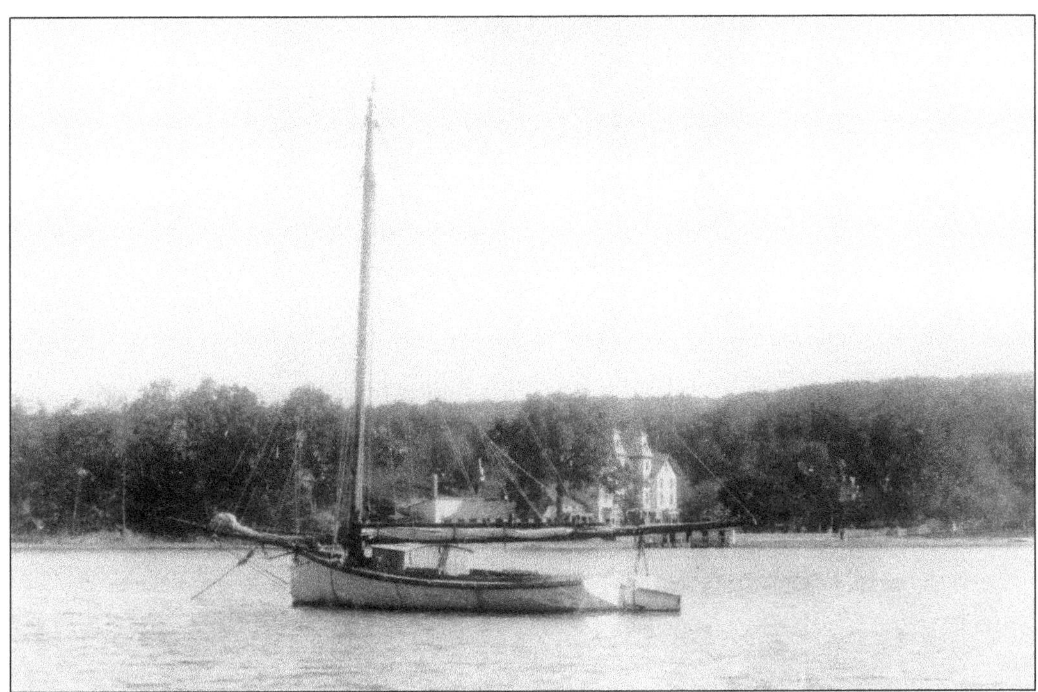
The catboat *Dame Trot* was owned by Capt. Joseph Scudder and anchored in front of his house on the upper west side of the harbor around 1906. Captain Scudder's sons John, George, and J. Whitney acted as his crew. (William Townsend Perks.)

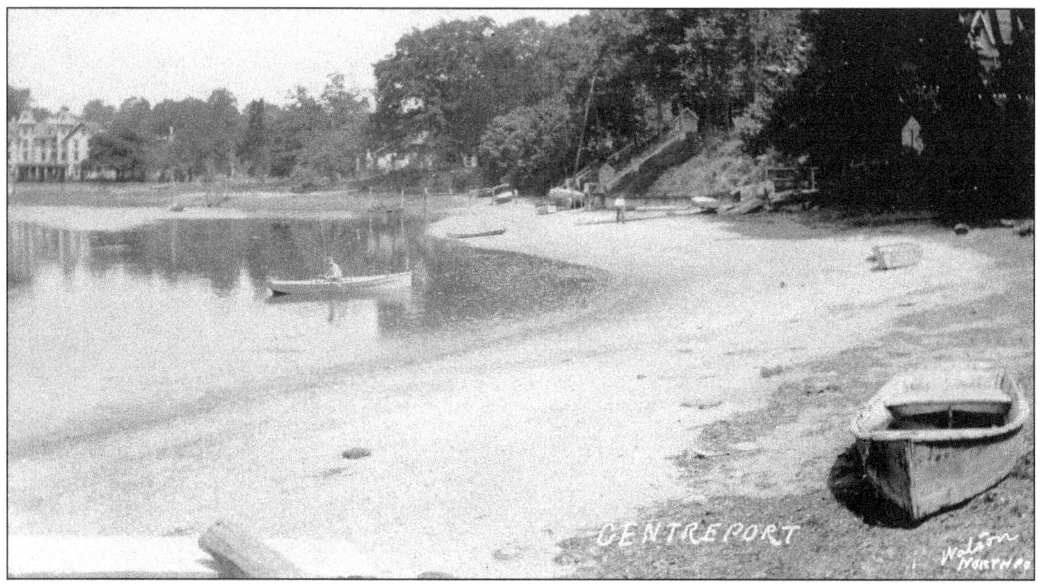

This is a view of the eastern shoreline of the harbor looking north toward Camp Alvernia. A close examination reveals several rowboats, a small sloop, and a motor launch. Almost every household in Centerport owned at least one boat.

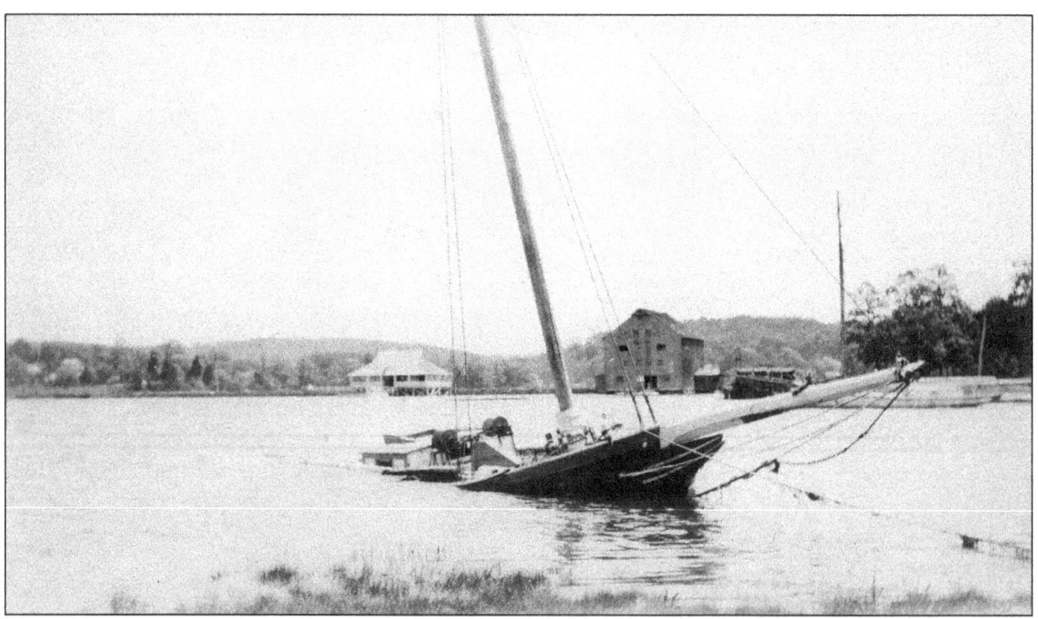

A derelict oyster sloop languishes near the shore of the upper harbor. In the first quarter of the 20th century, as the schooner trade and the oyster fisheries declined, the harbor was filled with more and more pleasure craft. (Huntington Historical Society.)

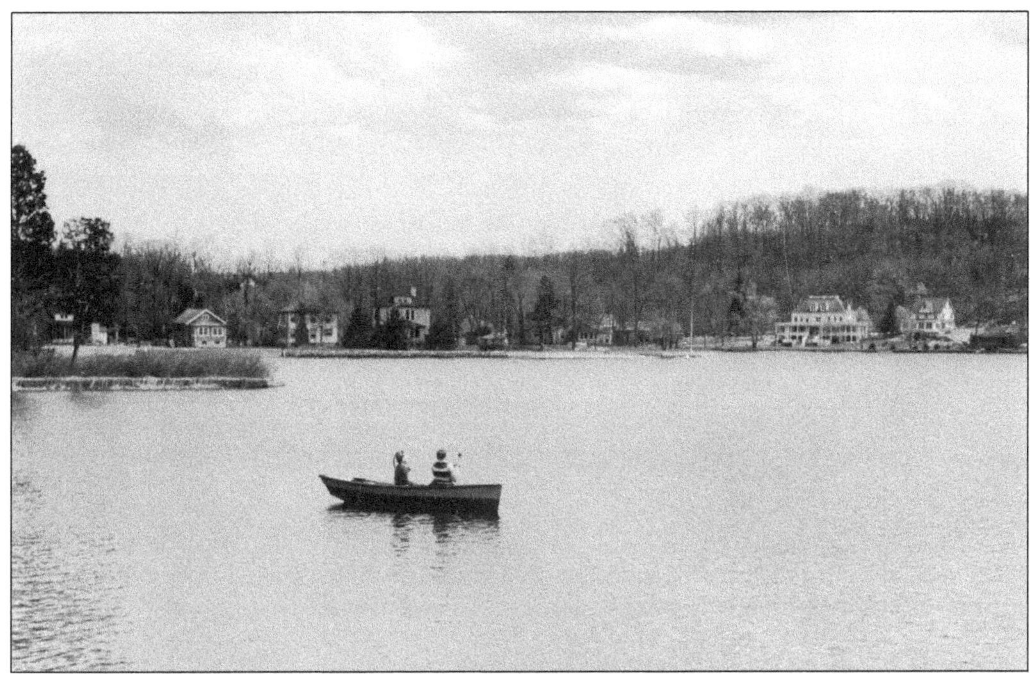

Here, two young people in a boat are engaging in a popular Centerport pastime at the millpond: fishing. It is interesting to compare the scenery in the background of this 1930s photograph by Robert Stone with the same view today. (Huntington Historical Society.)

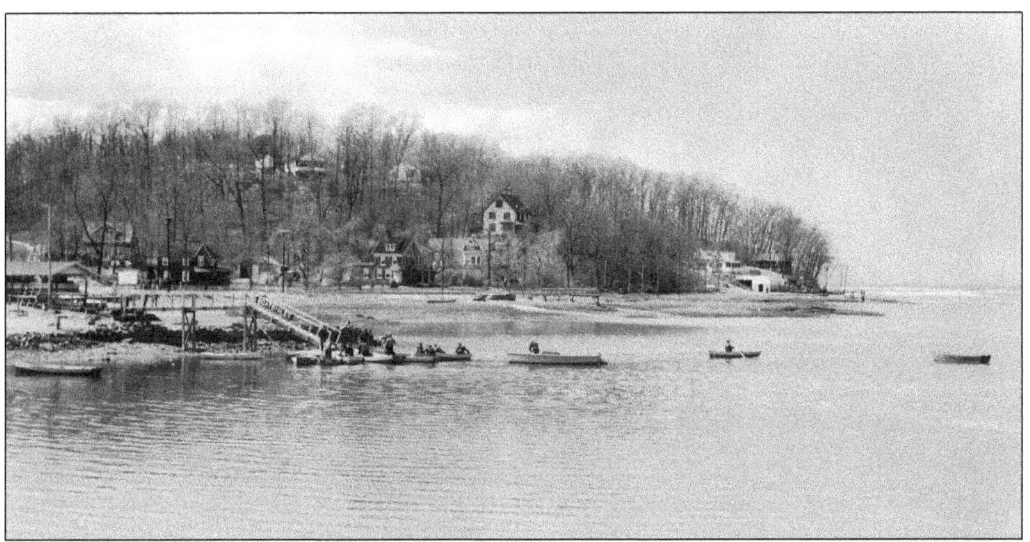

This 1939 photograph of the boatyard dock and the small boats in the upper harbor was taken by Robert Stone. These boats are different from their ancestors and their descendants, but boating activity in the harbor remains constant. (Huntington Historical Society.)

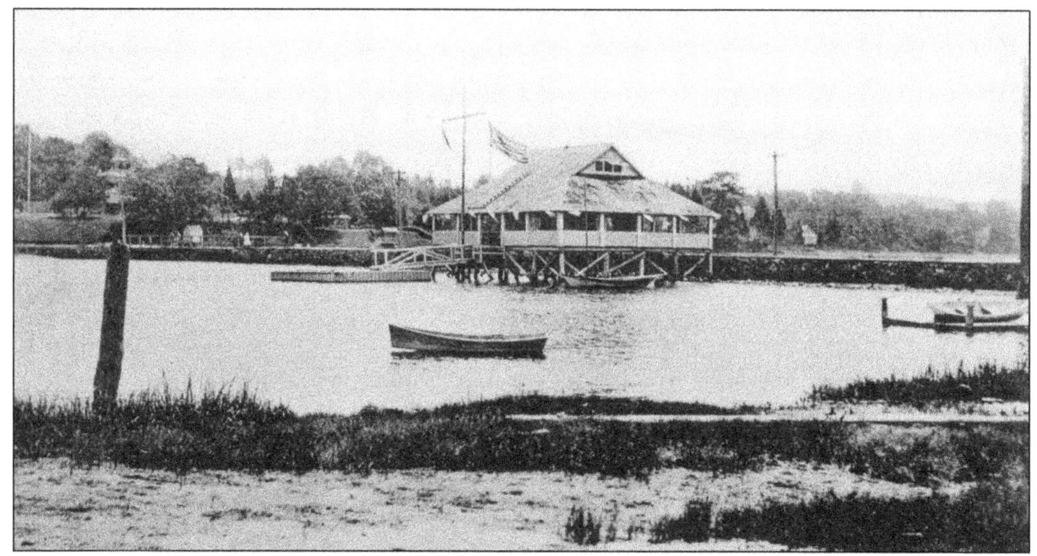

The Centerport Yacht Club was founded in 1906 by a group of local men. The first officers were George Swope (who later changed his surname to Rice), commodore; George Rinhart, vice commodore; F.P. Burt, treasurer; and Charles Whitney, secretary. Members included a virtual who's who of Centerport: H.H. Denton, John J. Robinson, George Miller, L.L. Lockwood, Lyle Andrews, Ed Morbach, D.P. Morse, A.H. Morrell, A.W. Stewart, C.R. Van Iderstine, and Archie Hall. The building was erected on piers driven into the south end of the harbor, and the mill dam causeway of the float and ramp on the harbor side provided access. The 50-by-50-foot building was completed in time to open on July 4, 1906.

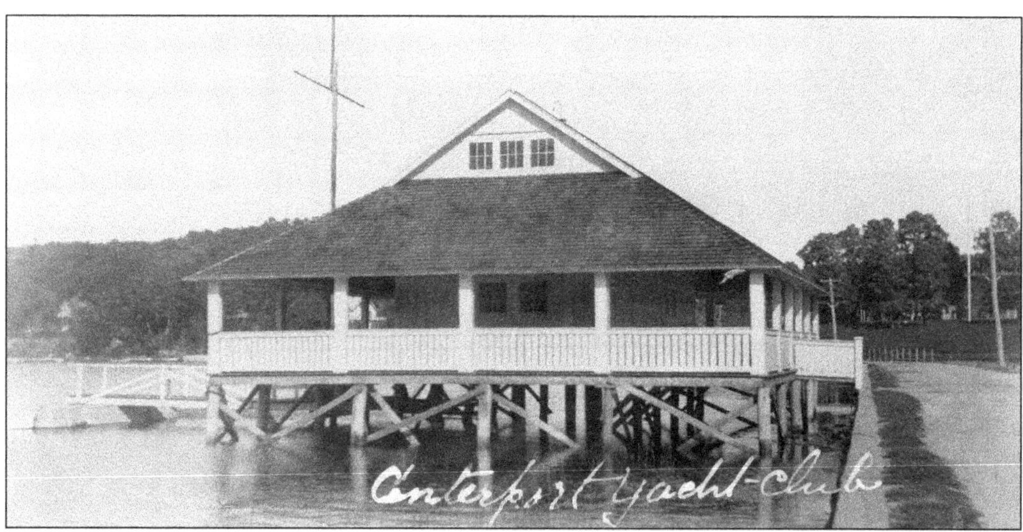

The yacht club provided music and dancing every Saturday night during the summer, and the sound of the music would carry up and down the harbor for all to hear. In 1908, the Centerport Yacht Club held a benefit called by the local newspaper "the theatrical event of Huntington's summer season." So many members of the yacht club who were associated with vaudeville offered their services that a playbill could not be announced in advance. (William Townsend Perks.)

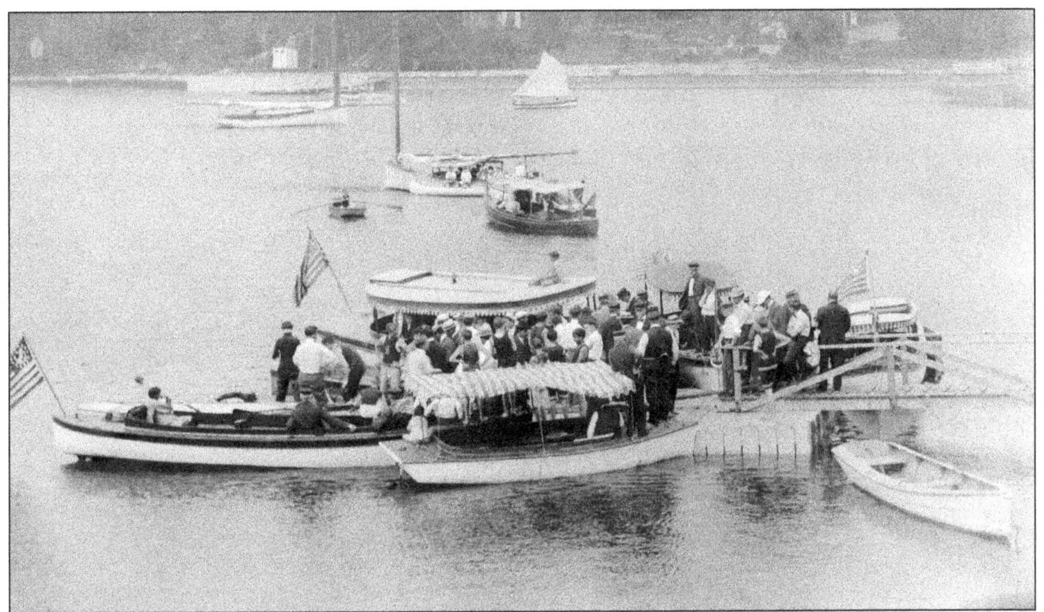

The Centerport Yacht Club's floating dock is a hub of activity during the club's Regatta Day in 1906. No less than five of the new and expensive motor launches of various sizes are shown in this picture. (Greenlawn-Centerport Historical Association.)

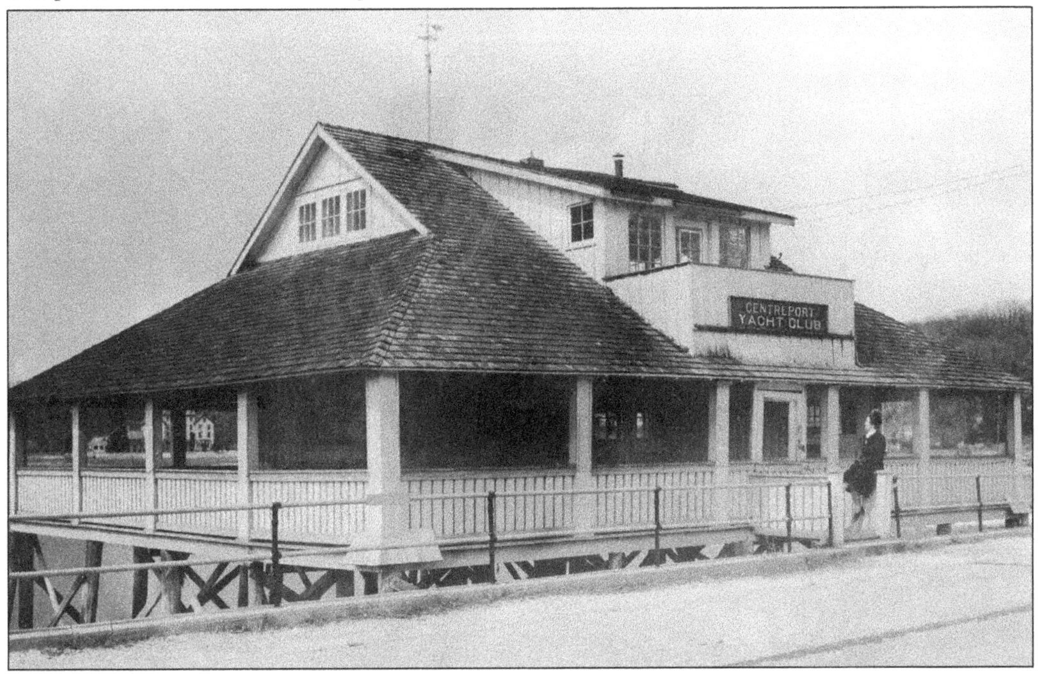

The club was active through World War I and the 1920s but succumbed to the Great Depression. The yacht club dispersed, and the building became vacant in 1931. Locals still used it for swimming and mooring boats. It was used by the community on some occasions, like the Ladies Aid rummage sale in June 1942. However, without maintenance, the building continued to deteriorate, and it was boarded up to prevent children from using it as a playground. It was destroyed by fire in October 1946. (Huntington Historical Society.)

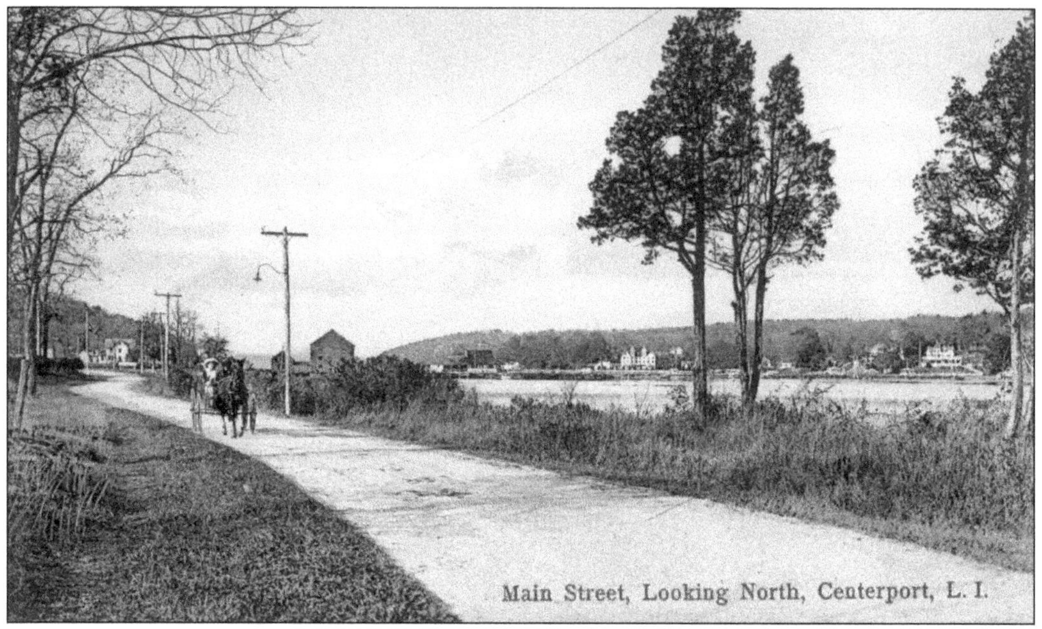

Centershore Road was known as Main Street when James Bunce published these cards about 1908. The Centerport Improvement Society had recently paved the road, but there is not much activity. Looking north (above), a horse and buggy with a woman onboard are approaching the photographer, while to the south (below), a cow is grazing by the millpond. The buildings on the pond are seen in the distance. At this time, Centerport had about 450 residents, and there were 17 telephones.

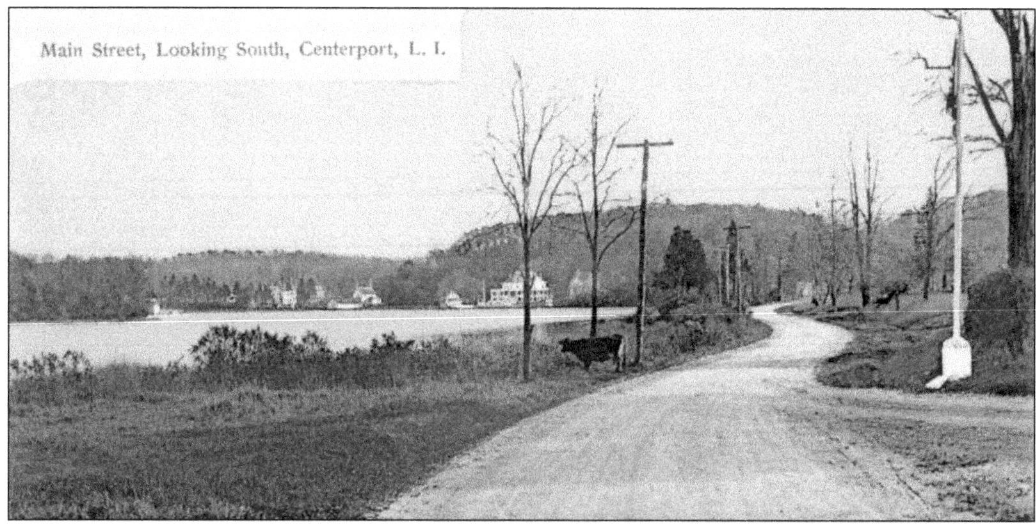

Three

Foundations of Our Community

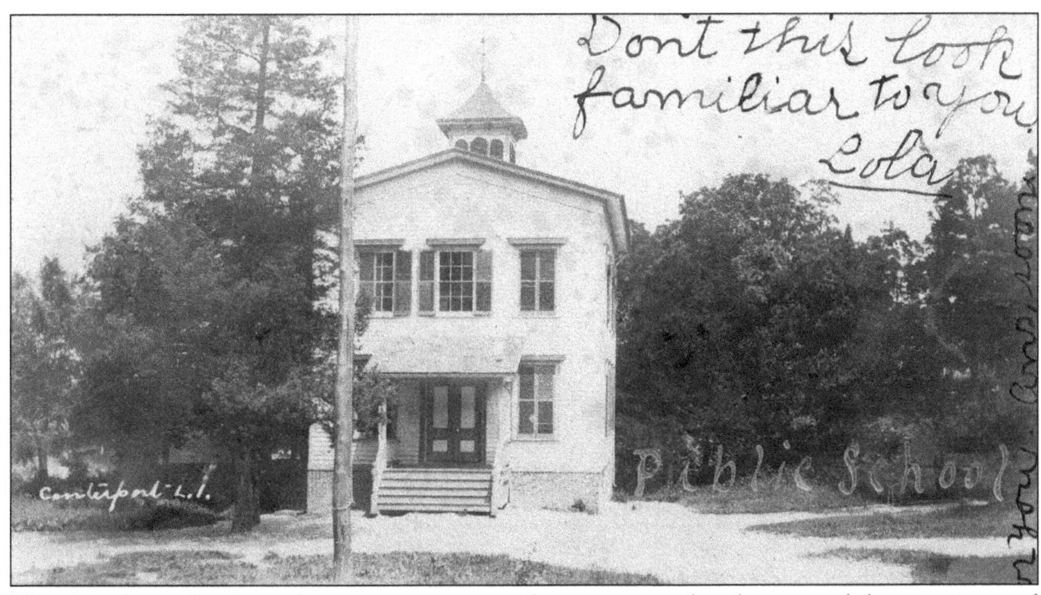

The churches, schools, and community services have supported and protected the town in good times and not-so-good times. They have brought residents together and encouraged everyone to work for the common good. (Greenlawn-Centerport Historical Association.)

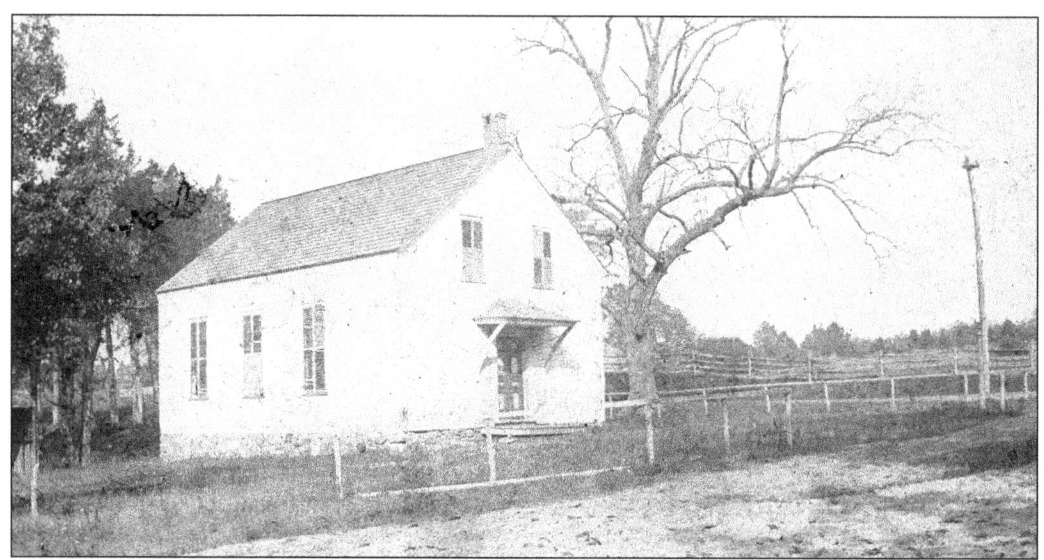

Methodist circuit riders visited Centerport before the Revolutionary War and established a class led by Nathaniel Bunce, but it was short-lived. Circuit preachers returned on a regular basis after the conflict ended. In 1806, a more permanent class was formed at the home of Joseph Higbie. That same year, a camp meeting was held in the area known as Kelsey's Woods, which is now the Eastbrook development. The Methodist congregation grew to more than 70 members by about 1840, when the Presbyterian and Methodist residents of Centerport petitioned the Huntington Town Board for land to build a Union church for the use of both societies and to be "open and free for all denominations of Christians in good standing in society." This church was built soon after and used until it was replaced in 1901. The large black walnut tree at right was taken down by the town highway department in 2019. (Huntington Historical Society.)

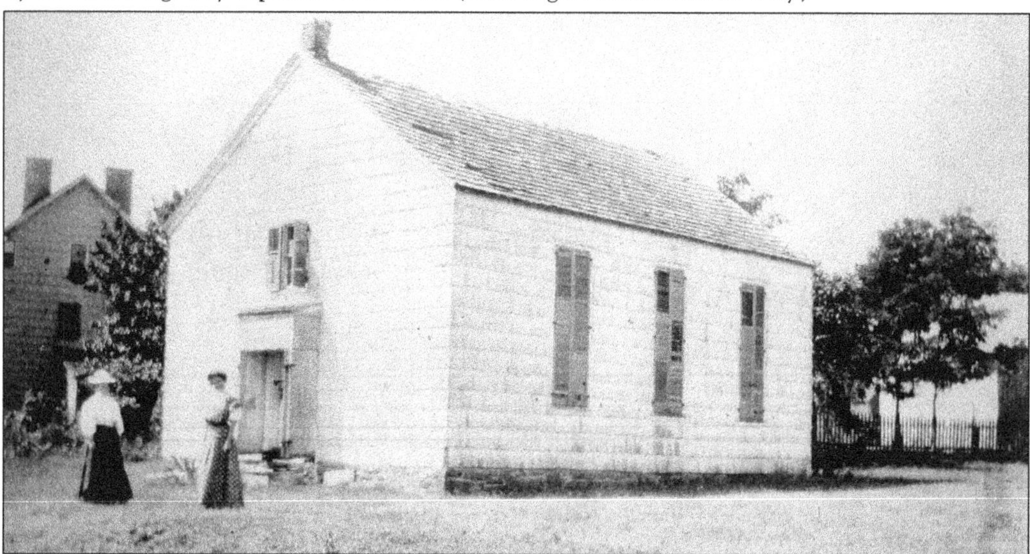

This Methodist church was erected at Woodbine Avenue and Washington Street in Northport about 1833. When the Northport congregation decided to build a new church 20 years later, the building was offered to Centerport. A group of Methodist residents participated in a fund drive, and the old church was moved to the west side of the millpond on land donated by William Titus and others. Trustees were elected, and the Centerport Methodist Episcopal Church was established.

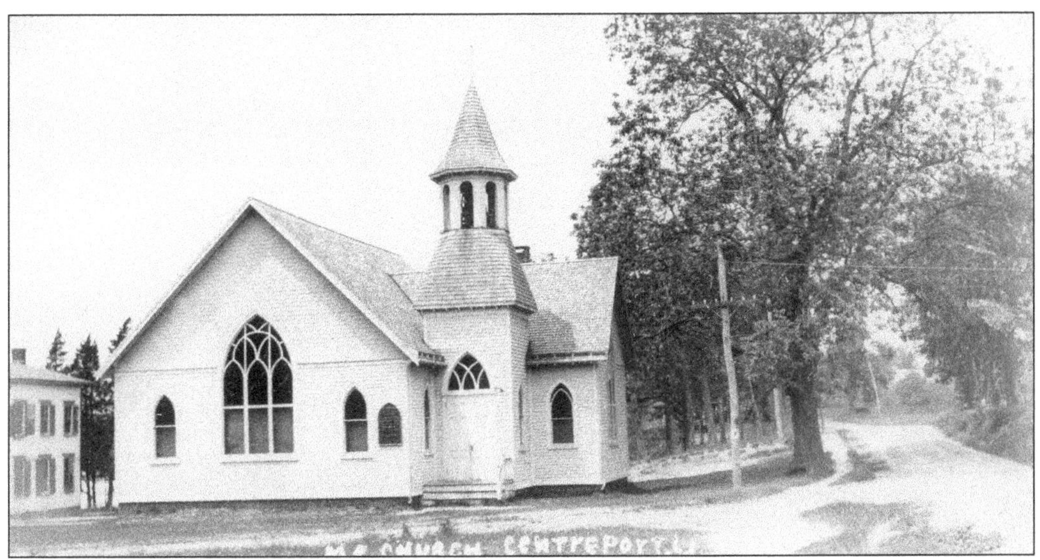

Centerport's two churches, Methodist Protestant and Methodist Episcopal, existed less than a half-mile apart until 1900. On August 21 of that year, the people of the two societies united into the Centerport Methodist Episcopal Church, and the joint congregations elected nine new trustees. It was decided to build a new church on the site of the Methodist Protestant church. The exchange of Methodist church buildings with Northport was completed when the old Union church building was moved to the rear of Woodbine Avenue at Main Street adjacent to Mill's Sail Loft.

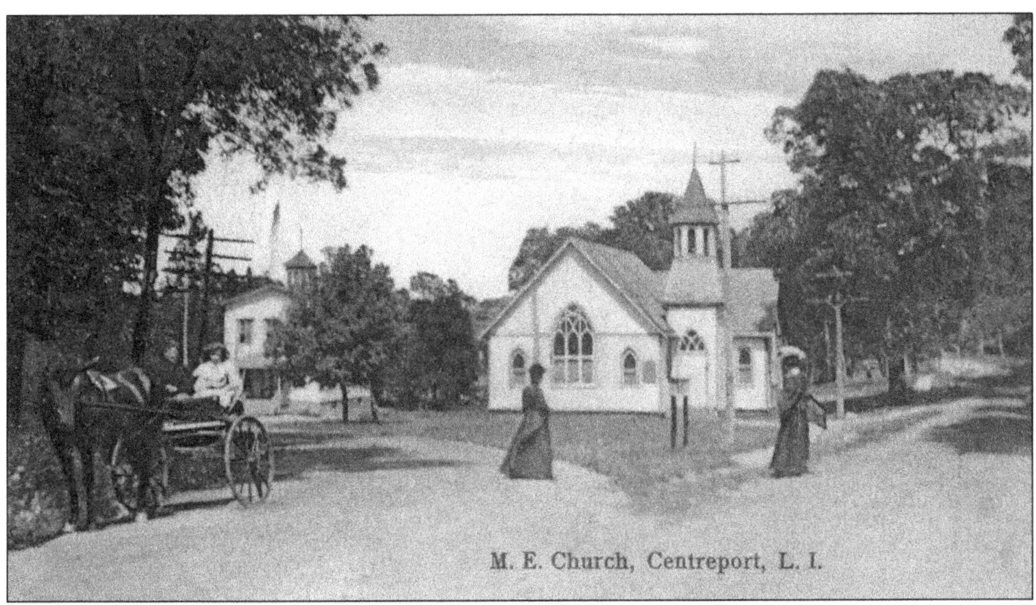

Local builder and church member Theodore Sammis was the lowest bidder for the construction of the new church, with a bid of $2,333. He was awarded the contract on November 9, 1900, and the new church was dedicated on May 12, 1901. Thanks to financial support from the congregation and the community as well as generous donations from Charles Burling and Joseph Morrell, the building was free of debt.

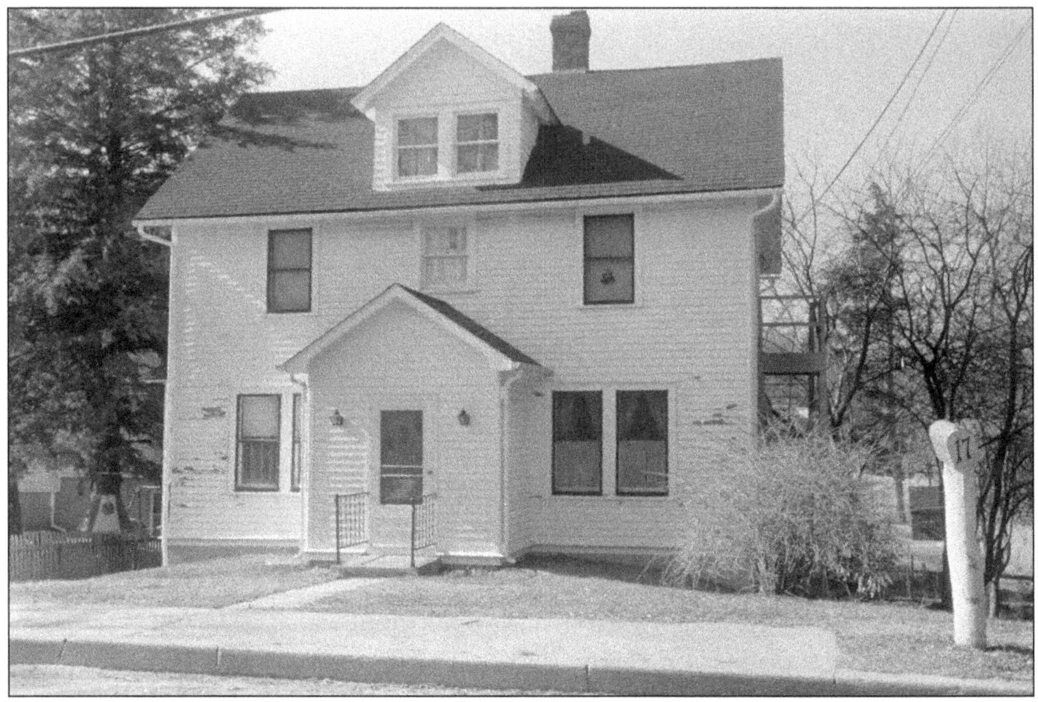

The parsonage was built behind the Methodist church in 1910, and was paid in full by 1914. William K. Vanderbilt II donated the landscaping, including a large evergreen tree in front of the church, and contributed generously toward the cost of the building. (Centerport United Methodist Church.)

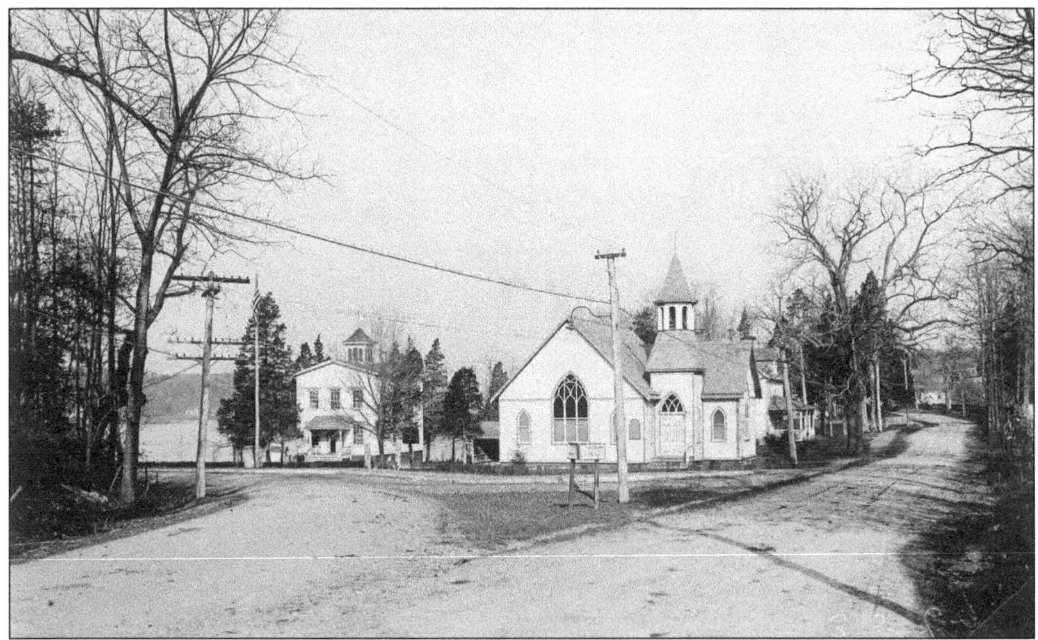

Here is Centerport's "square" about 1920; State Route 25A bends from right to left in the foreground, with Little Neck Road branching to the right. Neither road was paved at that time. The two-story building on the left is the second Centerport school, built during the 1860s, and on the right is the 1901 Methodist Episcopal Church.

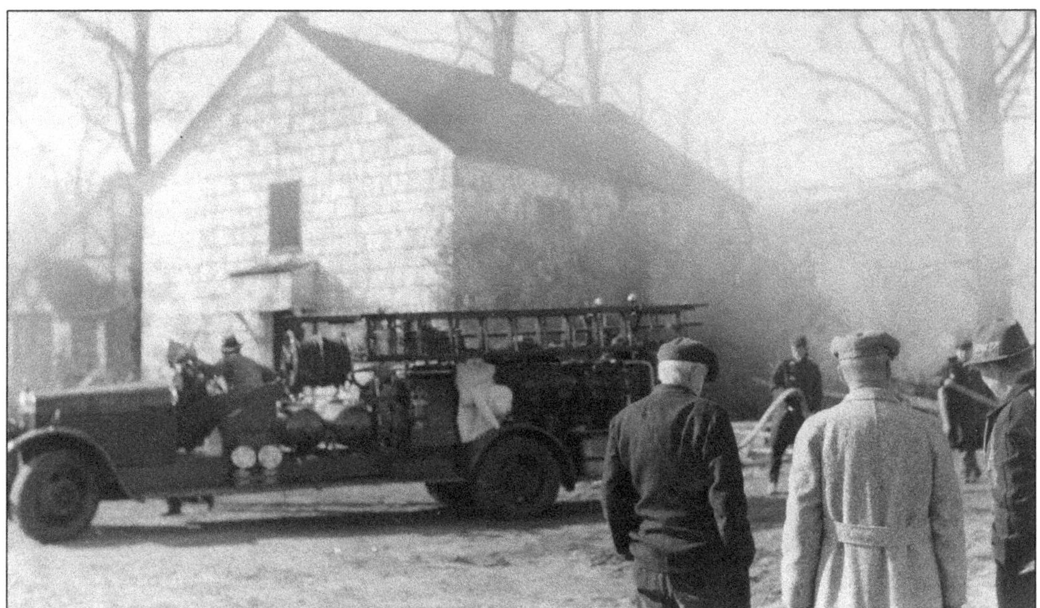

The former Methodist Episcopal Church on the millpond was used as a practice hall by the local vaudeville performers for the next two decades. In the fall of 1940, it was set on fire by sparks from the razing of the nearby Ward's Rest Inn. The Centerport Fire Department responded to the scene, but the building was heavily damaged and had to be demolished. (Greenlawn-Centerport Historical Association.)

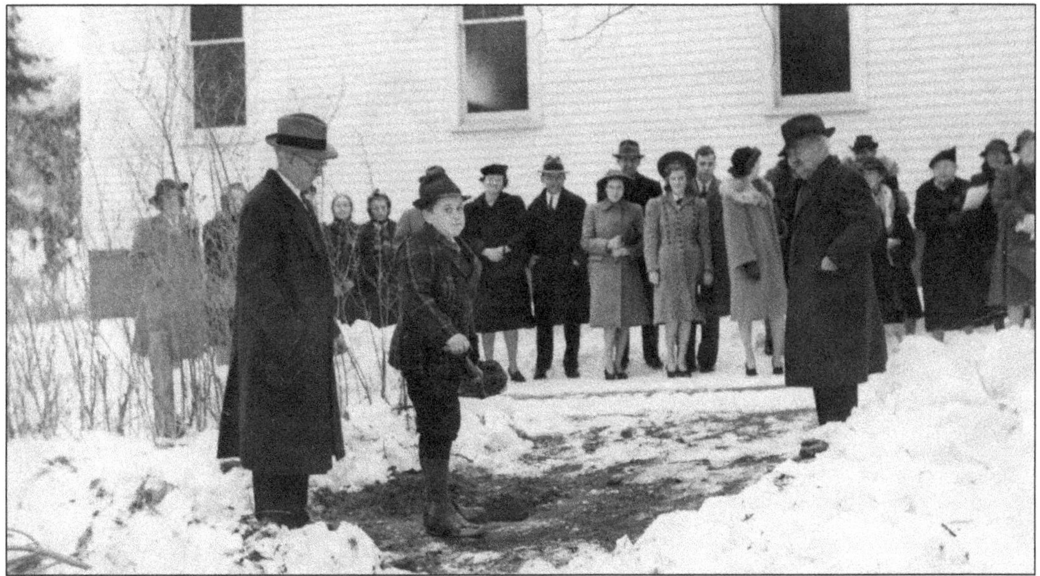

The congregation of the Methodist Episcopal Church grew significantly in the four decades after its construction. The church needed more space and local architect and church member James VanAlst donated his services to design a new parish house. The groundbreaking ceremony in this photograph took place on January 30, 1941. Pictured are Ken Swan, the youngest member of the congregation, breaking the ground, and to the left George Bunce, a church trustee and chair of the building committee who volunteered his time to supervise construction. (Greenlawn-Centerport Historical Association.)

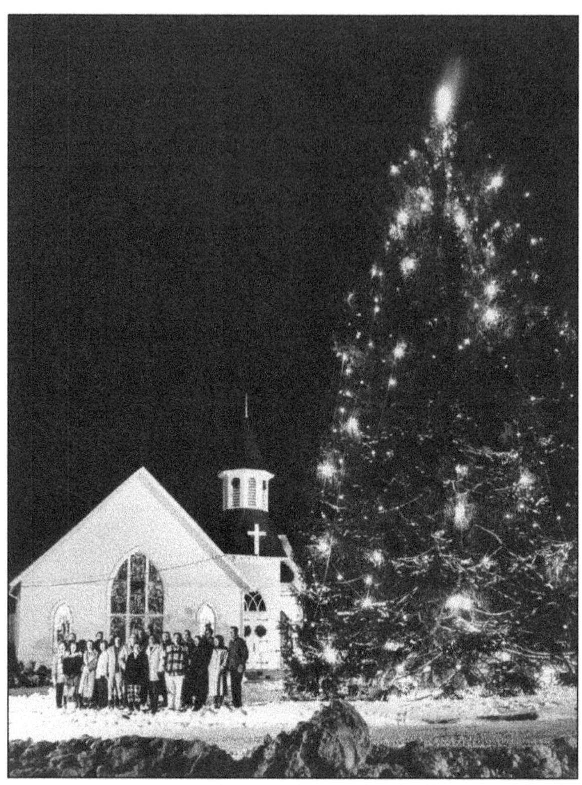

The first community Christmas tree lighting took place in 1922, and the annual holiday event continues to this day. The tree donated by Vanderbilt was used until it was destroyed by a hurricane. Its replacement is used to this day. (Photograph by Harvey Weber, Greenlawn-Centerport Historical Association.)

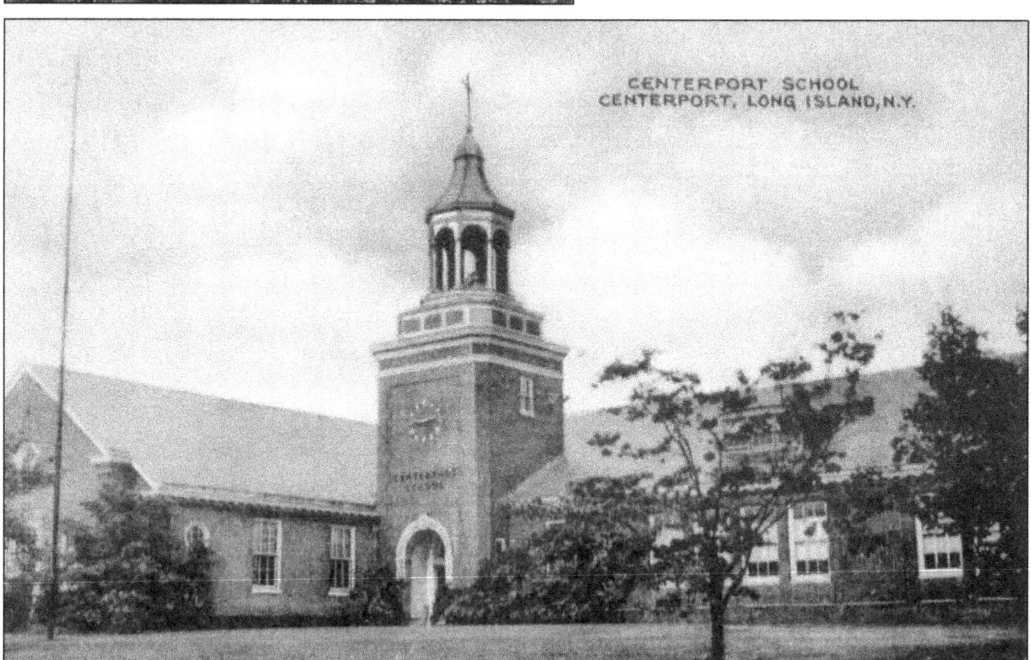

Additions and modifications to the Parish House/Sunday school were made during the 1960s, but the need for more space persisted. The situation was solved when the Harborfields School District closed the Centerport/Little Neck School and put it up for sale. On March 28, 1979, district residents voted to approve the sale of the Little Neck School to the Centerport Methodist Church.

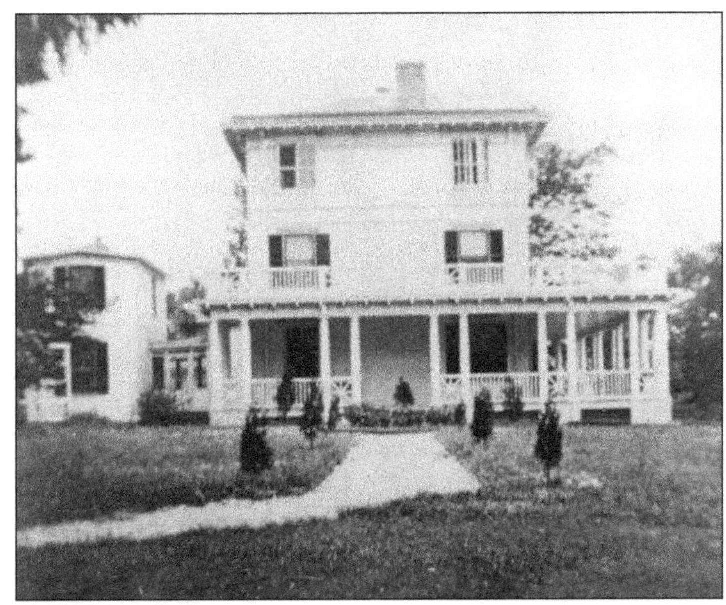

The Lowndes house, located on the millpond at the intersection of Mill Dam and Prospect Roads, was built about 1870 and operated for a time as a boardinghouse, accommodating 15 guests. Allison Lowndes was a lawyer. In the 1950s, the house belonged to Regina Brunswick, a parishioner of St. Philip Neri in Northport. The parish acquired the house for $1 in 1965. It is now the rectory of Our Lady Queen of Martyrs Church. (Greenlawn-Centerport Historical Association.)

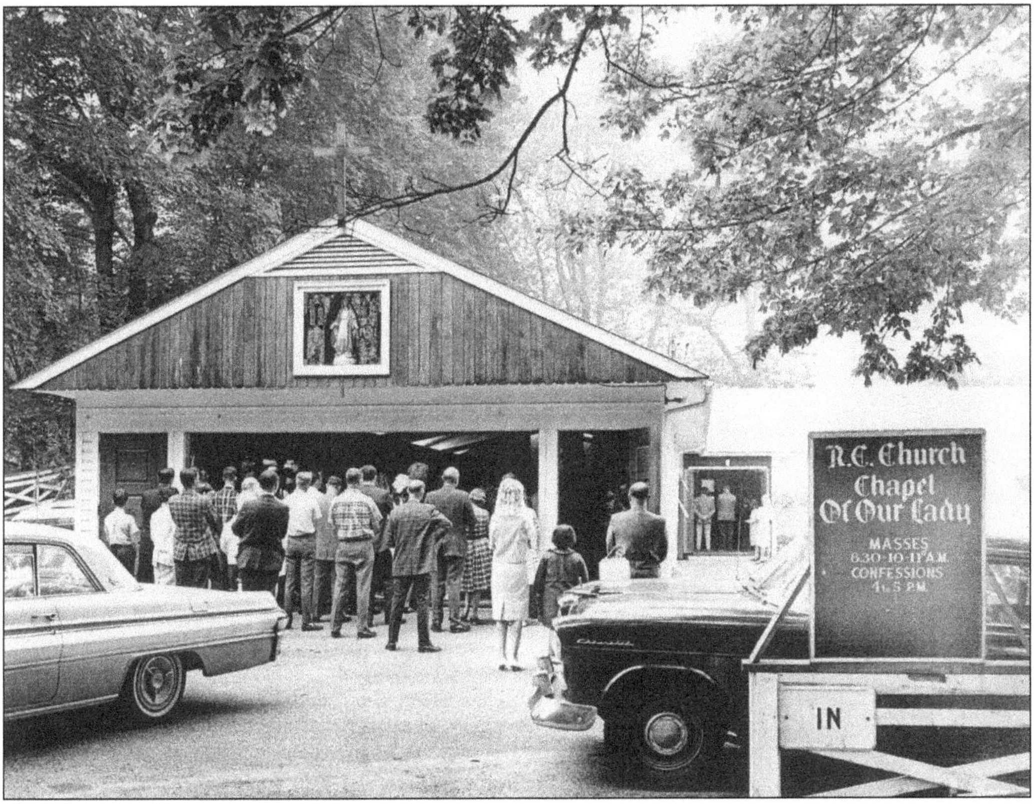

Before 1953, Centerport residents of the Catholic faith attended Mass with the Franciscan Brothers at Camp Alvernia or traveled west to St. Patrick's in Huntington or east to St. Philip Neri Church in Northport. In that year, Regina Brunswick donated her large boat garage, which was built in the 1920s, to St. Philip Neri for use as a chapel. St. Philip Neri established "Our Lady's Chapel" in the building. (Our Lady Queen of Martyrs Church.)

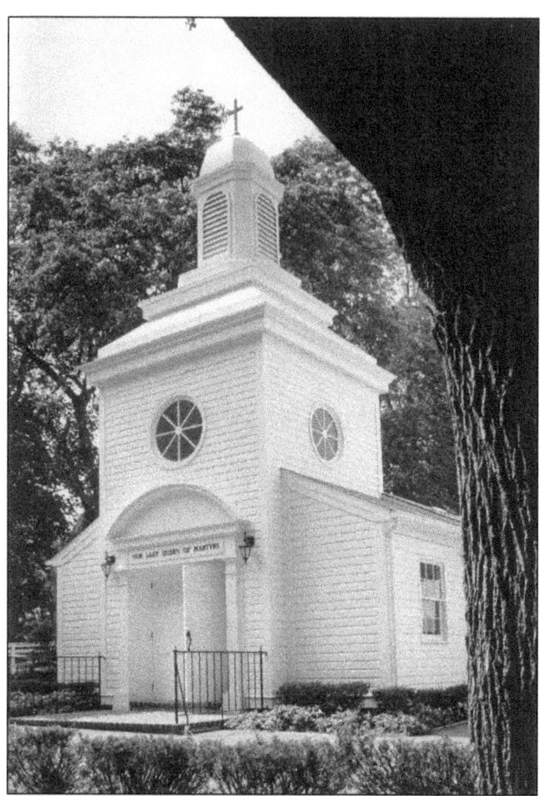

The parish grew, and in 1961, the boathouse was repaired and expanded. A new entrance with a tower and carillon were added. On June 18, 1966, the first Mass at Our Lady Queen of Martyrs was celebrated. Fr. James A. Green was chosen as the founding pastor. An entrance and steeple were added, and the building was used until 1985. A new building for Our Lady Queen of Martyrs was erected in 1985. Part of the old steeple can now be seen on the lawn of the former Lowndes house, now the parish rectory. (Photograph by Harvey Weber, Greenlawn-Centerport Historical Association.)

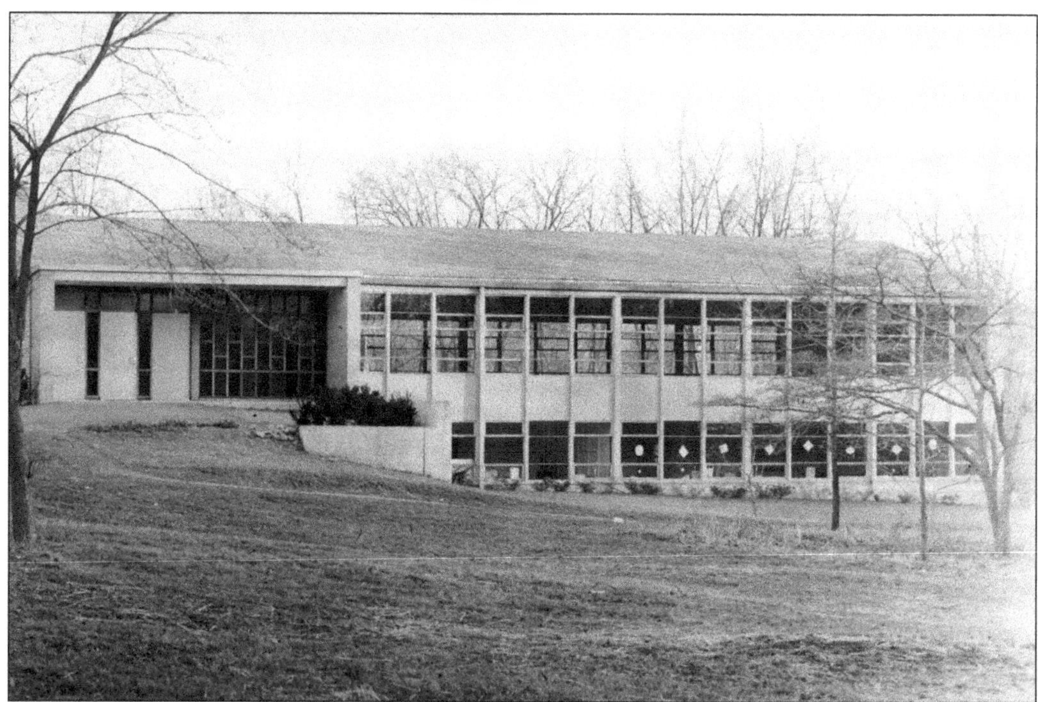

The first Congregational church was built on Washington Drive in the 1950s, designed by James Van Alst. A modern sanctuary (not pictured) was added in 1965. (Huntington Historical Society.)

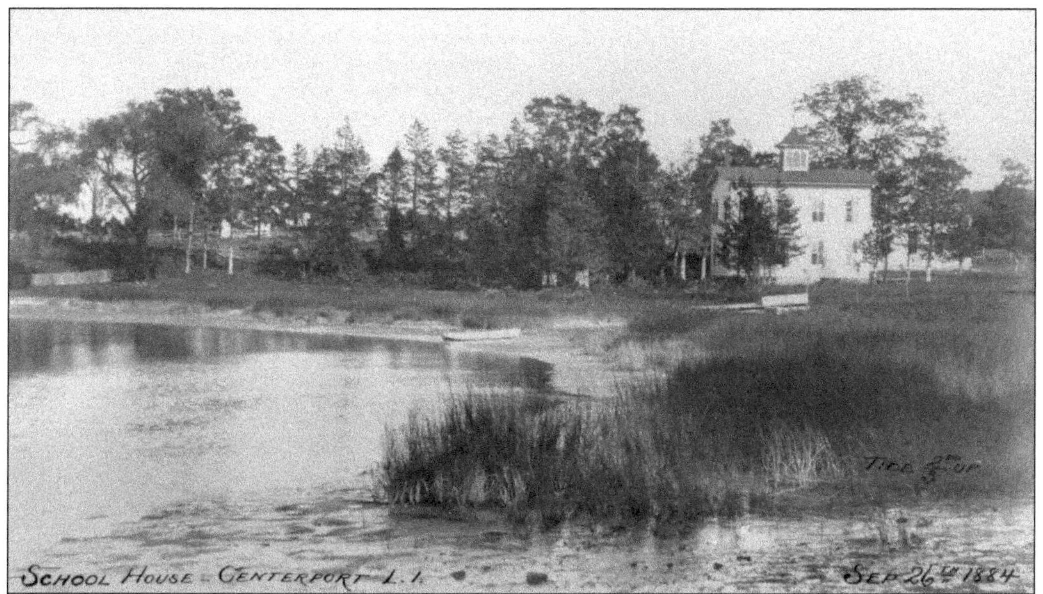

Although no photograph exists of Centerport's first school, it was reported to have 54 pupils enrolled in 1836. Flora Velsor was the teacher in 1861 when the building was sold and a new school was constructed. William H. Deming took this bucolic photograph of the second Centerport School and the south end of the millpond in 1884. (Queens Borough Public Library, Archives, Illustrations Collection–Centerport.)

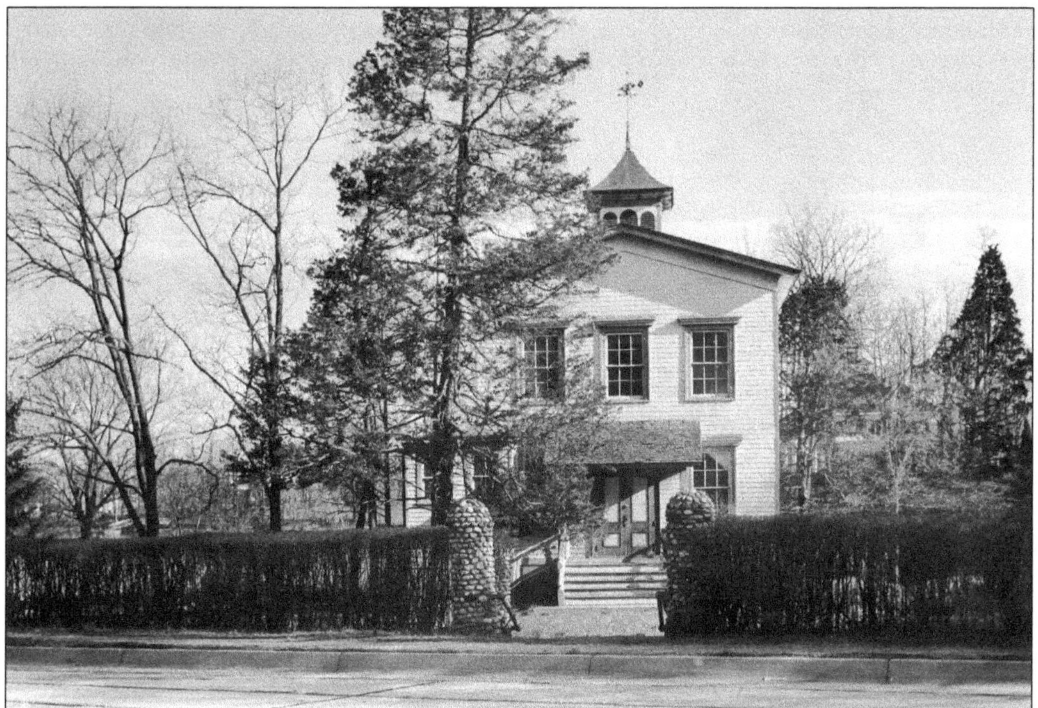

Unlike most school buildings on Long Island at the time, the new school's two classrooms were on two floors, with grades one to four on the lower floor and five to eight above. (Huntington Historical Society.)

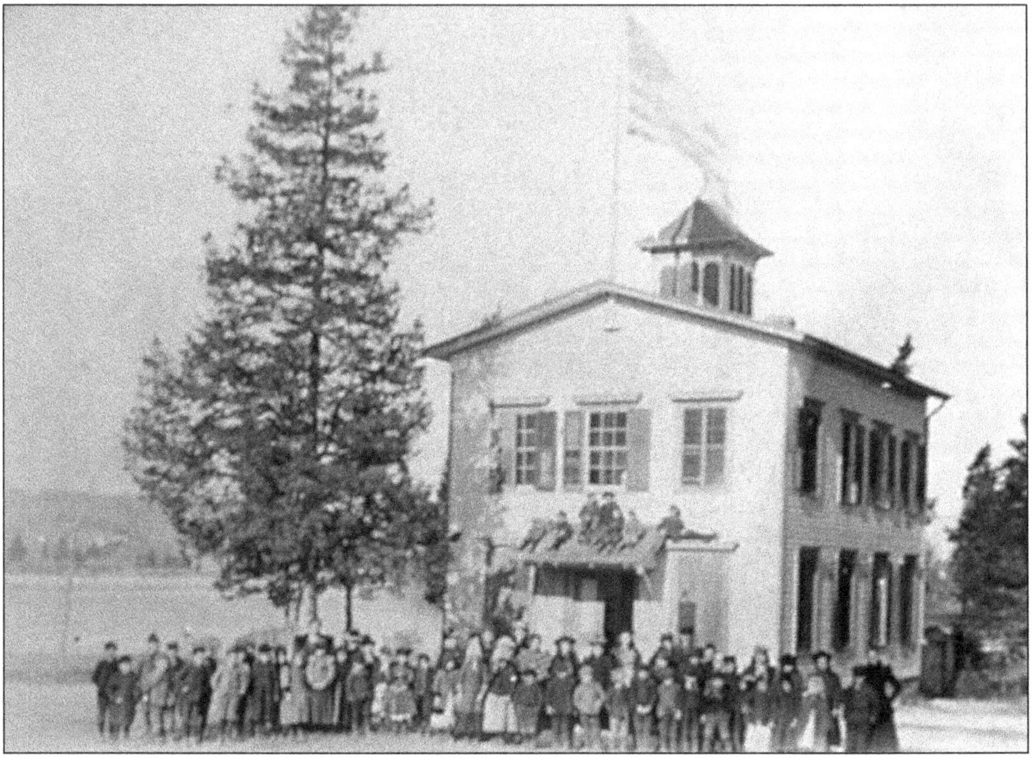

This image of the school and its students includes the entire student body. There is no historical record as to why some of the boys were allowed to climb on the roof. (Greenlawn-Centerport Historical Association.)

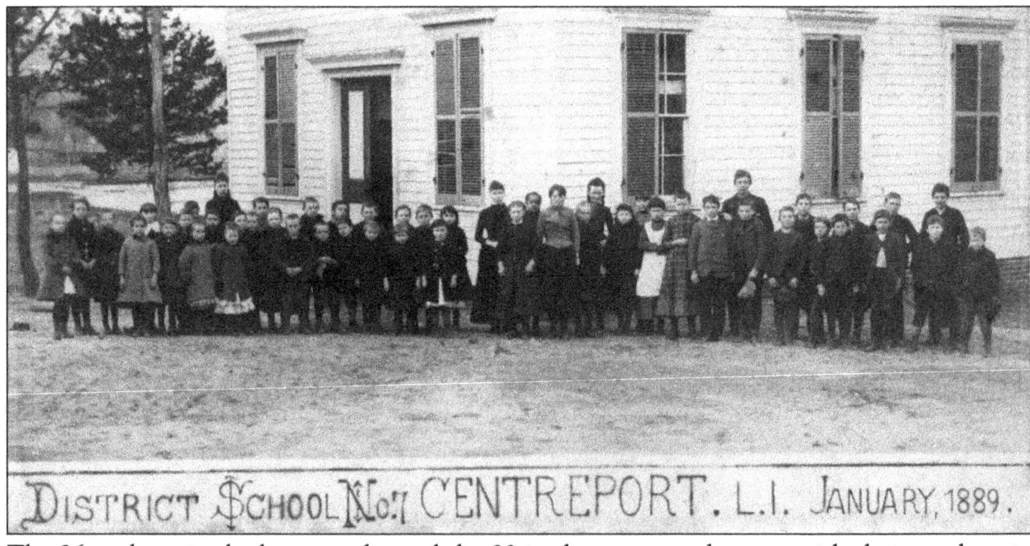

The 26 students in the lower grades and the 20 in the upper grades pose with their teachers in this photograph. Taken in January 1889, it shows the south and east sides of the building.

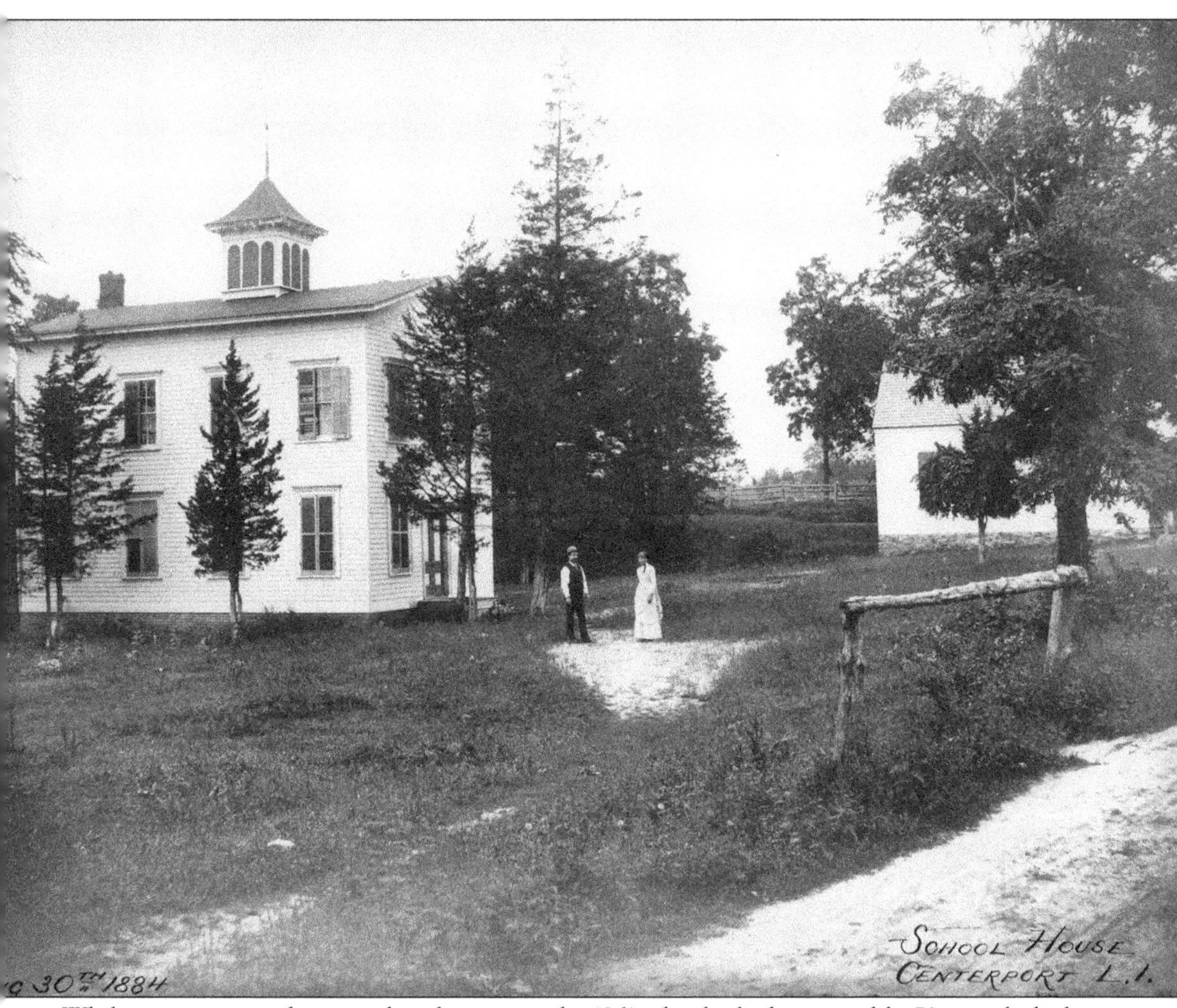

While picturesque and very modern for its time, the 1861 school, which operated for 70 years, lacked modern plumbing and heating, and was overcrowded. Neighboring Greenlawn had constructed a new school in 1924. The Centerport Board of Education chose four prospective locations for a new school and a site on Little Neck Road was ultimately chosen by public referendum. The new school building was completed in 1933, and a few years later, this building was demolished and the land divided between the Centerport Fire Department and the Centerport Methodist Church. This photograph is by William Deming. (Queens Borough Public Library, Archives, Illustrations Collection–Centerport.)

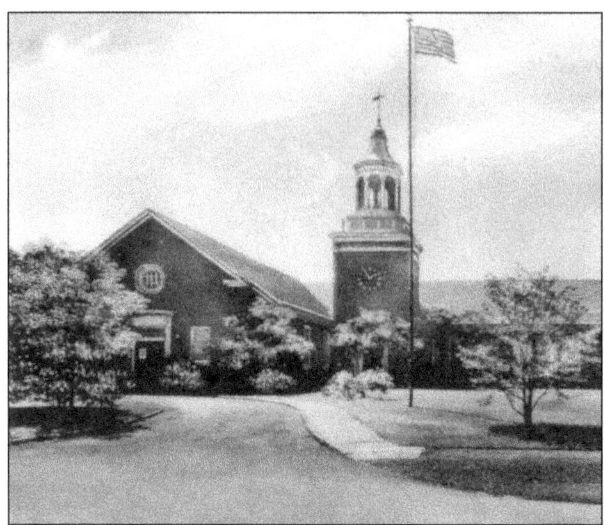

Ground was broken for the construction of Centerport's new four-room school late in January 1933. The Little Neck School building was completed before the following school year and dedicated on October 6, 1933. The architect was James Van Alst, a World War I veteran who studied at Pratt Institute in Brooklyn, the University of Pennsylvania, and Harvard University. His commissions included many public works projects throughout Long Island. He died in 1970. Contrary to community legend, William K. Vanderbilt II made no financial contributions to this project.

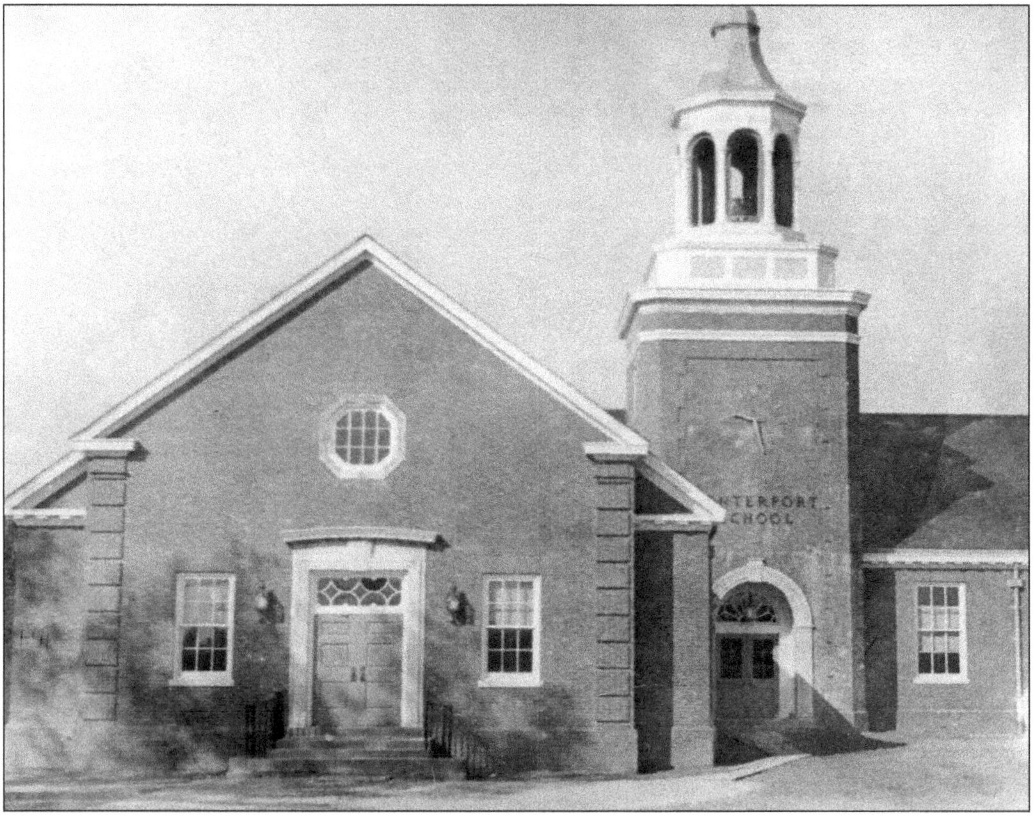

The new school building included four classrooms, a large auditorium that could also be used as a gymnasium, large bathrooms, space for a clinic, and a library. The bell from the 1861 school was installed in a four-story bell tower. The residents approved the construction of a new wing for the school in July 1947, and it was dedicated in September 1949. The Centerport School had grown to include eight classrooms, a kindergarten room, a 150-seat cafeteria with a modern kitchen, assembly room/gymnasium with stage, clinic, library, teacher's room, and an office for the principal. (Centerport United Methodist Church.)

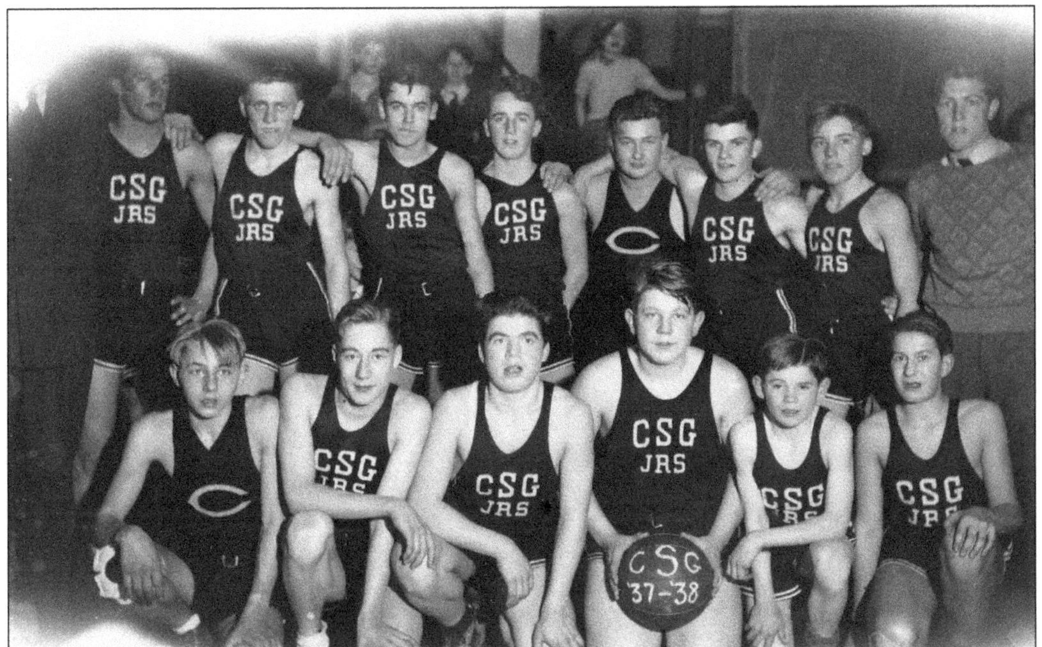

The Centerport School was the home court for this Centerport Sea Gulls basketball team in 1937–1938. The junior team pictured here won the Suffolk County Boys Association first-place trophy in March 1938. (Huntington Historical Society.)

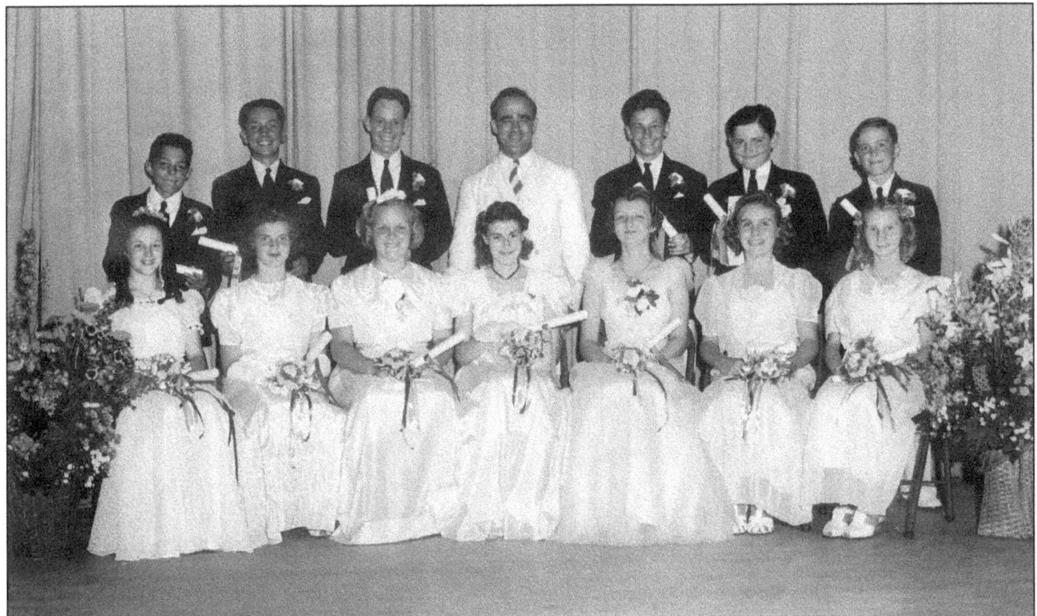

The graduating class of the Centerport School is seen here around 1939. The Centerport and Greenlawn School Districts were combined to form the Harborfields School District in 1956. As new families moved into the district, all of the school buildings became overcrowded. Centerport School closed in 1976, and the students and faculty transferred to the new T.J. Lahey School in Greenlawn. The Centerport United Methodist Church purchased the building and grounds in 1979. (Huntington Historical Society.)

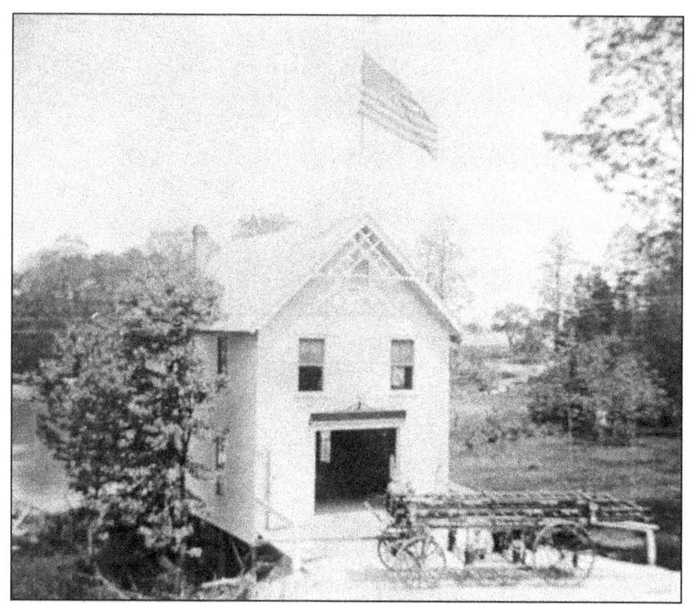

The first meeting of the men who created the Centerport Fire Department was held in the Centerport School on September 7, 1898, and the department was incorporated in November that year. Funds were raised, and lumber ordered. As many of the volunteer firemen were carpenters, construction of the new Centerport firehouse was completed by December 1898. A Mr. Gilderstone of Halesite donated an American flag to the department, and a used hand engine was purchased in 1902. (Greenlawn-Centerport Historical Association.)

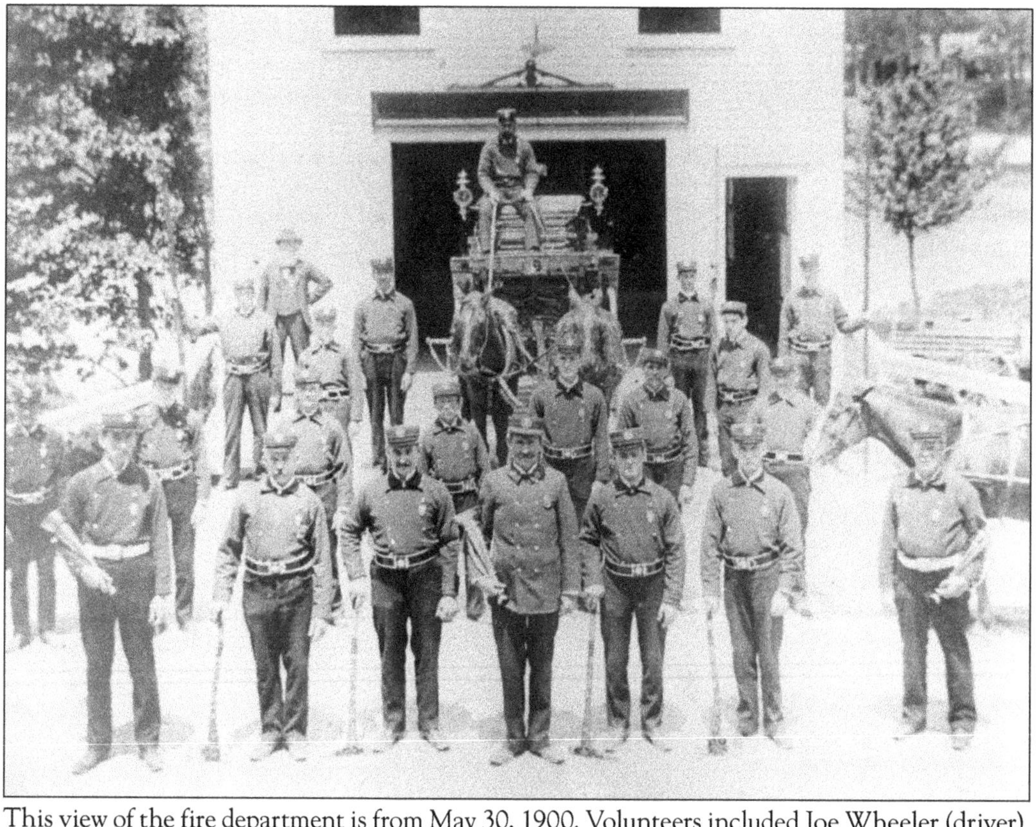

This view of the fire department is from May 30, 1900. Volunteers included Joe Wheeler (driver), William Benham, W.L. Nichols, Frank Morris, Frank Sonnee, Norm Baylis, Ed Soper, Platt Monfort, "Lone" Mott, "El" Bunce, Ed Mott, Tom Stein, Fred Chalmers, Charles Higbie, Frank Zuchowski, Frank Suydam, William Mott, Walter Rowland, Chief H. Denton, Milt Rowland, Jim Howard, and John Bunce. (Greenlawn-Centerport Historical Association.)

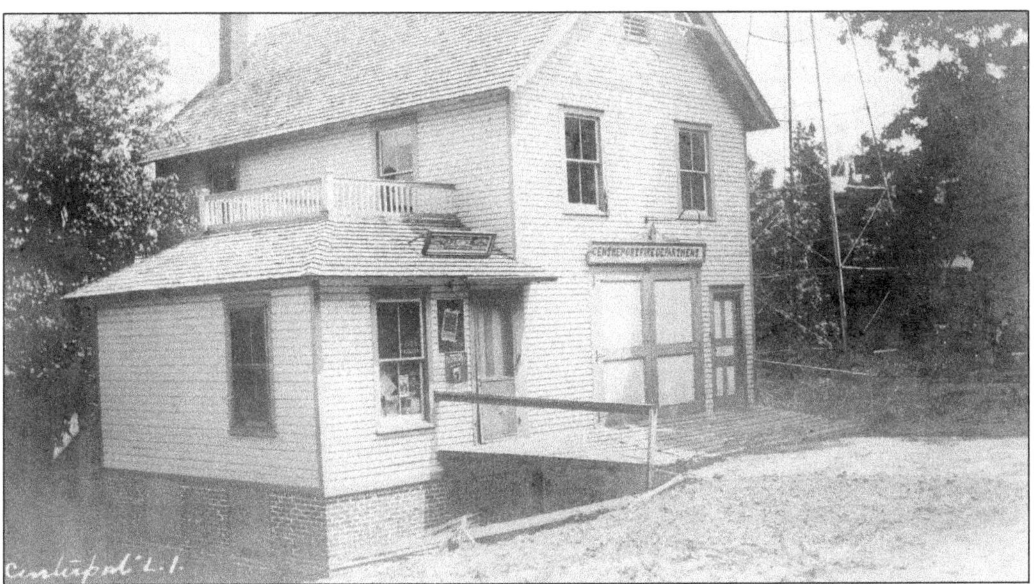

James J. Bunce requested permission to install a barber's chair in the truck house in 1902. Two years later, the members built an addition onto the west side of the firehouse and sublet it to him.

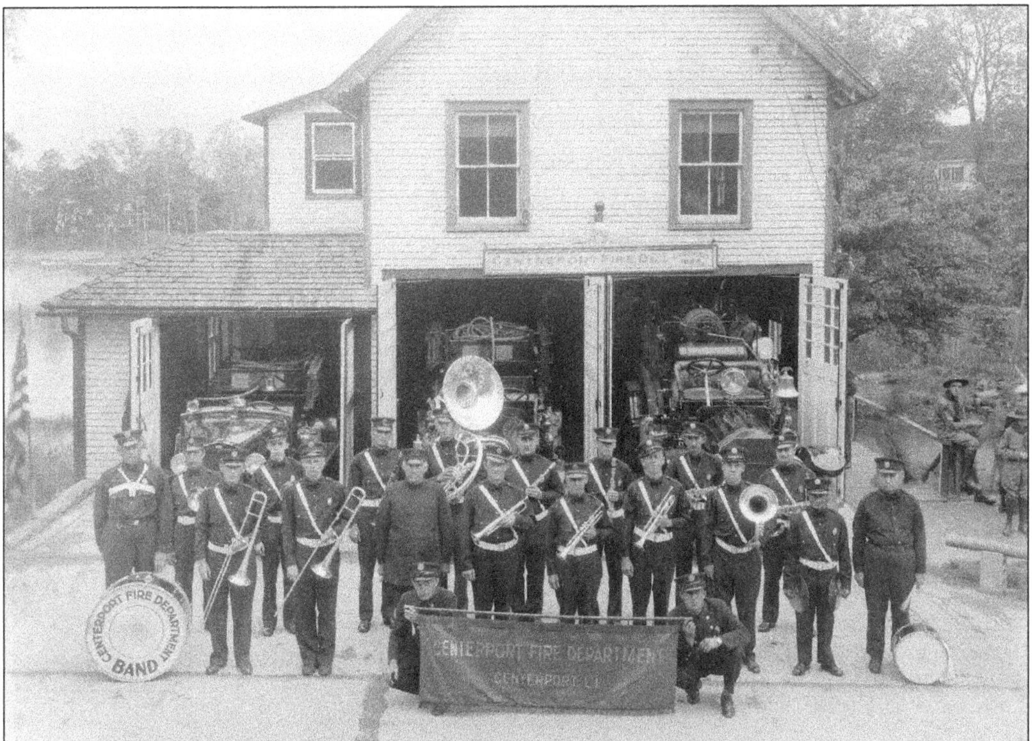

The Centerport Fire Department band is shown here ready for a parade in 1940. This was probably taken just before the parade around the millpond on the day the new firehouse was dedicated. (Greenlawn-Centerport Historical Association.)

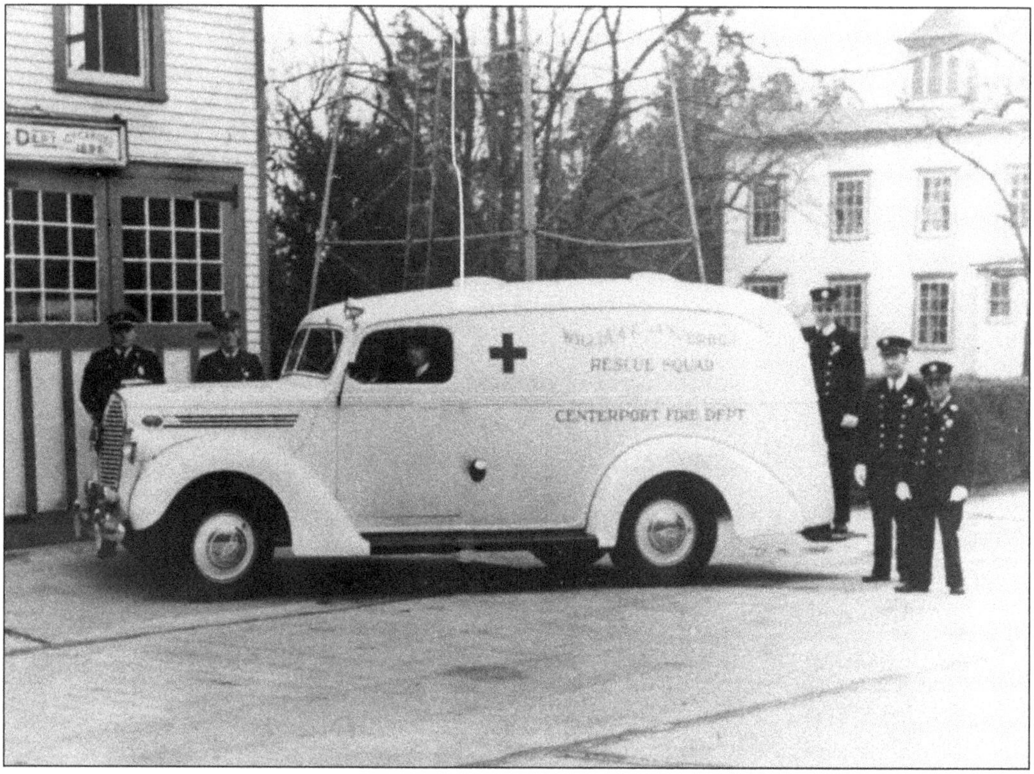

This 1938 Ford panel truck was donated in 1937 by William K. Vanderbilt II for use as an ambulance, the first and only ambulance in the town of Huntington. The second Centerport school, which served the community from 1848–1933, can be seen on the right. It was torn down in 1939. (Huntington Historical Society.)

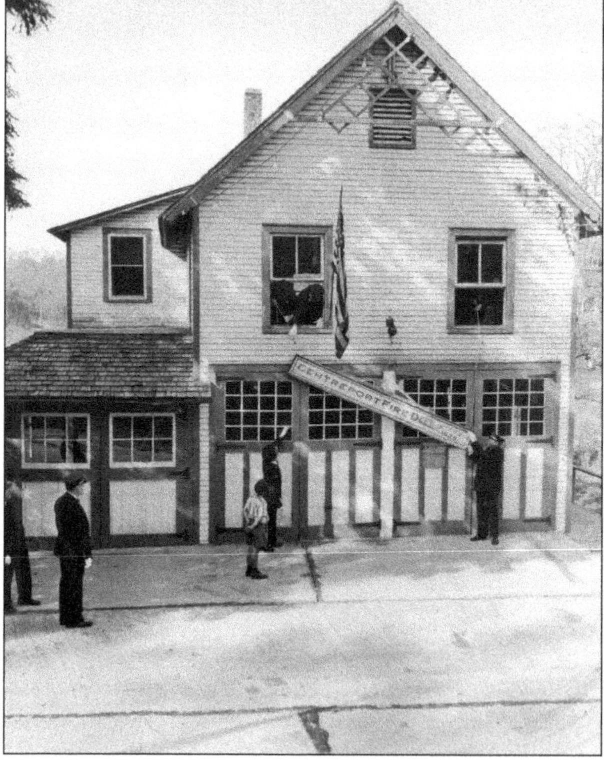

The sign came down from the old firehouse on Dedication Day, September 29, 1940. This relic of the original firehouse is still proudly displayed in the new building. (Huntington Historical Society.)

The new firehouse is under construction in April 1940 on land formerly occupied by the school, which was torn down in 1939. James Van Alst designed the building. The construction budget was set at $60,000 but was reduced to $45,000, and the building was completed at a cost of only $40,000. (Huntington Historical Society.)

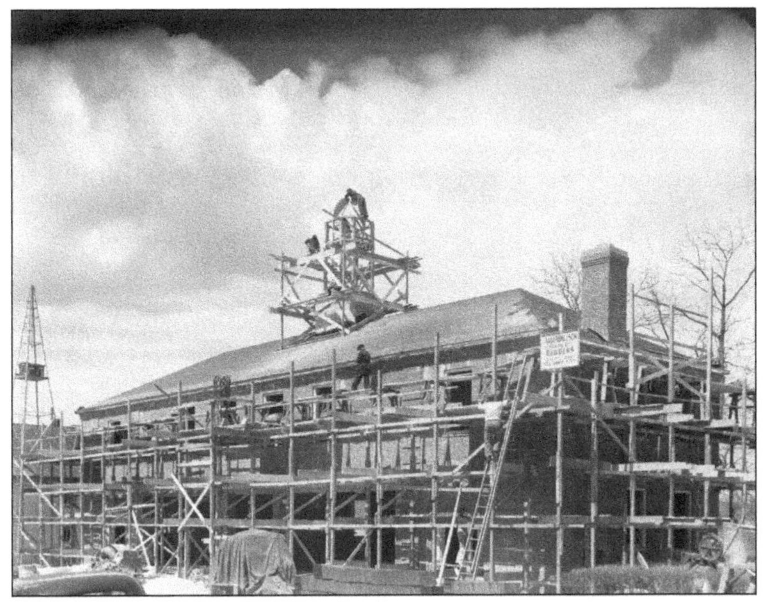

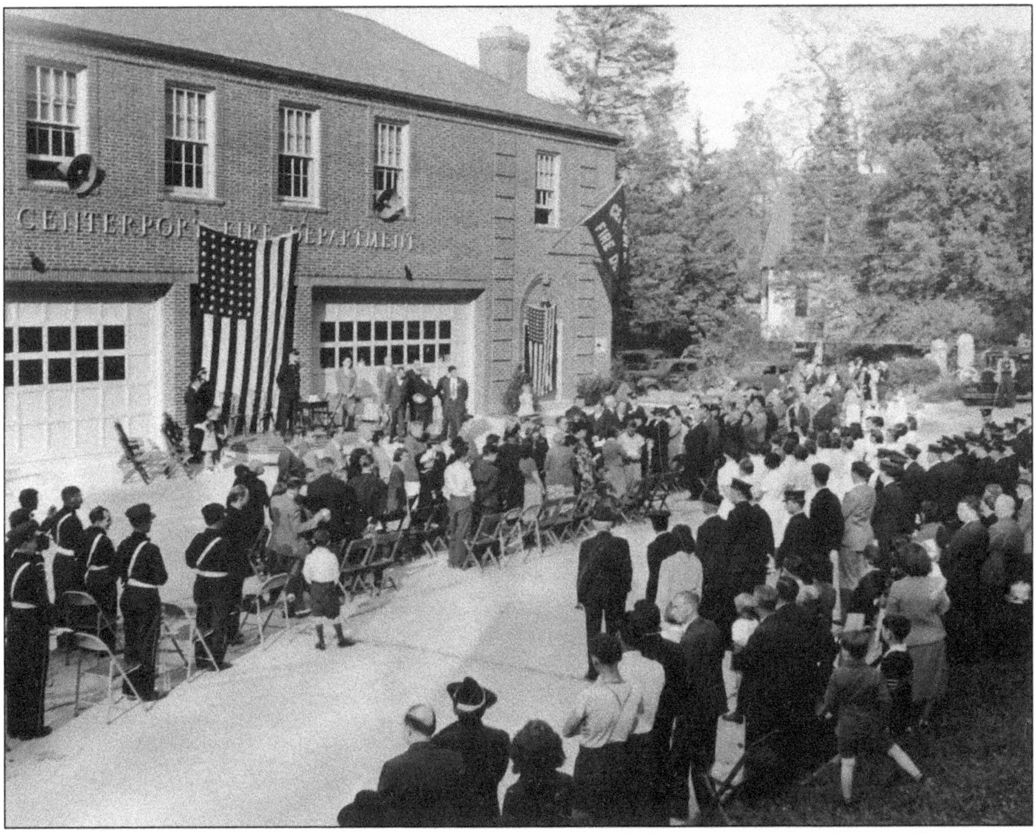

The new firehouse dedication ceremony was attended by William K. Vanderbilt II and his second wife, Rose Warburton. In addition to the new firehouse, the new ambulance donated by Vanderbilt was dedicated. Centerport was the first fire department in the Town of Huntington to have an ambulance. (Huntington Historical Society.)

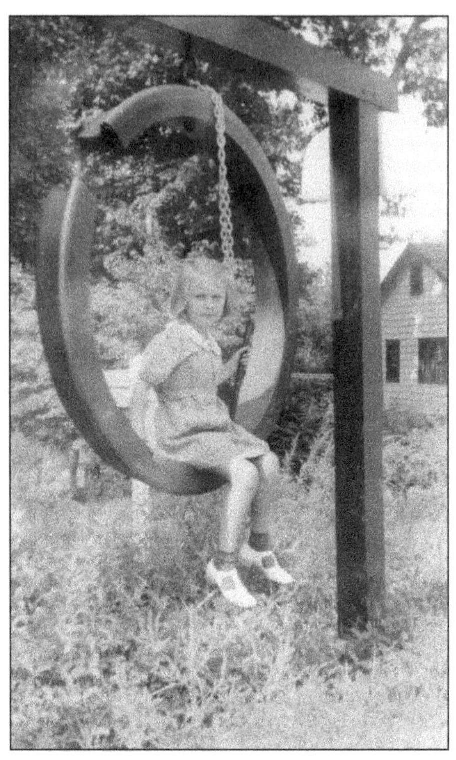

This gong, which functioned as the fire alarm from the earliest days of the department, was a retired Long Island Rail Road wheel rim. Seated in the gong is Lorraine Jelinek Vanecak, age six, in September 1938. Nearby today is the old bell from the second Centerport School, which stood next to the fire department from 1861 to 1939. Three foundations of the community intersected when the bell from the Centerport School was removed from the Methodist church and placed in front of the Centerport Fire Department. (Greenlawn-Centerport Historical Association.)

The Centerport Post Office is shown here in Benham's store on the east side of the millpond. The first postmaster, Shuebel M. Nichols, was commissioned on March 10, 1831, and served until 1852 except for the years 1840–1841. In 1938, this building became the home of the artists Arthur Dove and Helen Torr. (Greenlawn-Centerport Historical Association.)

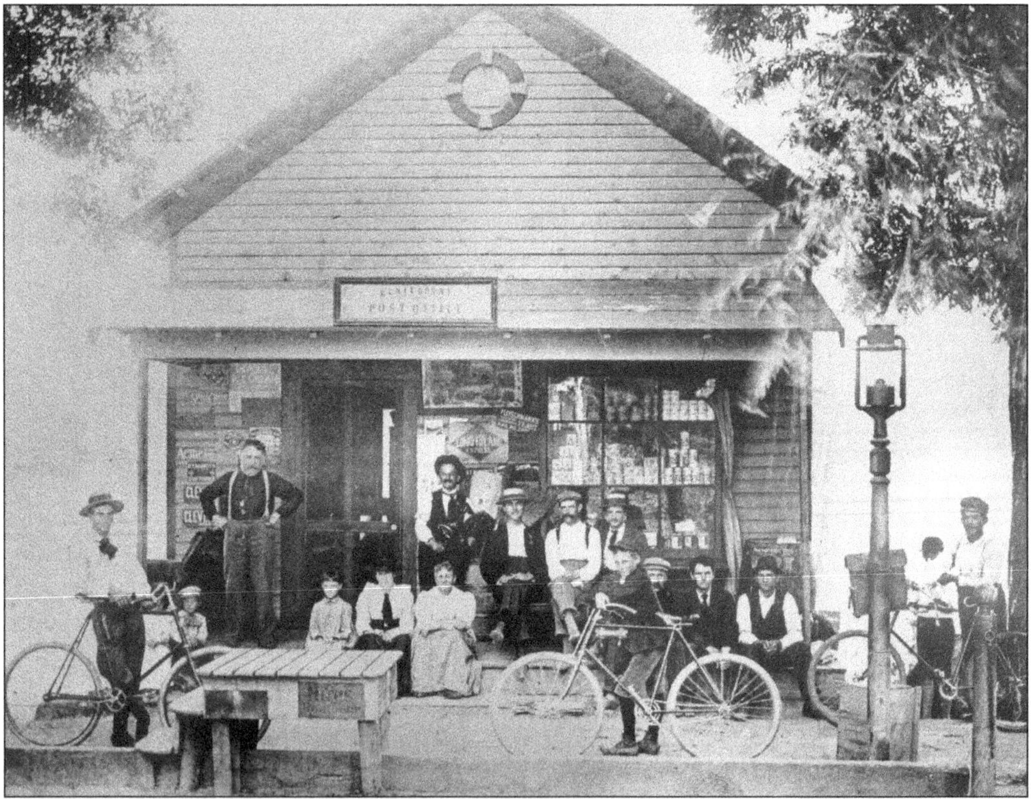

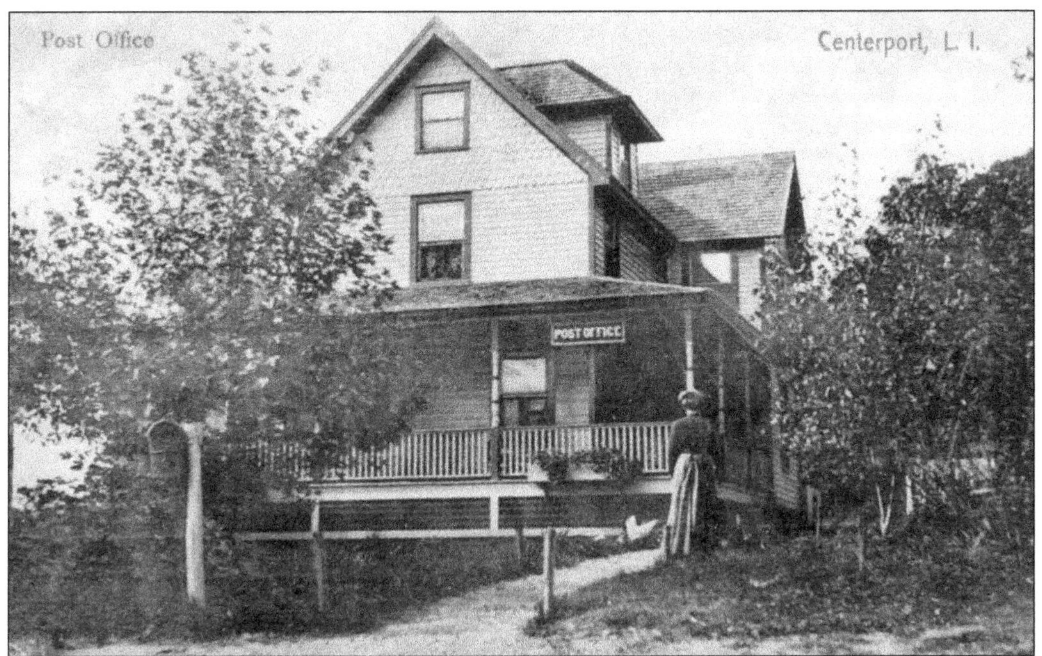

The Dickinson house on the west side of Centershore Road near the intersection of Mill Dam Road was the site of the Centerport Post Office from 1899 to 1911, when Louise Dickinson served as postmistress. This house suffered a fire due to arson in October 1991. A new house was constructed on the site. (Greenlawn-Centerport Historical Association.)

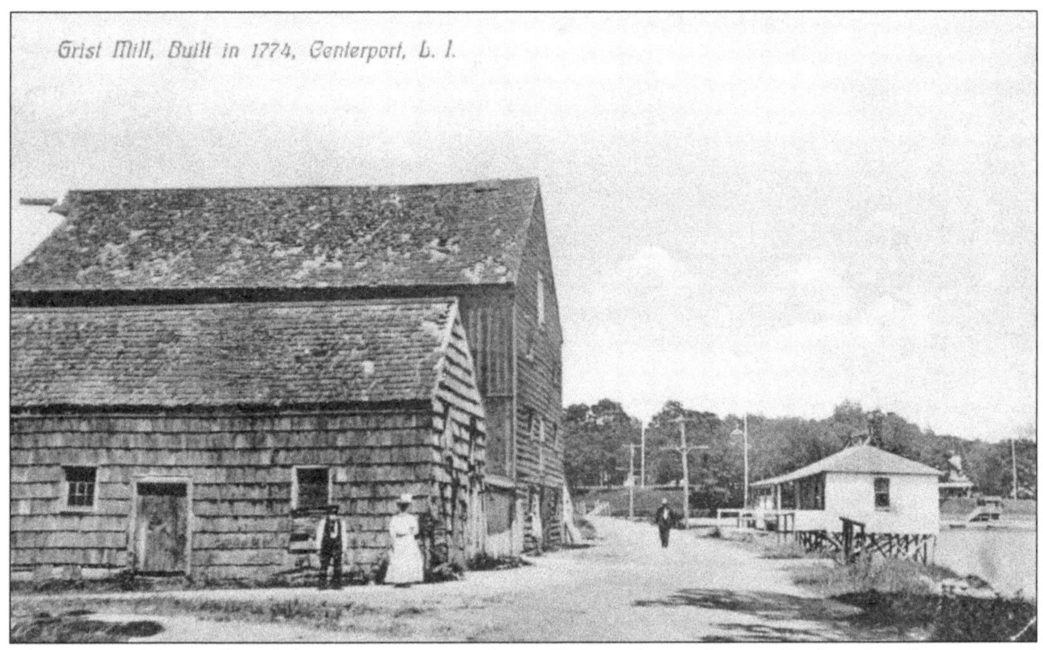

This view of the mill and the causeway over the mill dam shows the small white building erected on pilings over the millpond by James J. Bunce in 1908. It served as the Centerport Post Office from 1911 until 1934.

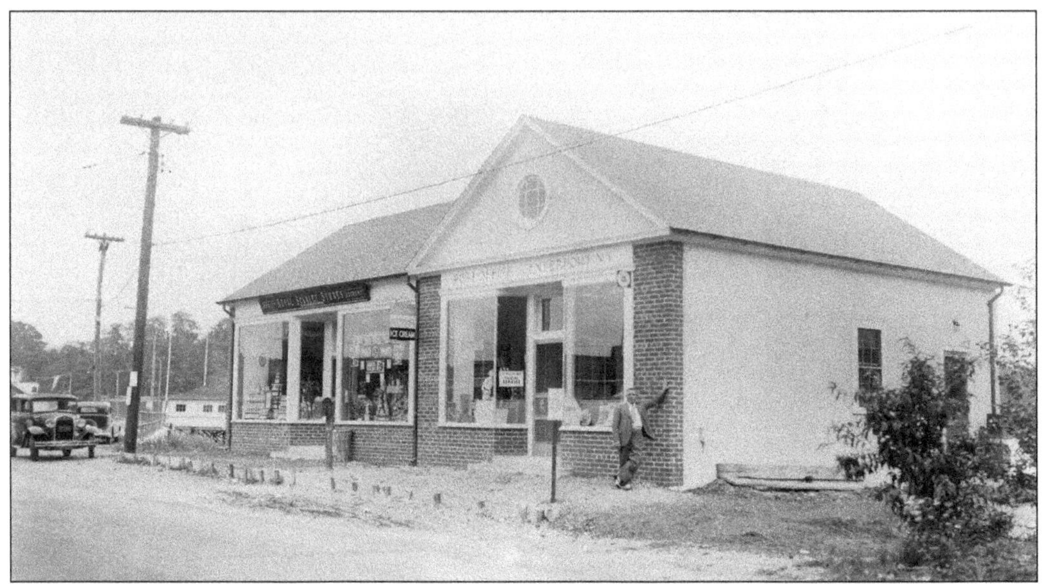

Postmaster James J. Bunce constructed this new building on the southwest corner of the mill dam in 1934 to accommodate both his store and the Centerport Post Office. Bunce is seen standing in the foreground at the corner of the building, while the former post office building and a 1931 Ford Model A can be seen at far left.

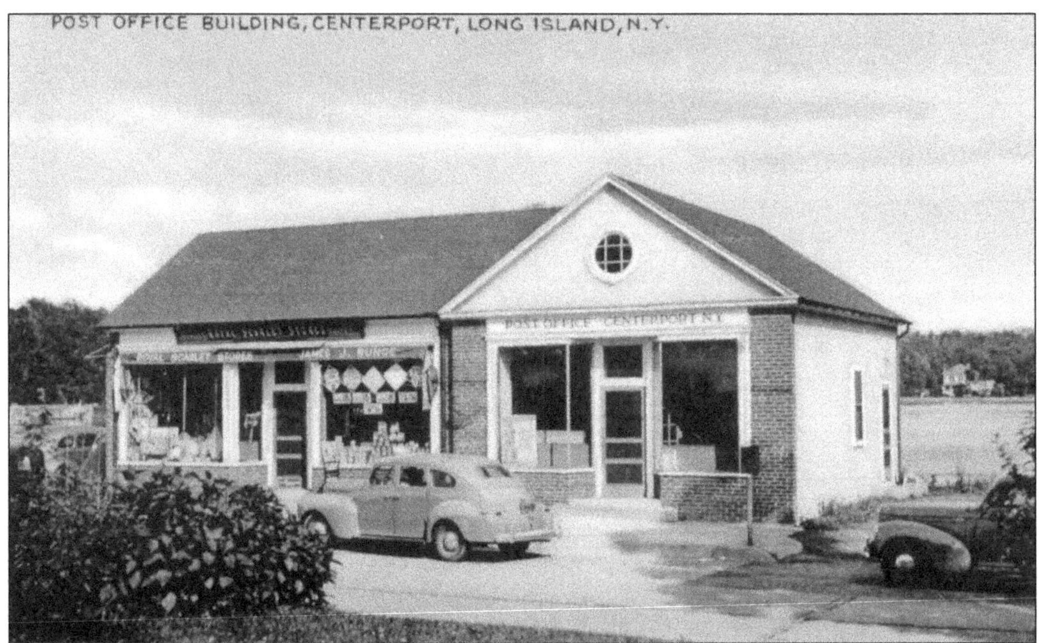

Bunce retired in 1936, and this building remained the post office during the entire tenure of his niece, Postmistress Elizabeth "Bessie" Zoeller, who served from 1936 to 1959. Her successors included Fred Hussong, who served from 1959 to 1961, and Jim Hill, who was postmaster in 1962 when the post office was moved south to a location along Centershore Road. Many residents know this building as the location of a popular delicatessen known as Rudy's Store, run by Rudy Rzehack. It is now used as an office building.

Four

Seasonal Visitors

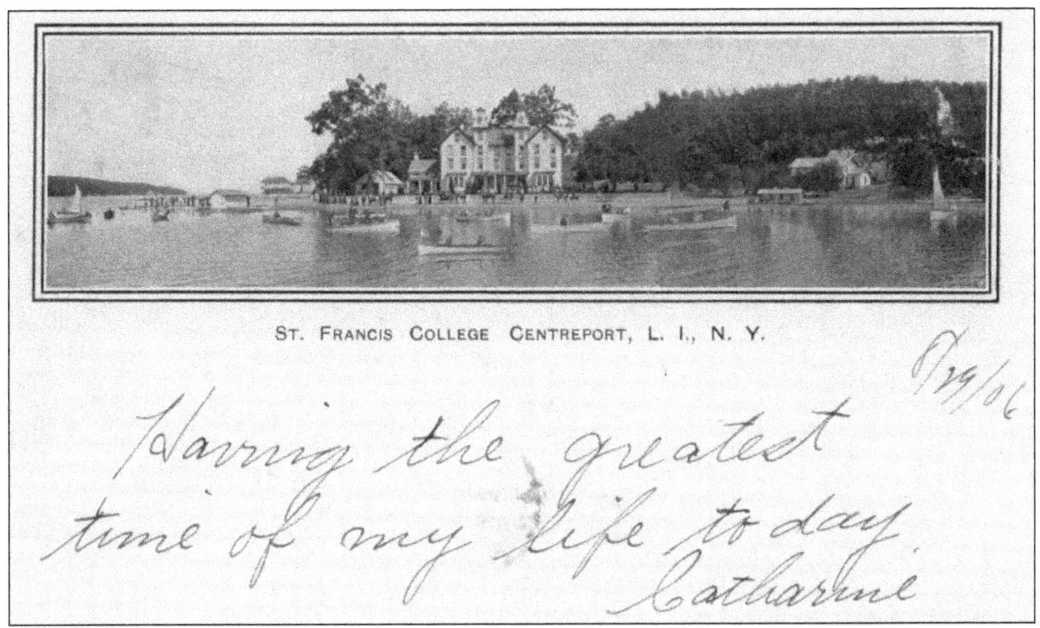

The beautiful harbor, pond, and lake have enticed summer visitors to come to Centerport for generations. People have come to their cottages large and small, boarders have come to guesthouses, and young people have come to camps.

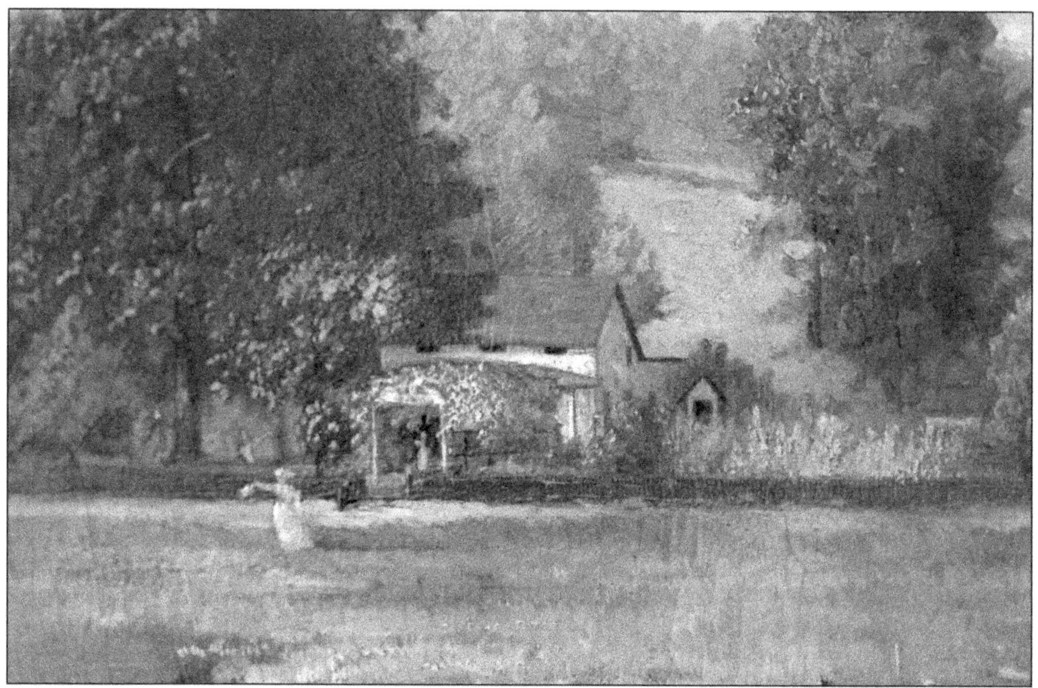

In 1879, David B. Chalmers and his wife, Ruth Ann Burr Chalmers, from Brooklyn, bought a farm on the east shore of Centerport harbor from Capt. Isaac Sammis. This detail of a painting by 19th-century landscape painter Alessandro Mario shows the 1840 house that started the boardinghouse days in Centerport. (Photograph by James Clemens, private collection.)

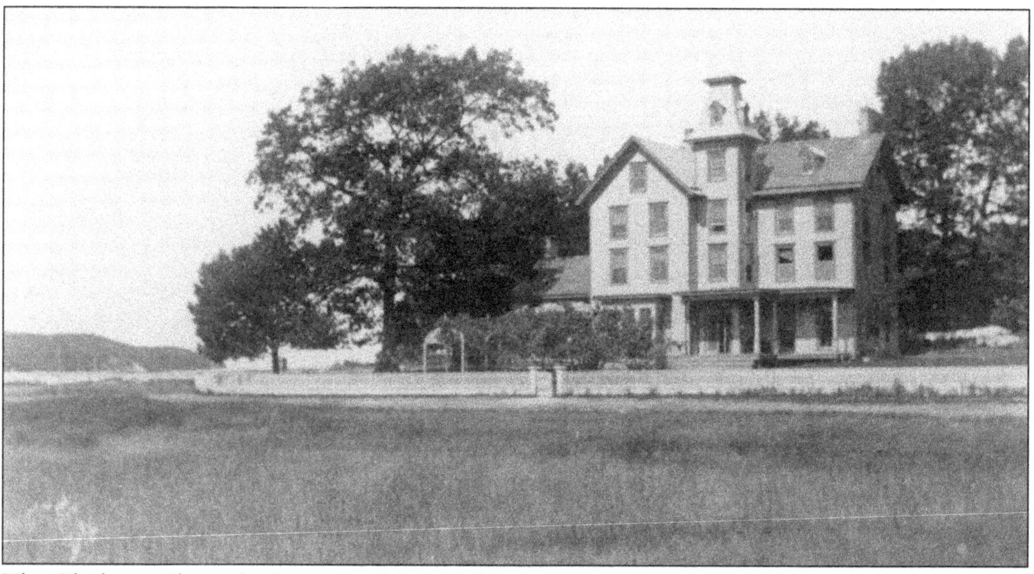

The Chalmers Place, the largest and finest of Centerport's summer hotels, was run by Ruth Ann Burr Chalmers (1821–1897). The Chalmers family added a two-story wing on the west side in the French Mansard style. One of their six children, Mary Emma Chalmers, (1843–1927), assisted her mother. Its location, 37 miles from New York City, could be reached by the Port Jefferson branch of the Long Island Rail Road at Greenlawn. It featured 20 large and airy sleeping rooms. This photograph is by William Deming. (Queens Borough Public Library.)

This advertisement for the Chalmers Place describes the hilly surroundings with "beautiful landscape and water views and perfectly healthy." Bathing (swimming) and rowboats were offered free of charge. Guests at the Chalmers Place stayed for several days or weeks. It could accommodate 75 guests.

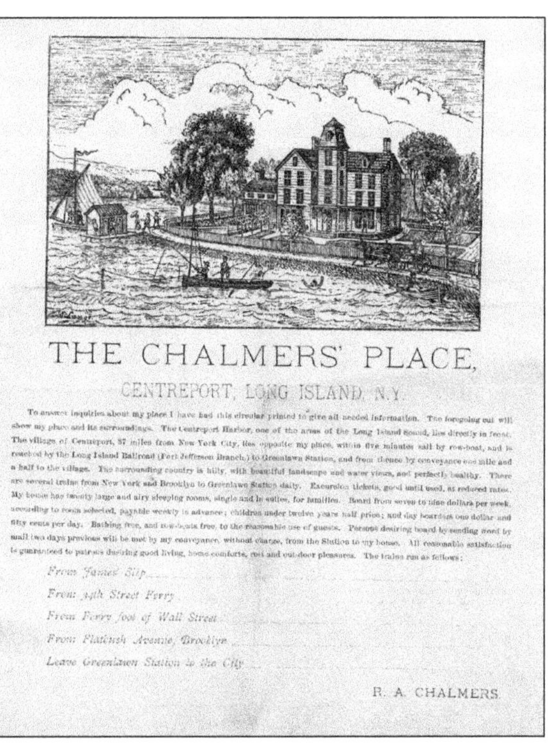

THE CHALMERS' PLACE,

CENTREPORT, LONG ISLAND, N.Y.

To answer inquiries about my place I have had this circular printed to give all needed information. The foregoing cut will show my place and its surroundings. The Centreport Harbor, one of the arms of the Long Island Sound, lies directly in front. The village of Centreport, 37 miles from New York City, lies opposite my place, within five minutes sail by row-boat, and is reached by the Long Island Railroad (Port Jefferson Branch,) to Greenlawn Station, and from thence by conveyance one mile and a half to the village. The surrounding country is hilly, with beautiful landscape and water views, and perfectly healthy. There are several trains from New York and Brooklyn to Greenlawn Station daily. Excursion tickets, good until used, at reduced rates. My house has twenty large and airy sleeping rooms, single and in suites, for families. Board from seven to nine dollars per week, according to room selected, payable weekly in advance; children under twelve years half price; and day boarders one dollar and fifty cents per day. Bathing free, and row-boats free, to the reasonable use of guests. Persons desiring board by sending word by mail two days previous will be met by my conveyance, without charge, from the Station to my house. All reasonable satisfaction is guaranteed to patrons desiring good living, home comforts, rest and out-door pleasures. The trains run as follows:

From James Slip

From 34th Street Ferry

From Ferry foot of Wall Street

From Flatbush Avenue, Brooklyn

Leave Greenlawn Station to the City

R. A. CHALMERS.

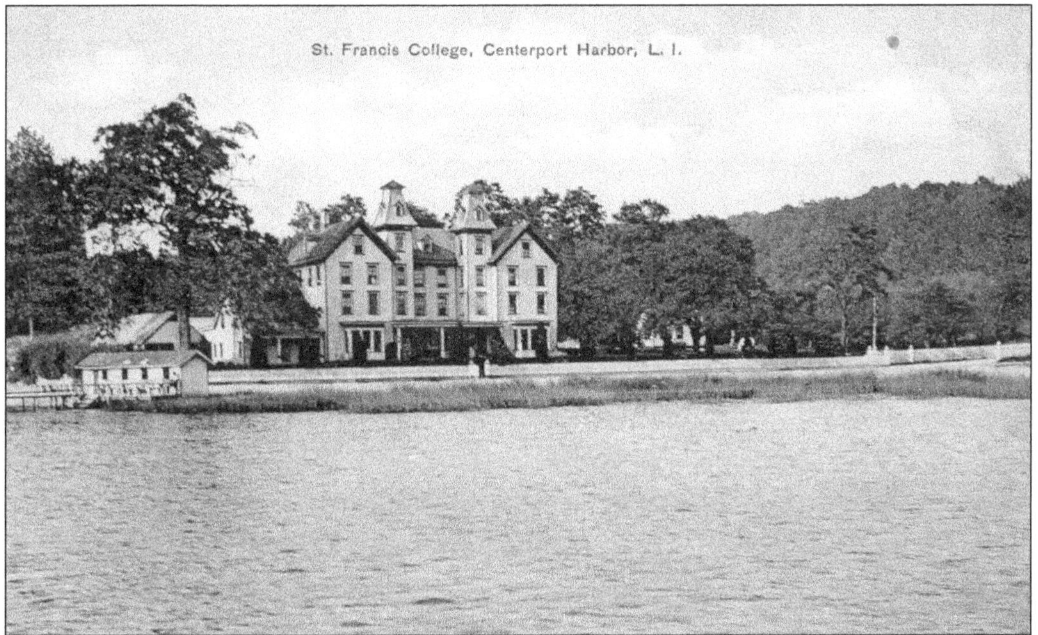

David Chalmers died in 1885. The Chalmers Place was purchased from the Chalmers family by the Franciscan Brothers of the Brooklyn Diocese in 1888 for $10,500. The seminarians, founders of Saint Francis School/College, were searching for a quiet country place where they could find peace to rest and study during their break from teaching. They noted the similarities to their homeland in Ireland. They originally called their summer home the Monastery at Mount Alvernia. They immediately doubled the size of the Chalmers House by adding a new wing and a second tower.

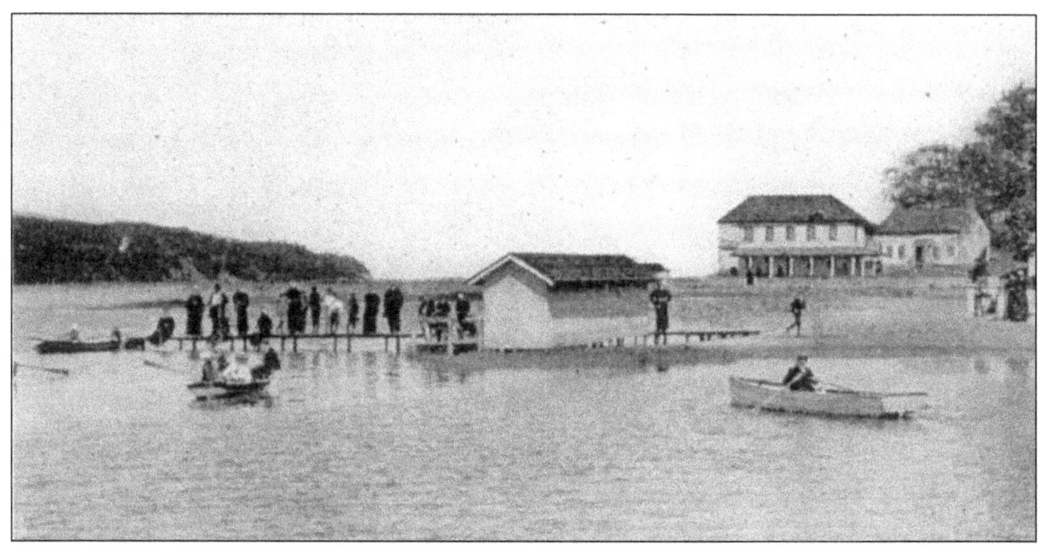

The Franciscan Brothers enjoyed the cool fresh air and the opportunities for boating and swimming that the summer boarders had enjoyed. This view shows the brothers on their dock. The building in the background on the right is the Klinker house, a late-18th-century structure that was on the property when they purchased it from Ruth Ann Chalmers. It was torn down in 1935.

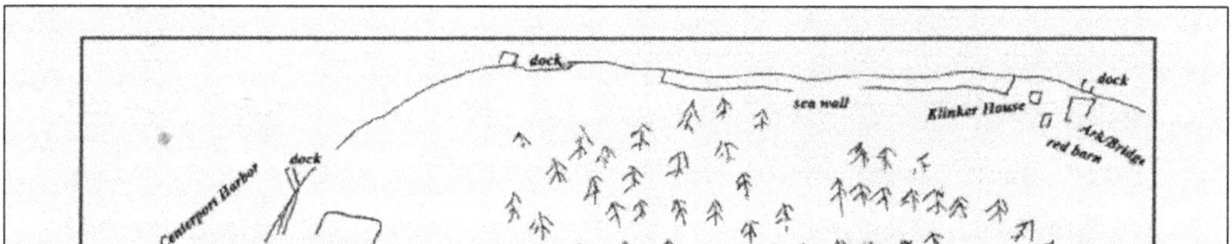

dock
sea wall
Klinker House
dock
Ark/Bridge
red barn
Centerport Harbor
dock
Chalmers House
St. Francis Monastery
Long Dorm
toilet
pump house
baseball field
pup tents
Bayview House
Martin House
apple orchard
cemetery
Prospect Road
This map is not drawn to scale.
Mt Alvernia
Alvernia, circa 1890

Alvernia, circa 1890

This map of the site from a camp history by Brother Edmund shows how the camp appeared in 1890. The camp was open from July 1 to September 1. In 1901, Brother Jerome, who had handled the purchase, was the first brother in charge. The brothers acquired the nearby Bayview boardinghouse from Susan Martin when additional housing was needed.

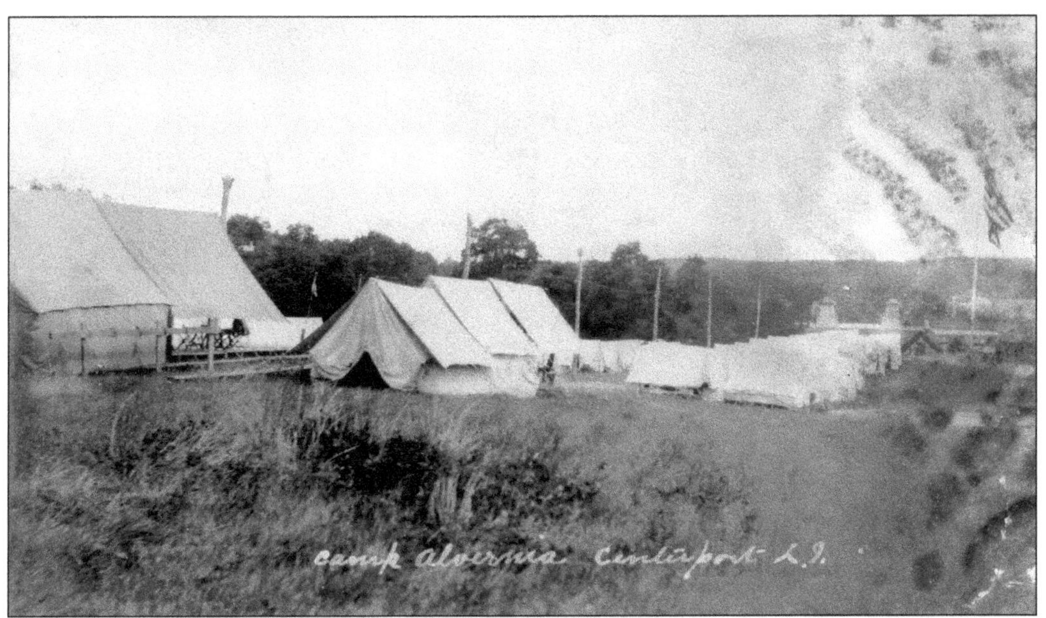

The campers stayed in small tents and used larger ones for dining and group activities. The towers of the monastery are visible in the background of this c. 1905 photograph. (Greenlawn-Centerport Historical Association.)

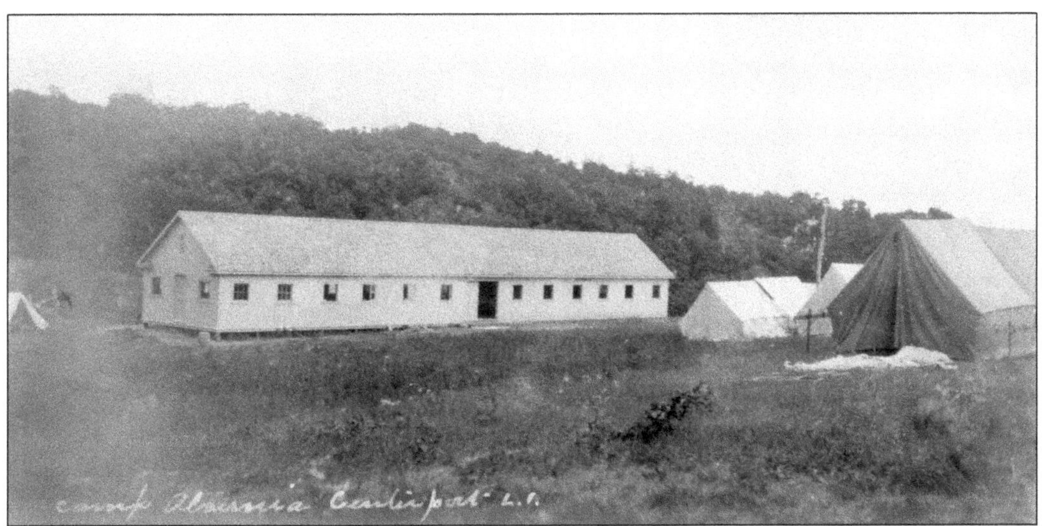

The Long Dorm building was constructed around 1888 to house some of the campers. It stood where the main building is now located. (Greenlawn-Centerport Historical Association.)

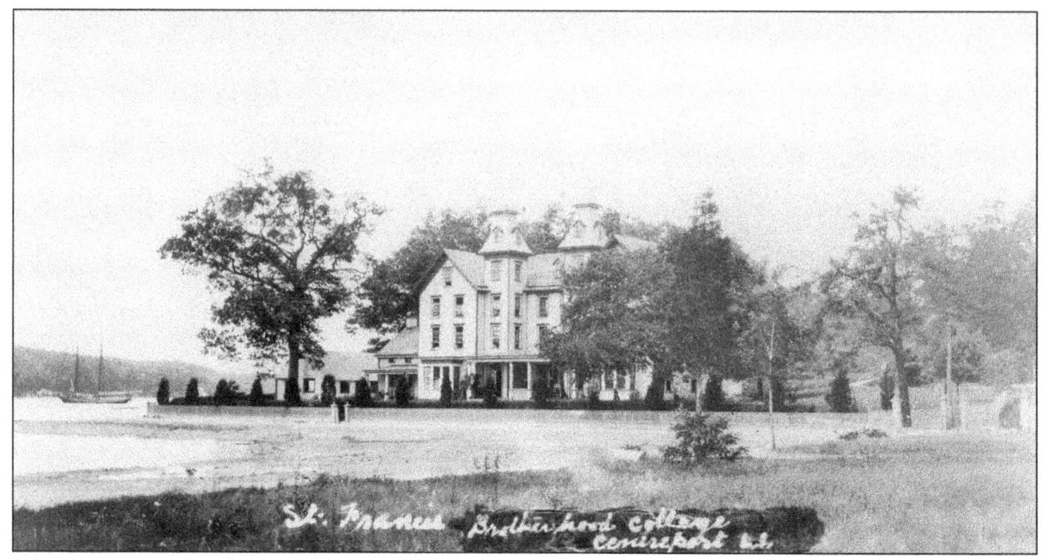

The Franciscan Brothers purchased the Chalmers House for the purpose of establishing a summer retreat. After a few years, requests from the parents of boys attending their 14 St. Francis parochial schools inspired the brothers to broaden their mission to provide a summer experience for younger boys, and thus Camp Alvernia was created. It was the first Catholic camp in the United States and could house 80 men and 100 young men.

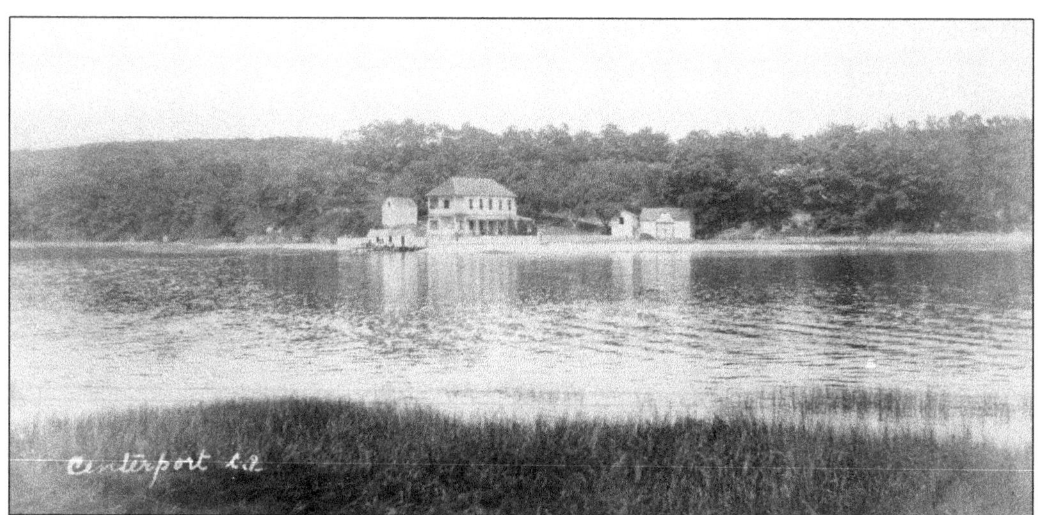

The northern shorefront buildings of the camp are seen here. The long two-story building is called the Ark, but it was previously known as the Pavilion. This photograph was taken after the building was raised up and a second story was added as a first story in about 1905. The Ark was renovated extensively in 1938 and several times more recently. It is still used today as part of the retreat center and as a primary grade classroom by Love of Learning Montessori School.

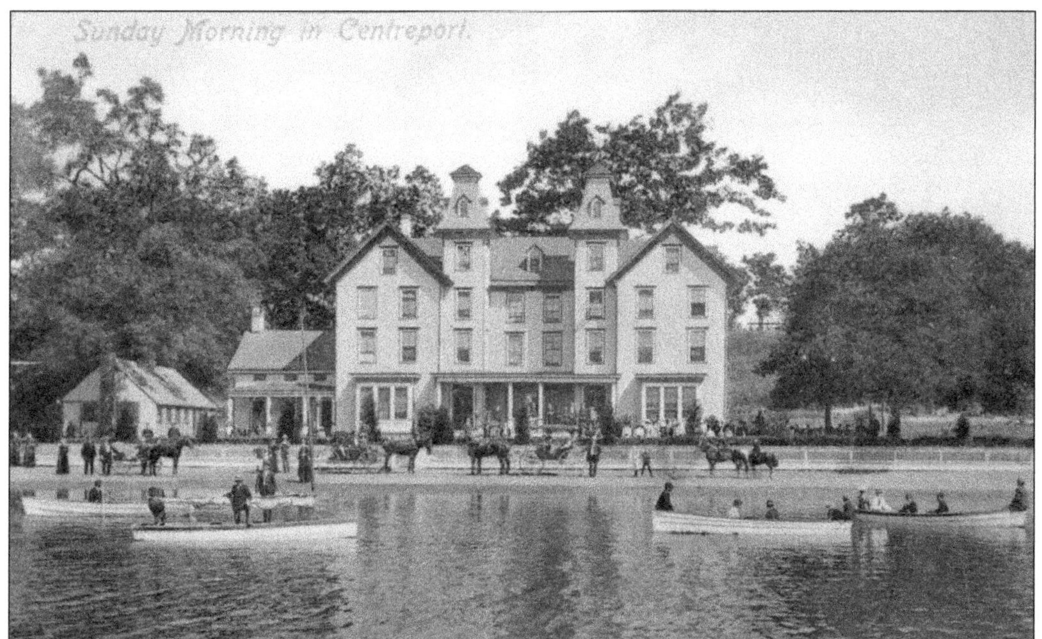

The Franciscan Brothers converted a part of the first floor of the former Chalmers House into a chapel named Our Lady of the Angels. They invited local residents who belonged to the parish of St. Philip Neri Church in Northport to worship with them. On Sunday mornings, the visitors arrived by carriage or by boat and sometimes found that a rising tide had left their horses standing in water and their boats adrift while they were attending Mass. The monastery was torn down on short notice in 1980 after being vacant for 10 years. (Greenlawn Centerport Historical Association.)

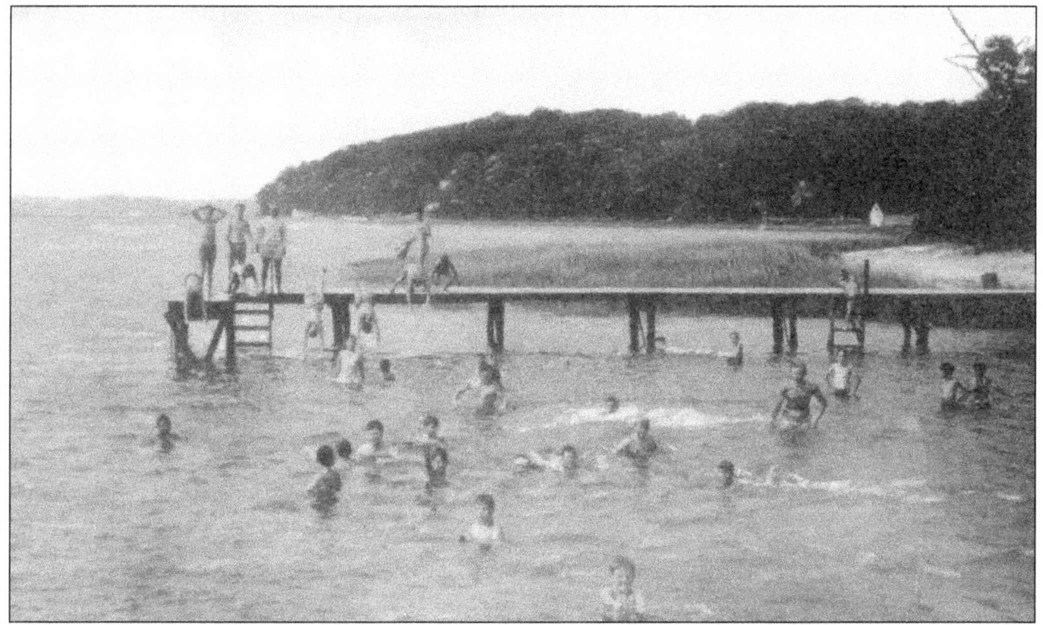

This image and the two on the following page were taken from a postcard folio of scenes from Camp Alvernia. Swimming was a popular and important activity for the boys. An annual water carnival was held featuring competition with other camps as well as local residents.

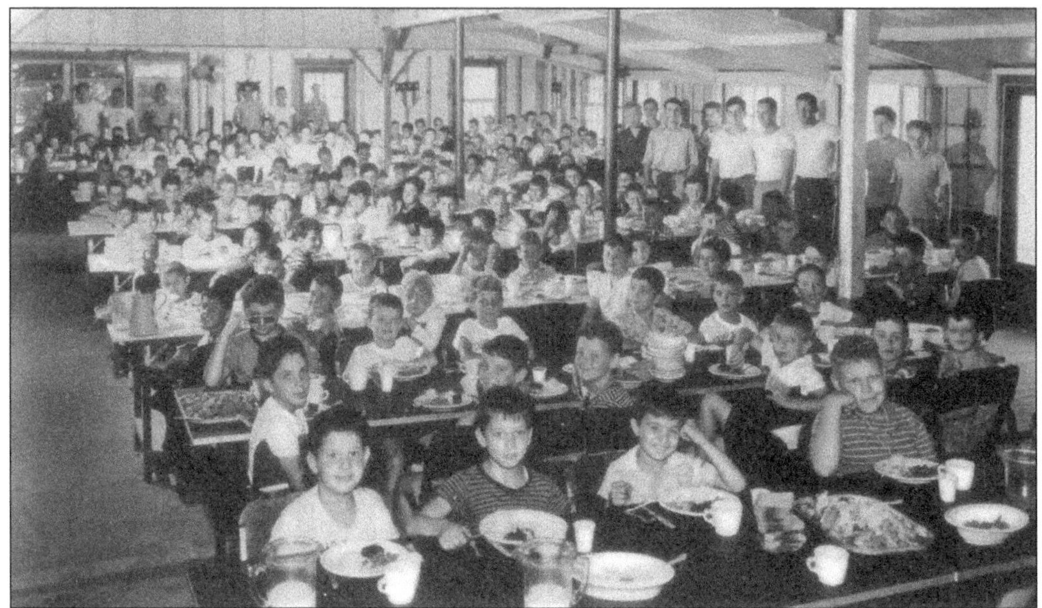

This is a view of the mess hall at Camp Alvernia. One young man wrote home on a postcard, "I'm having a good time. The place is lousy but the food is good!"

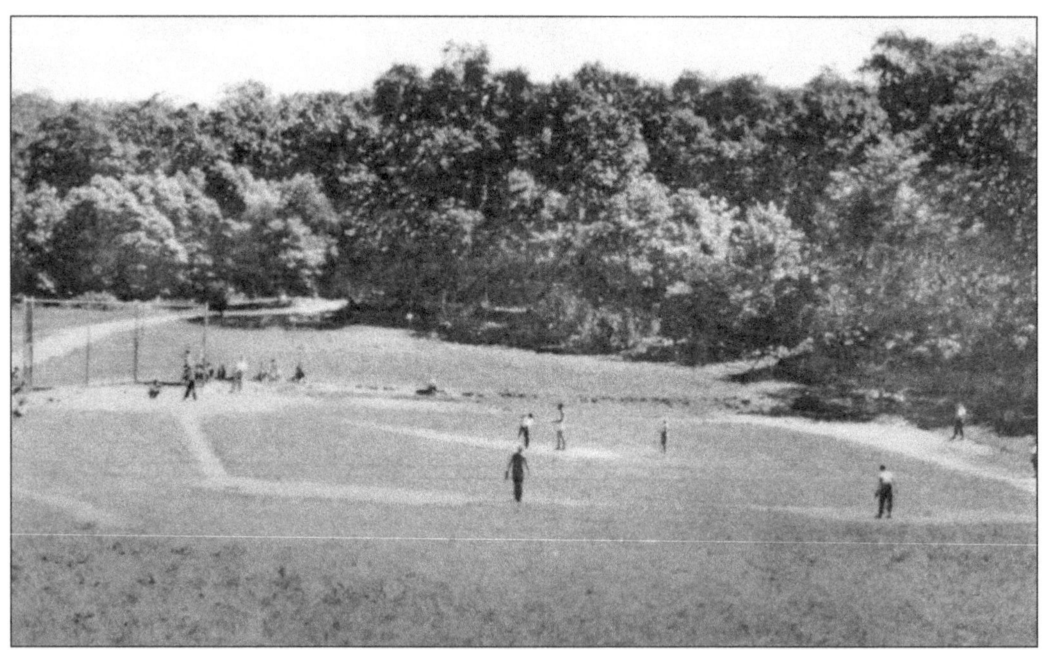

Boys play baseball at Camp Alvernia's field. A commemorative marker at the entrance notes that football coaching legend Vince Lombardi attended camp here in 1932 and 1933 while attending St. Francis Prep. The field is now named for him.

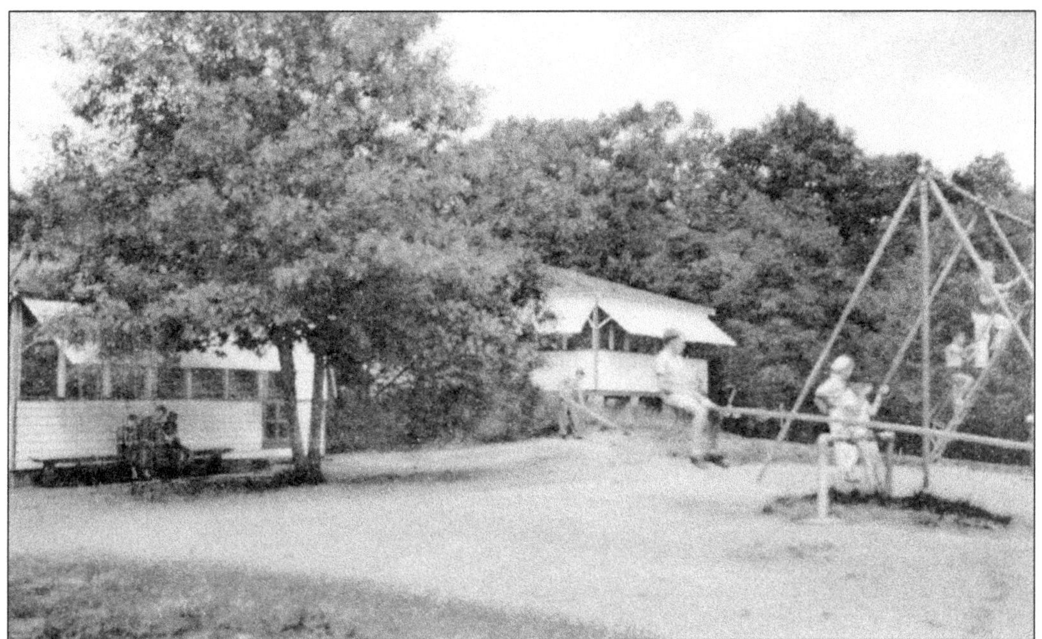

The playground at Camp Alvernia is still used today. The Franciscan Brothers sold their property on the east side of Prospect Road opposite the camp to Suffolk County in 1998; it is now maintained as passive parkland.

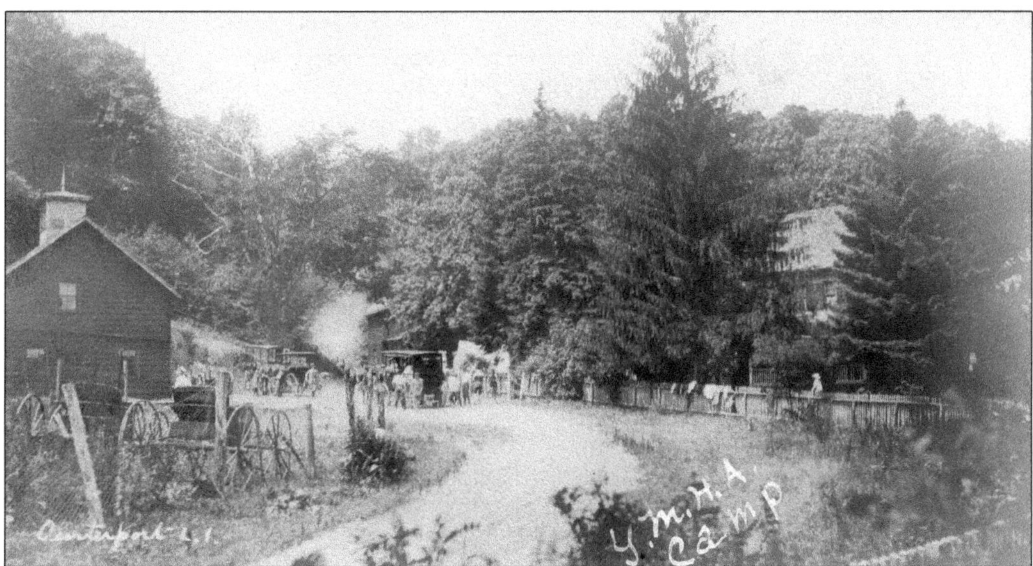

The Young Men's Hebrew Association (YMHA), based in Brooklyn, leased the Joseph Irwin farm, which was located on the west side of the harbor, in an area that is now Huntington Beach, between 1904 and 1909. They established a summer camp for boys and young men. Their activities included swimming, fishing, rowing, croquet, tennis, and baseball. The YMHA camp lasted for five years until the main house on the property was destroyed by fire in 1909.

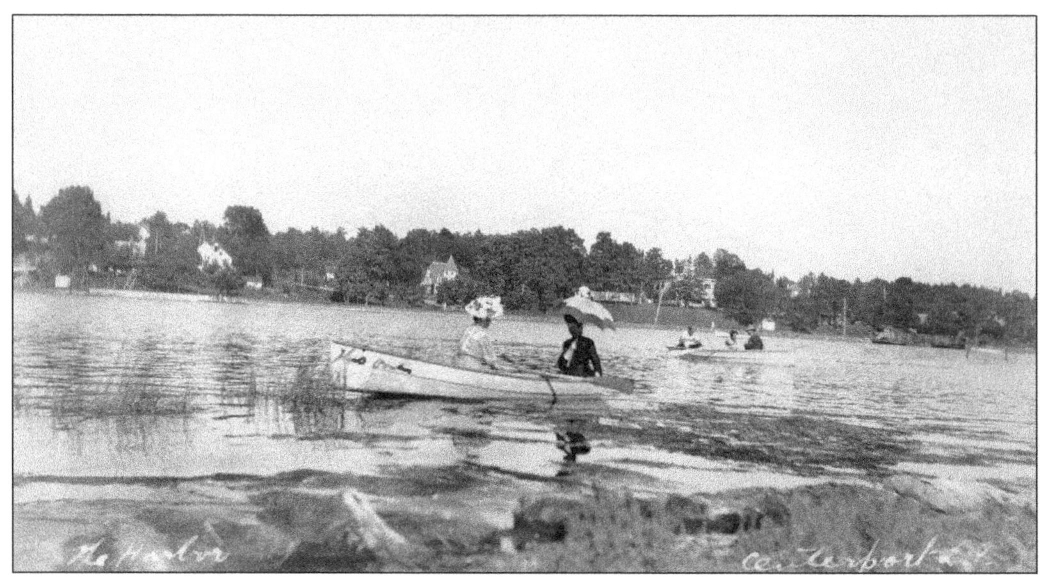

Rowing was always a popular activity with summer visitors. These fancy ladies enjoy an outing on the upper harbor. (Huntington Historical Society.)

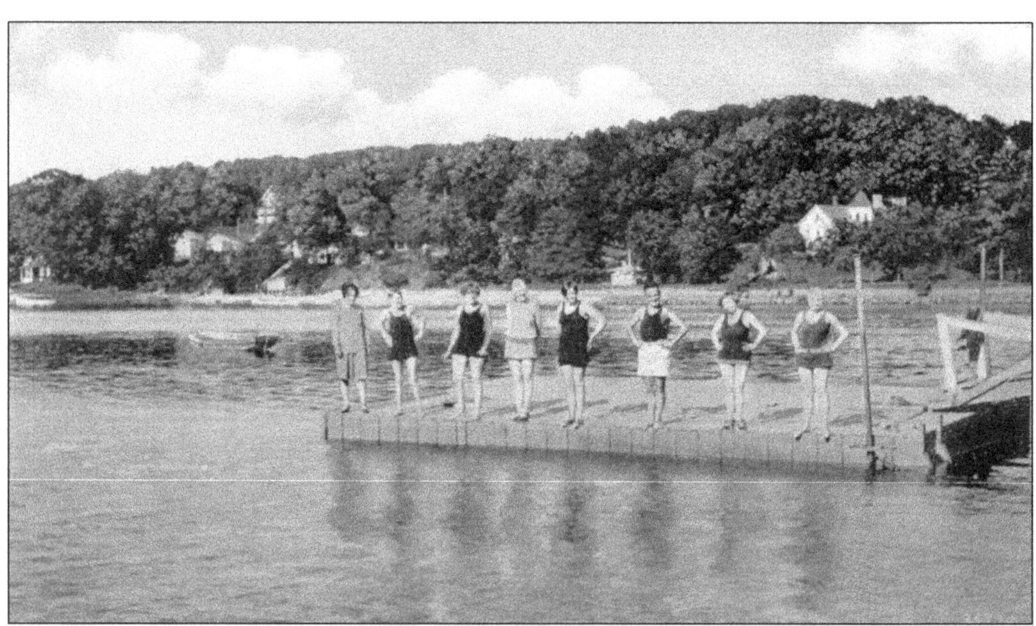

Local young ladies were recruited by the photographer to create this postcard of bathing beauties. They are standing on the floating dock in front of the original Centerport Yacht Club.

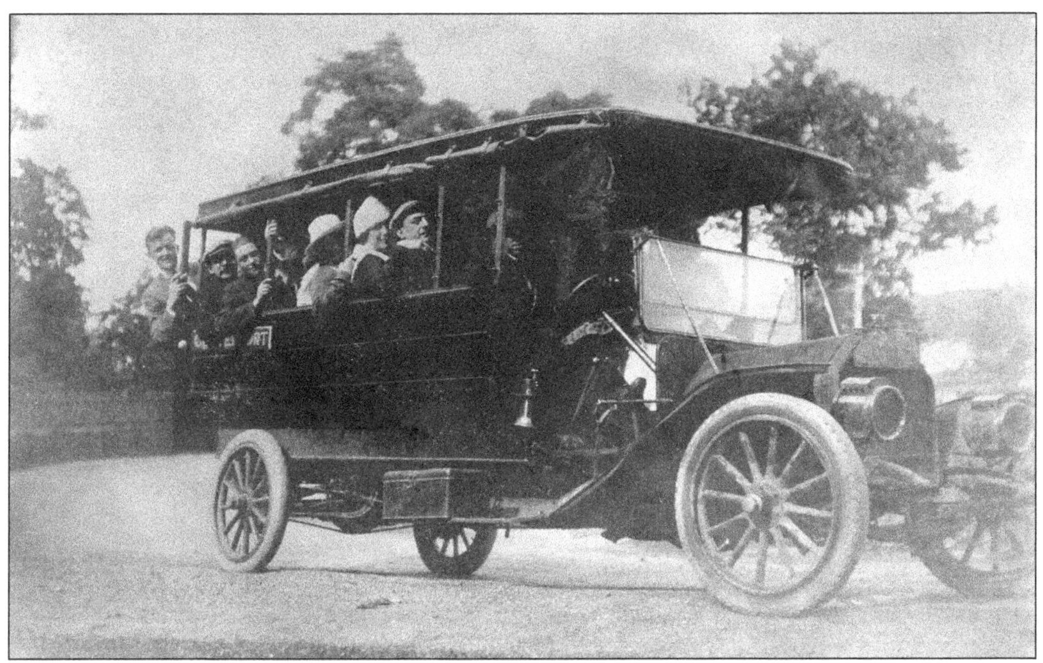

Summer visitors and boarders usually traveled by the Long Island Rail Road to the Greenlawn station and made the mile-and-a-half trip from there to the many boarding houses and hotels in Centerport by public conveyance. Samuel Ballton was born a slave in Virginia and served in a cavalry regiment during the Civil War, and operated a stage service between Greenlawn and Centerport at the turn of the 20th century. A bus drawn by two mules named Agnes and Nellie replaced the stage, and this motor bus replaced the one pulled by draft animals around 1907. (Greenlawn Centerport Historical Association.)

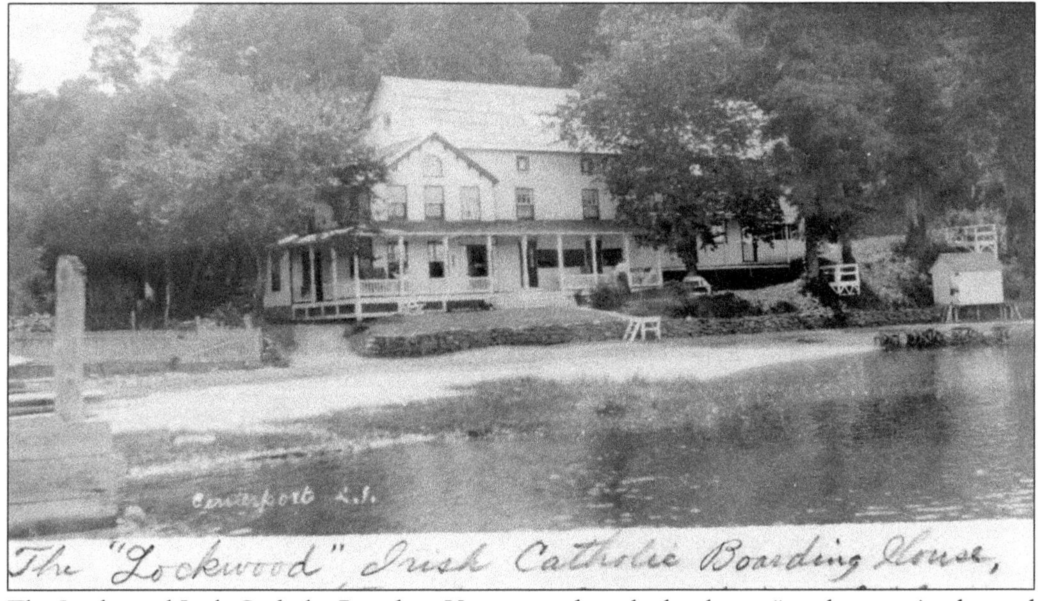

The Lockwood Irish Catholic Boarding House was described as being "on the water's edge and on the Sunrise Trail," open through September, "the ideal vacation month." Leon L. Lockwood was the proprietor. His wife, Mary, was Irish. It burned down in 1930 when a gas stove exploded.

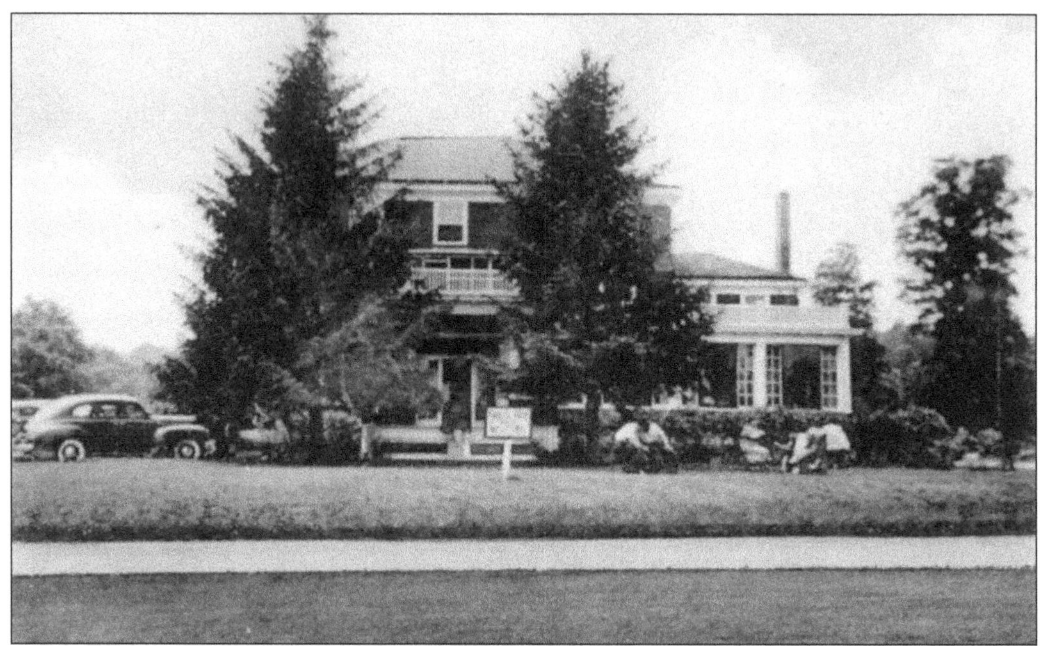

A former house on the west side of the millpond became the Parisi-Ann House Summer Resort, and later the Greenlawn Country Club, which advertised boating, fishing, and bathing. It was one of the last boardinghouses to operate in Centerport.

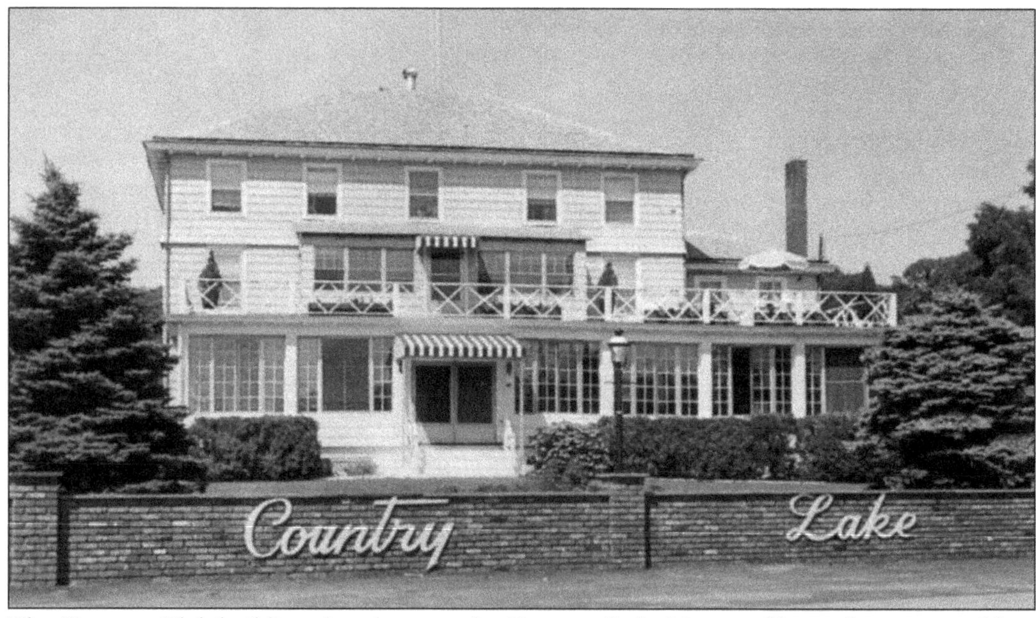

The Country Club building then became the Country Lake Nursing Home. It was one of four large houses along the shores of the millpond and harbor that became nursing homes in the 1950s and 1960s. It was closed and vacant by 2000, and has since been demolished and the land subdivided for housing.

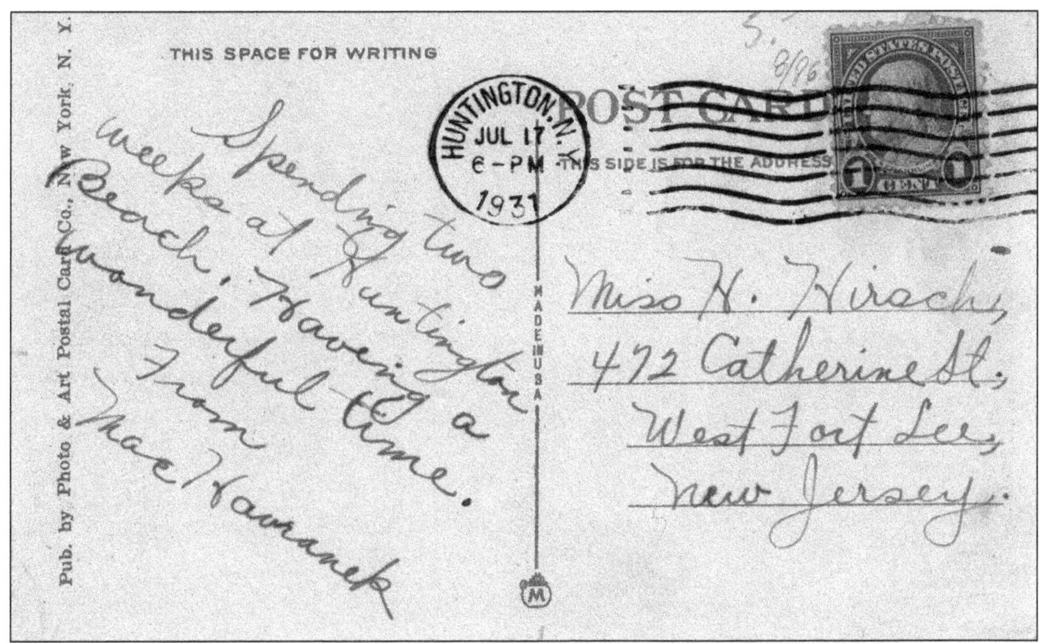

Huntington Beach was formed in 1927 as a summer community on property bought by developers Hall and Ruhland from the Fleet and Irwin estates. A network of streets named for presidents of the United States was laid out, and the land was divided into sections 20 feet wide. The first houses were built on the north end of McKinley Terrace in the spring of 1927, followed by a lot of building in the spring of 1928. In that year it was decided to hold a fireworks celebration for the Fourth of July. Funds were collected, and this cooperative activity led to the formation of the Huntington Beach Community Association that same year. (Above, Greenlawn-Centerport Historical Association; below, Huntington Beach Community Association.)

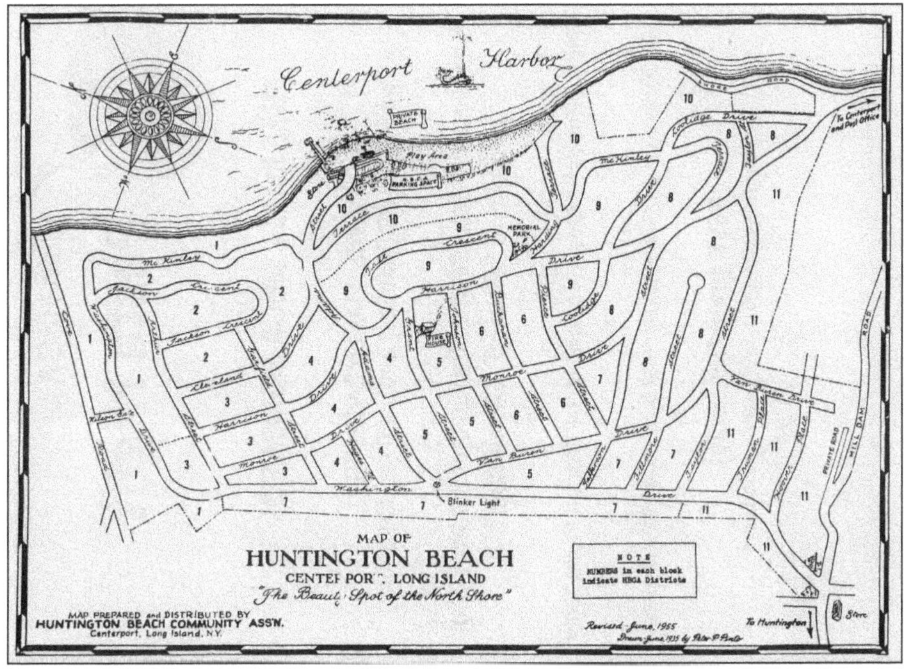

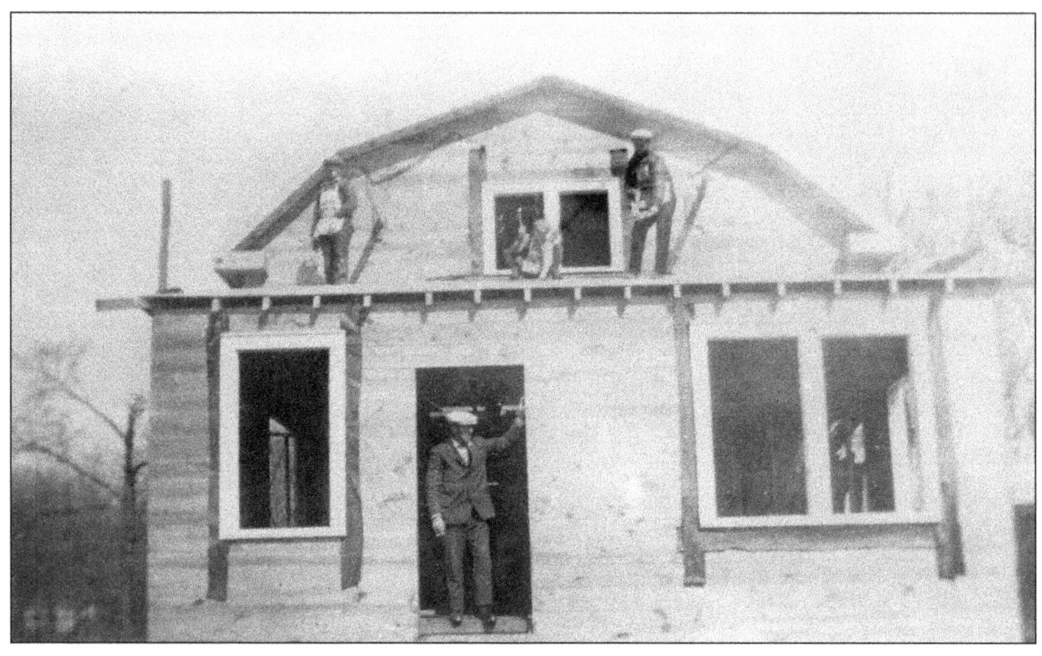

Above, carpenters are at work on a modest new home under construction in Huntington Beach. More lots were sold, and houses were built; in the end, about 750 houses were built in the community. Below, the same house today has new windows and doors, but the structure is unchanged. (Both, Huntington Beach Community Association.)

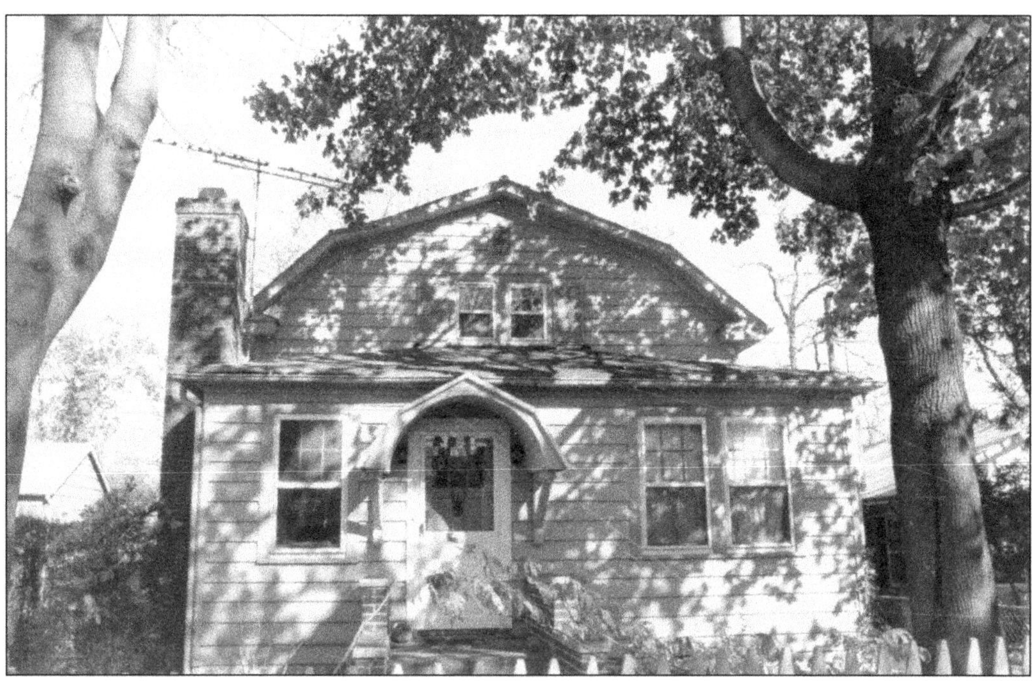

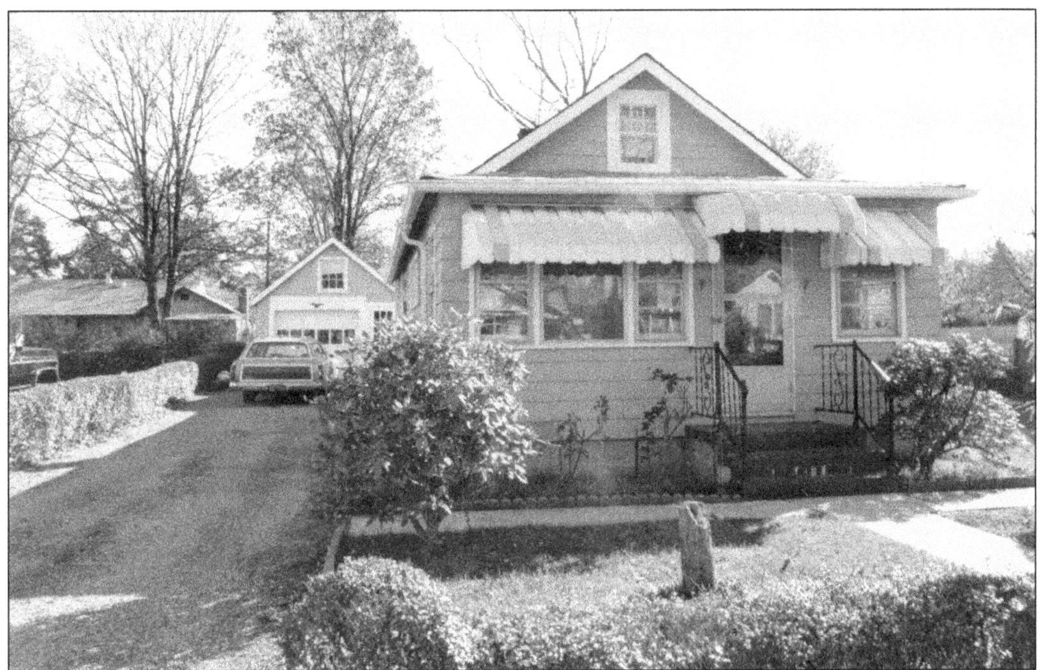

Here is a typical Huntington Beach cottage. Many of the original summer cottages were converted to full-time residences in the years following World War II. There are virtually no summer places anymore, but the tradition of constant home expansion and improvement continues. (Huntington Beach Community Association.)

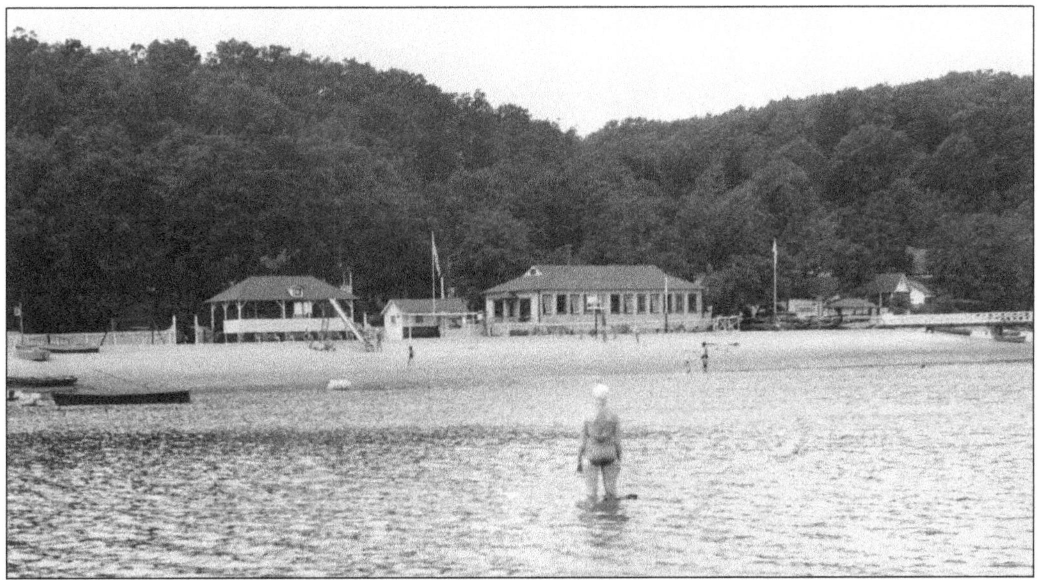

A lone swimmer enjoys the private community beach in mid-September 1940. Behind her are the original pavilion and casino buildings. The old casino was built as a general store, and gas pumps were soon added. After a short stint as a meat market, the building was reopened as the Beach Tavern in May 1943. (Huntington Historical Society.)

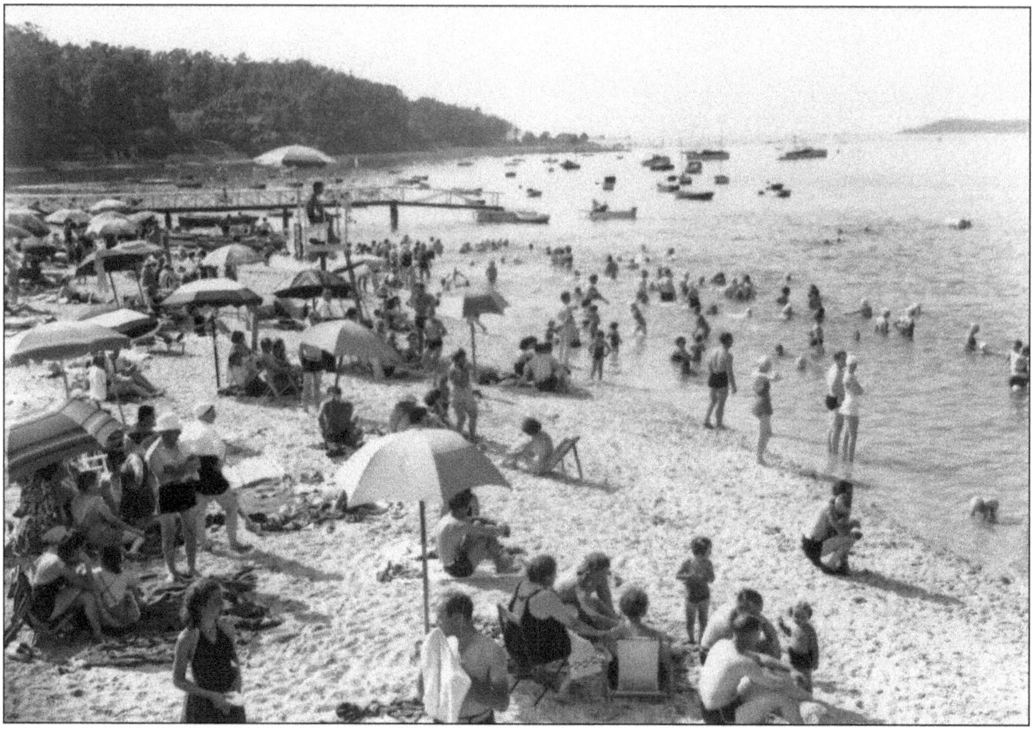

From the beginning, the private beaches were very popular with community residents and their guests. This is the crowd of beachgoers in August 1940. (Huntington Historical Society.)

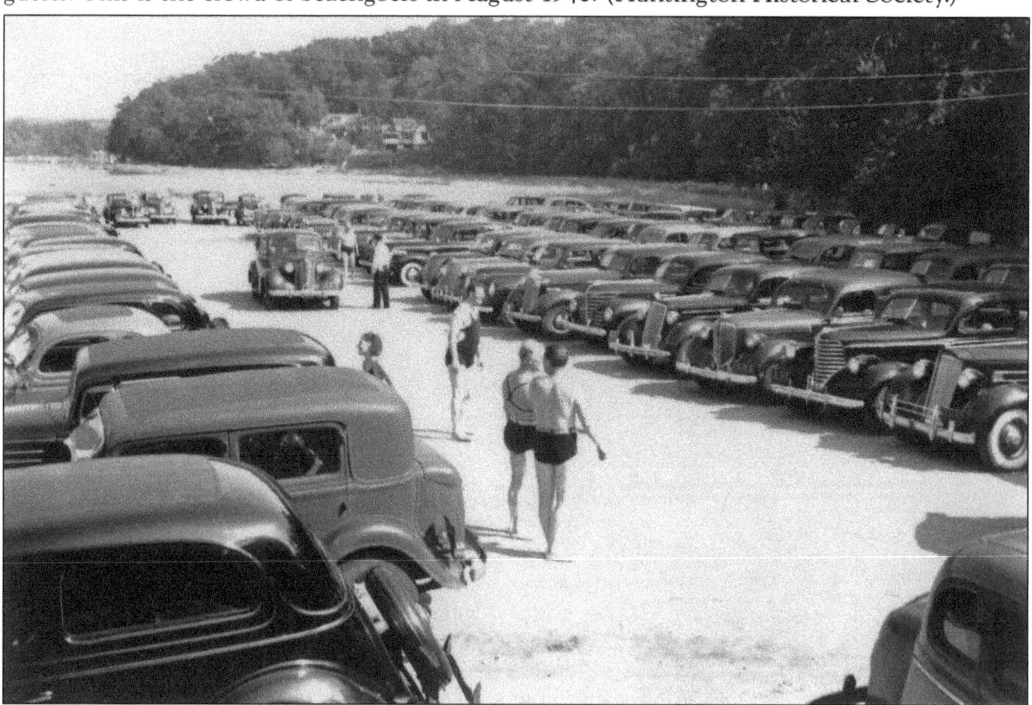

Lots of beachgoers resulted in an overflow of vehicles in the main parking lot. This photograph by Robert Stone was taken that same summer. (Huntington Historical Society.)

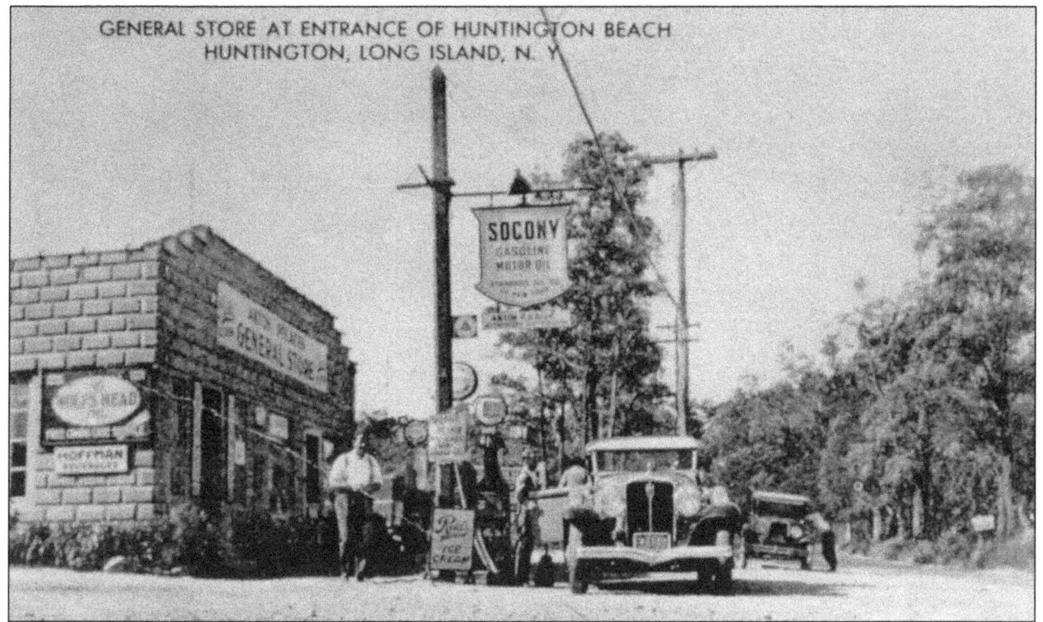

The growing number of cars and people presented an opportunity for Al Stanka, who had built the earliest summer homes in the community. In 1929, he built a general store across the street from the entrance to the community. The store was managed by Stanka's brother-in-law Anton Polacek. It sold groceries, hardware, and gasoline and featured a soda fountain. (Greenlawn-Centerport Historical Association.)

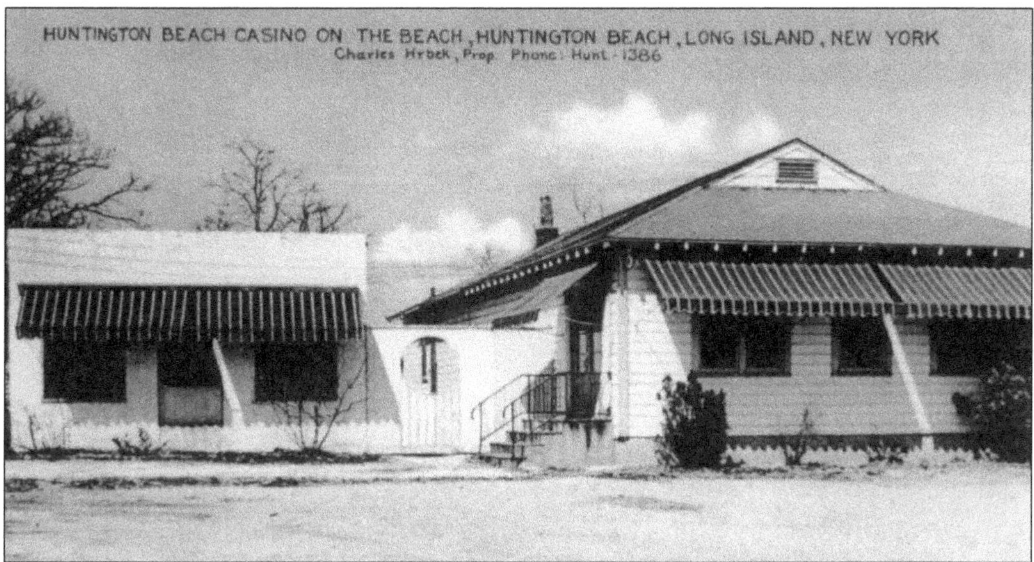

Here is the original casino building when it was operated by Charles Hrbek. The first casino was constructed in the 1930s and operated as a restaurant and bar for many years. It burned to the ground in 1953, and the bar was moved to what had been a storage building on Adams Street. The noise and traffic, as well as the behavior of the bar patrons, were constant problems for the nearby residents. When the association was required to install bathrooms at the beach for a cost of $18,000, a committee was chosen to meet with the casino owner. To resolve the issue, the Huntington Beach Community Association purchased the casino for $30,000 in 1962.

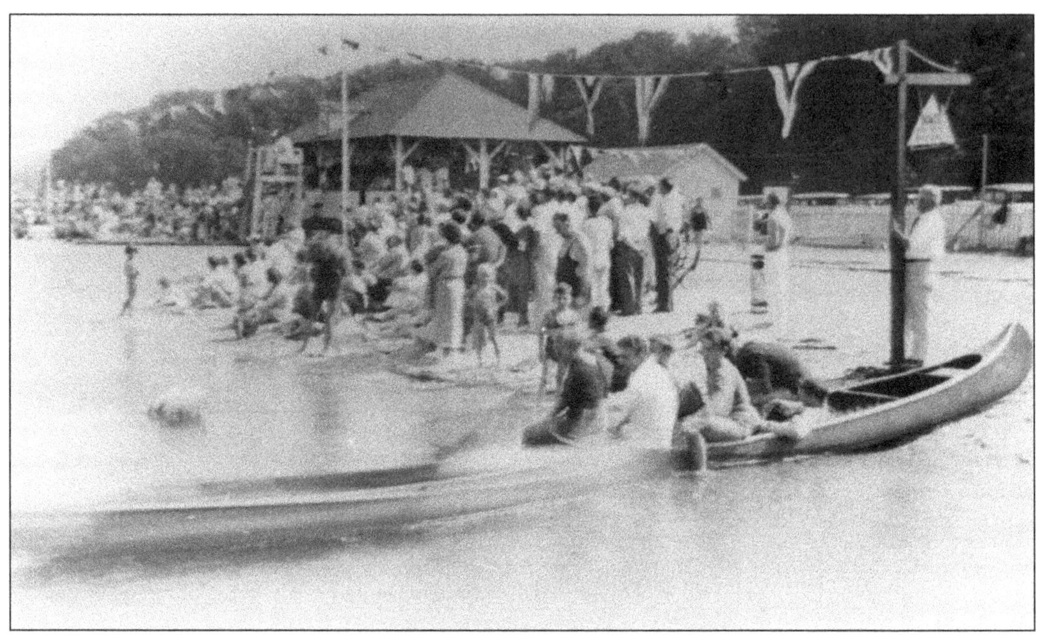

In the early years of the community, it was a tradition to celebrate Labor Day with a day of games and races for everyone before the summerhouses were closed and the summer rentals ended. Games included tug of war, a rolling pin toss, egg toss, canoe races, and a canoe tipping contest, but the highlight of the day was the swimming races. This tradition lives on as the community celebrates Family Day in mid-August. (Huntington Beach Community Association.)

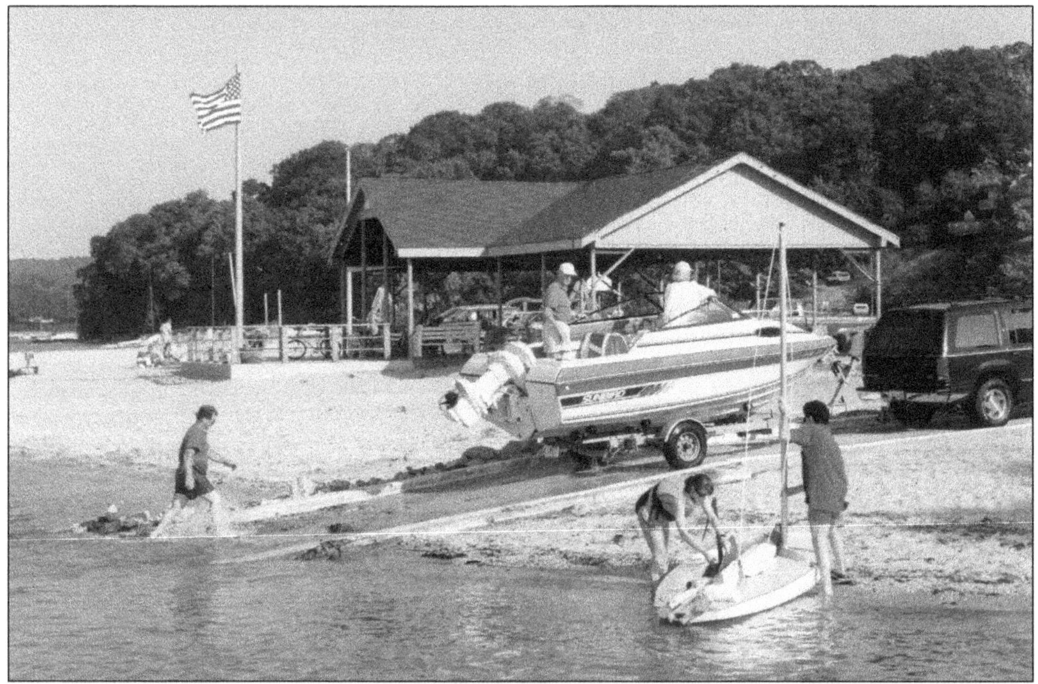

This recent photograph shows a typical beach scene. The original pavilion was replaced with a new and larger one in 1951. (Huntington Beach Community Association.)

Five

GOLD COAST ESTATES

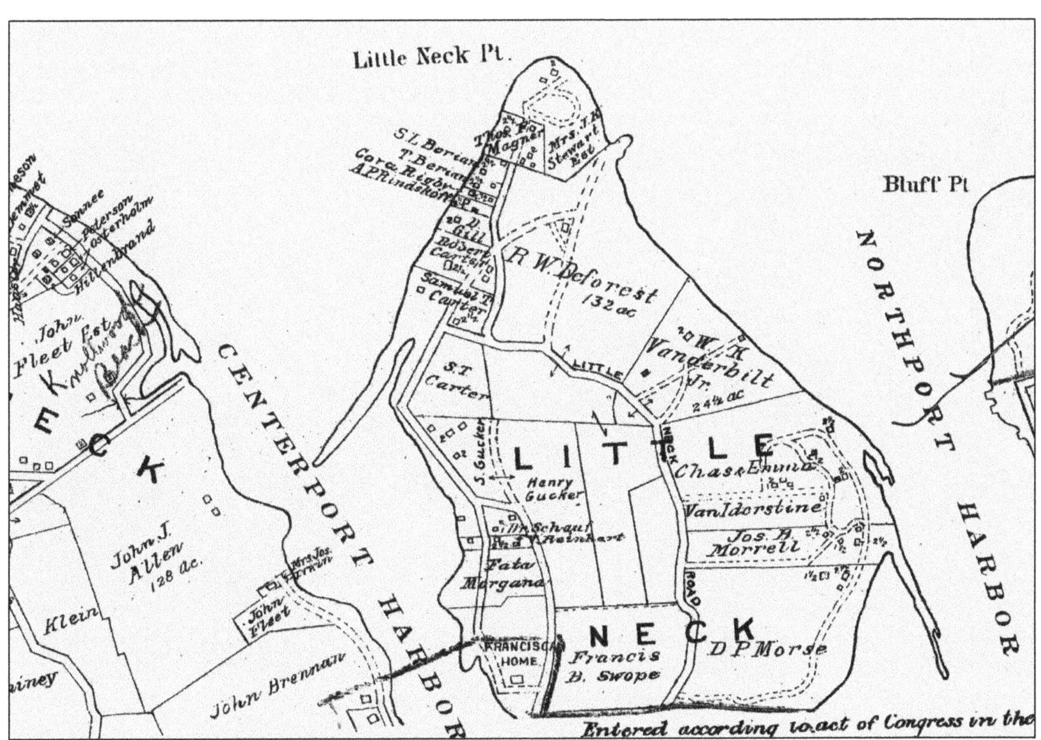

Seen here is a detail of a map of the Little Neck section of Centerport from 1917, published by E. Belcher Hyde Co. The owners of the large estates and fine houses had joined and supported the community. They formed and funded the Centerport Improvement Society in 1907. The society paved the road from Greenlawn Station to Centerport, as well as the roads around the millpond and to the end of Little Neck, established a lighting district, and improved the appearance of public places. In recent years, the civic associations have filled much of this role.

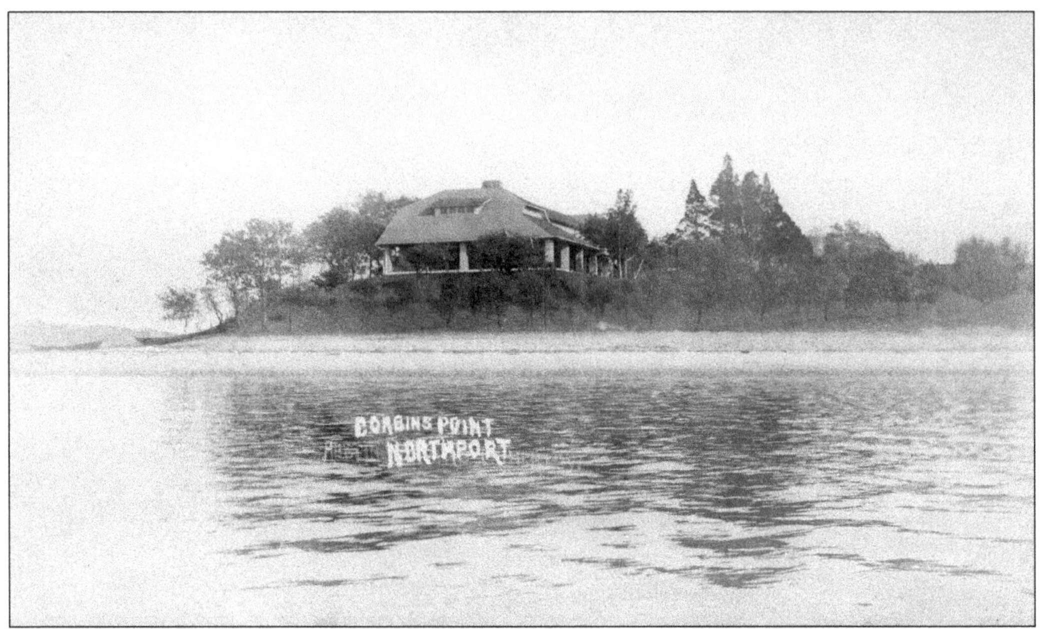

This postcard is incorrectly labeled "Northport," as it shows Austin Corbin's bungalow, at Austere Point or Little Neck Point in Centerport, built in the early 1900s. Corbin was the president of the Long Island Rail Road.

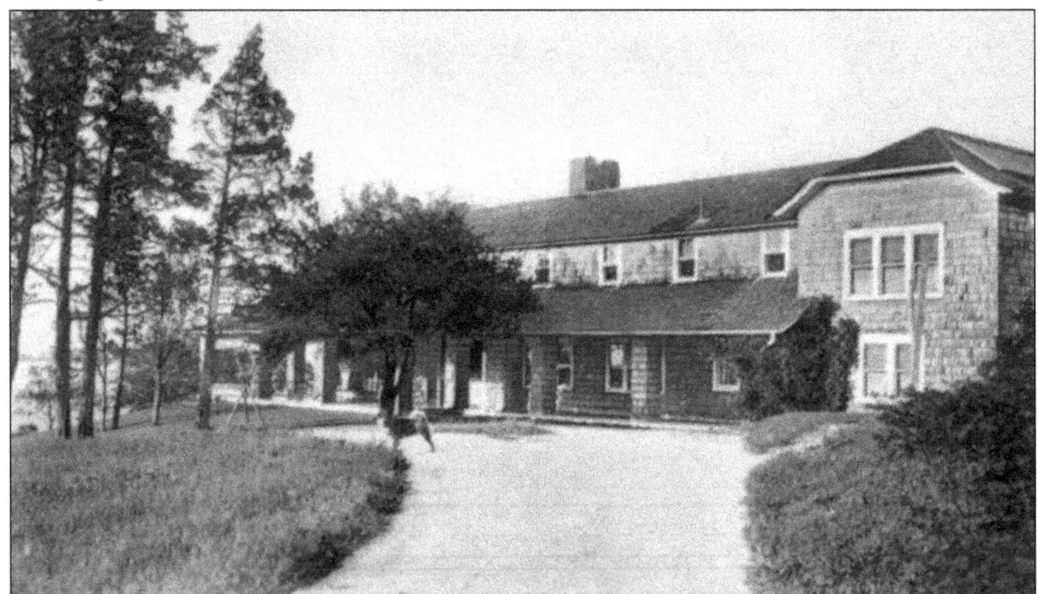

Corbin's 16-acre estate was later purchased by J.K. Stewart in 1915 for use as a summer home. (Stewart invented the speedometer, which was first installed in Ford Model Ts.) It was later sold to the R.B. Honeyman family and was sometimes called Honeyman Point. The Russian composer Sergei Rachmaninoff (1873–1943) and his wife, Natalia, spent two summers in Centerport in 1940 and 1941 in the Honeyman mansion overlooking the water. The composer needed to rest following minor surgery. It was here that Rachmaninoff wrote his final composition, *Symphonic Dances*, which was performed for the first time in 1942 by the Philadelphia Orchestra. The house burned down in 1960.

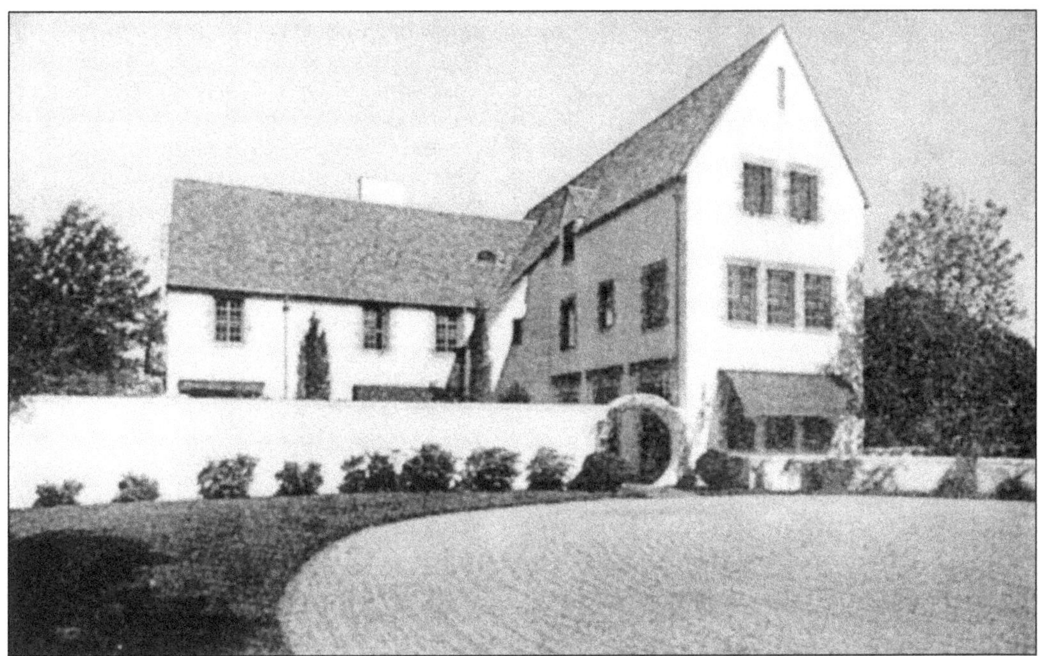

Plaisance, a Tudor estate built by Marius deBrabant around 1910, was designed by the noted architectural firm of Delano & Aldrich of New York. It featured a living room overlooking the pool and Northport Harbor. Marius deBrabant of Los Angeles was an administrator of the Union Pacific Railroad. His wife, the heiress Mary C. Clark, referred to as "Countess," was the daughter of US senator William A. Clark of Montana. Plaisance, the name they chose for their Long Island estate is French for "pleasantness," or a "pleasure ground laid out with shady walks, trees and shrubs, statuary, and ornamental water." The 84-acre site was subdivided in 1955. The mansion remained vacant, was vandalized, and was demolished in the late 1950s.

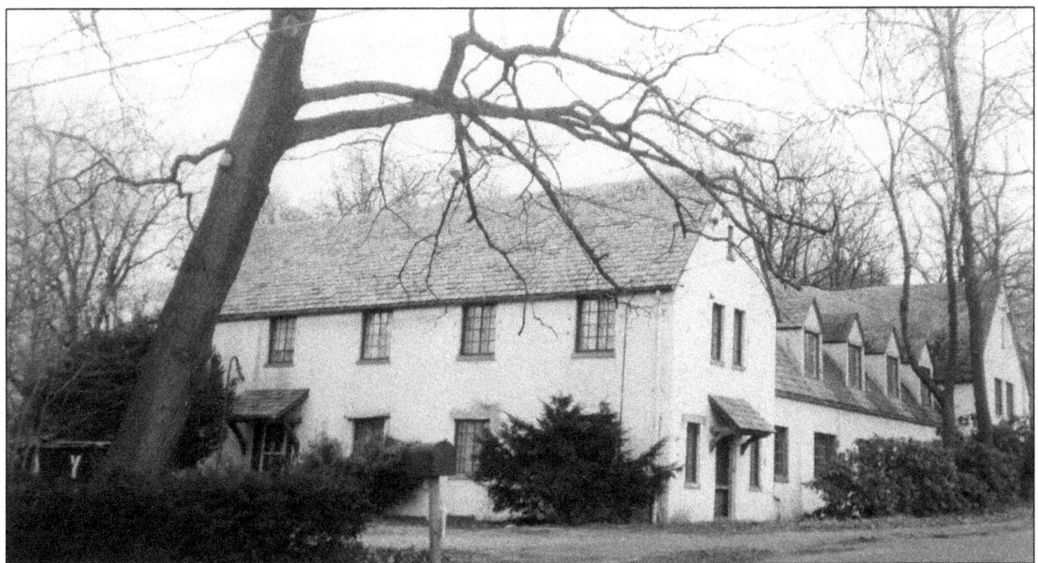

This house was the servants' quarters for the Plaisance mansion and is the last surviving structure of the 1910 estate. It is located on the southeast corner of Gina Drive and Little Neck Road. (Greenlawn-Centerport Historical Association.)

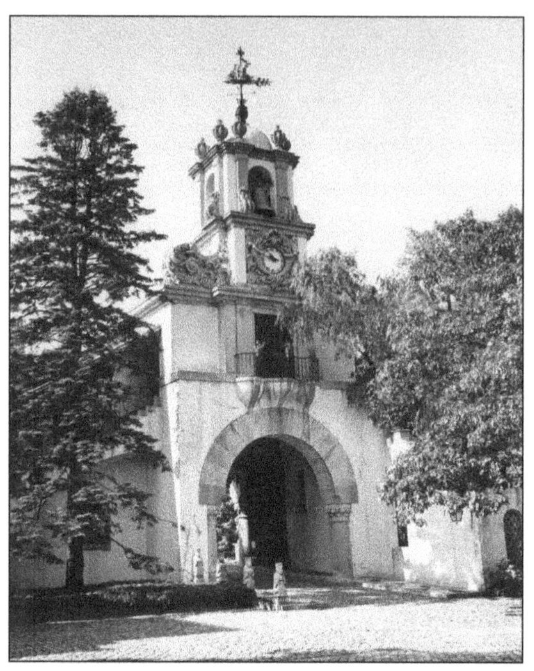

William Kissam Vanderbilt II (1878–1944) was Centerport's most famous resident. Vanderbilt purchased 24 acres of property on the Little Neck peninsula in 1910 and created Eagle's Nest, his summer home. The original mansion was a modest bungalow. Two iron eagles at the gate came from the old Grand Central Station in New York. There was a boathouse for his yachts and a hangar for his seaplane. He lived there happily with his second wife, Rose Warburton. In the 1920s, Vanderbilt bought more land, and the firm Warren & Wetmore enlarged and remodeled the mansion in the Spanish Revival style. Visitors today enter under the bell tower to the courtyard. It is believed that beams from the old Titus Mill purchased by Vanderbilt were used in the remodel. (Library of Congress.)

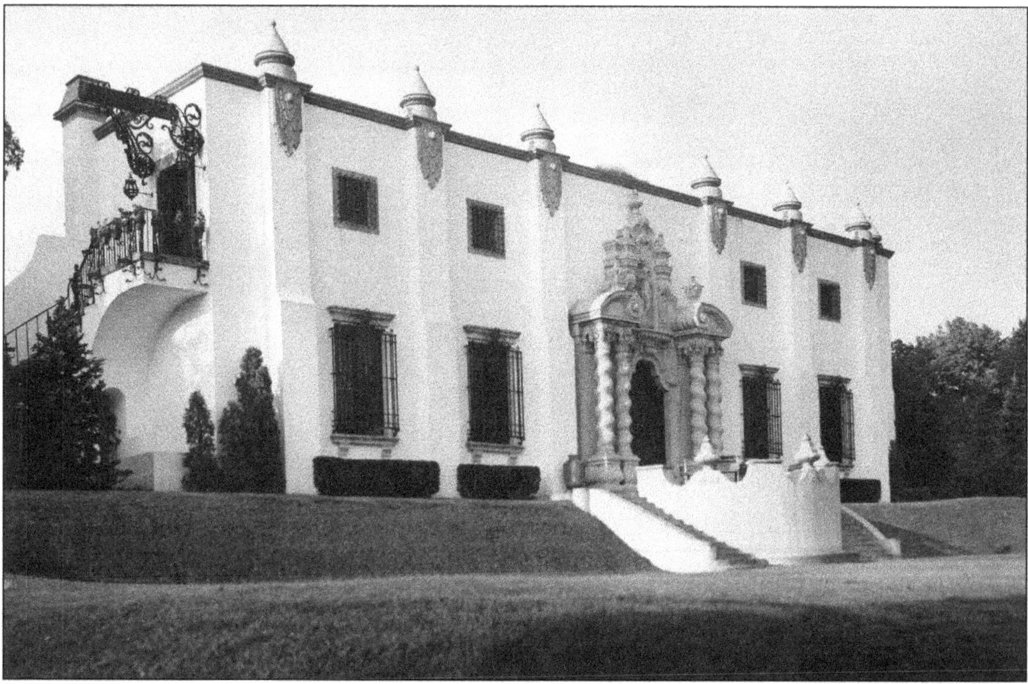

The Hall of Fishes Marine Museum was built in 1922, with an addition in 1929 to accommodate marine species Vanderbilt collected on his worldwide adventures. He also built a two-story Spanish-style garage with chauffeur quarters. Vanderbilt purchased 81 acres of the former DeBrabant estate in 1943. He died in 1944, leaving the Eagle's Nest estate to Suffolk County. It has been a natural history museum since 1950. A planetarium was added in 1971. The site was nominated to the National Register of Historic Places in 1985. Much more about the estate can be found in the 2015 book *Eagle's Nest* by Stephanie Gress. (Library of Congress.)

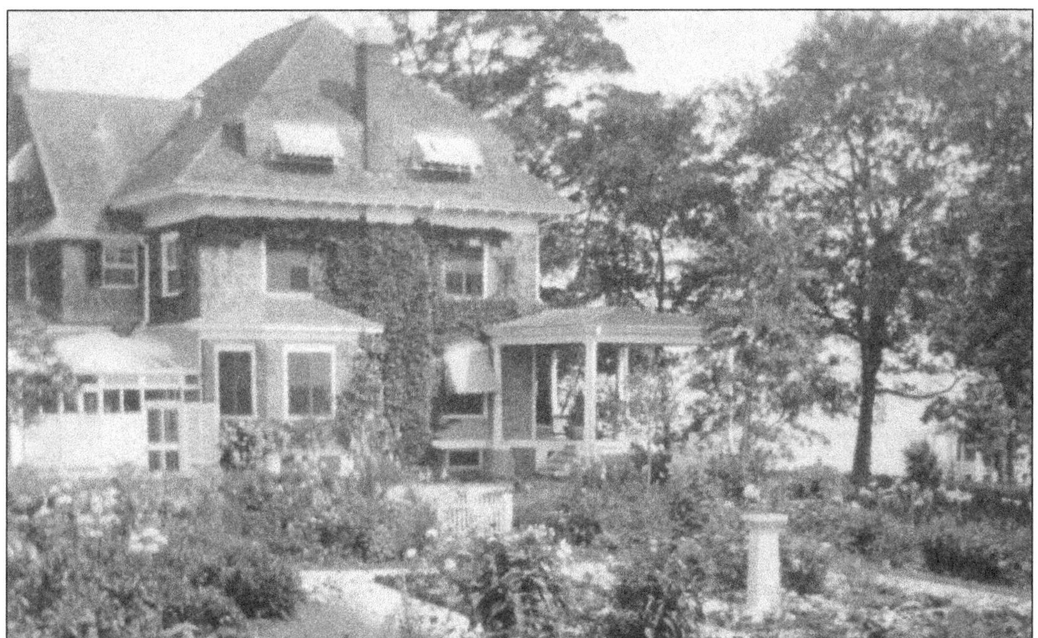

The Moorings, the estate of Joseph P. Morrell, is pictured here about 1906. Morrell purchased the home in 1901 from William Van Iderstine. Morrell was a charter member of Centerport Harbor Yacht Club; he died in 1930. His wife, Harriet Whiting Morrell, was a charter member of the Asharoken Garden Club and was active in the Methodist church. The Van Iderstine/Morrell mansion burned down in 1945 in one of the biggest fires in the history of the Centerport Fire Department. William Van Iderstine's brother Charles's mansion on Idle Day Drive was listed in the National Register of Historic Places in 1985. (Photograph by James Clemens, private collection.)

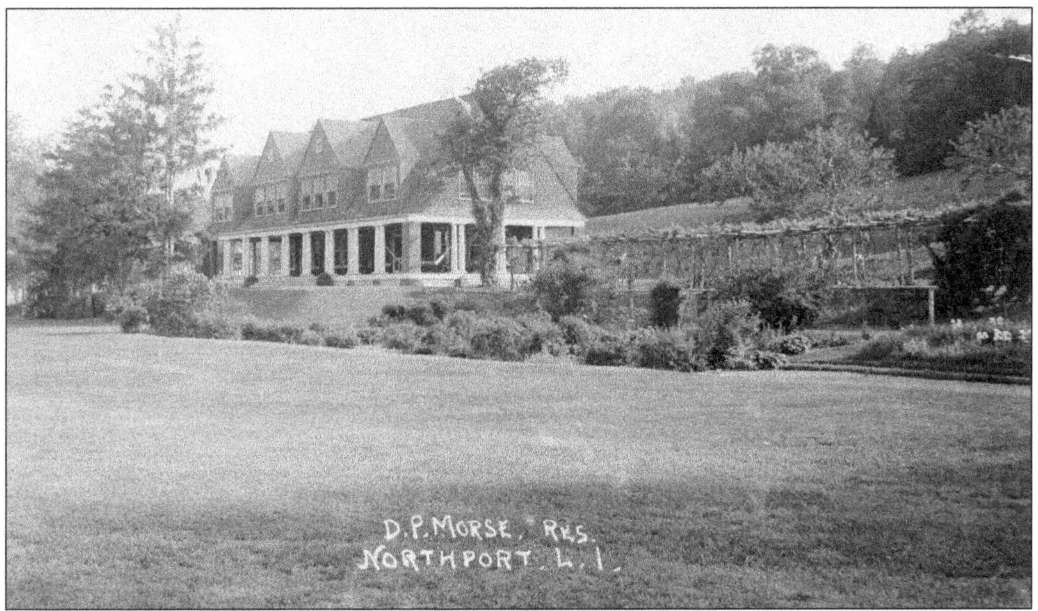

In 1901, Daniel P. Morse, a shoe manufacturer, purchased the 32-acre Thomas Donahue property on the east side of Little Neck. He began making extensive improvements to the buildings and graded and built new roads. This photograph of his house is by J.V. Feather, mislabeled as Northport.

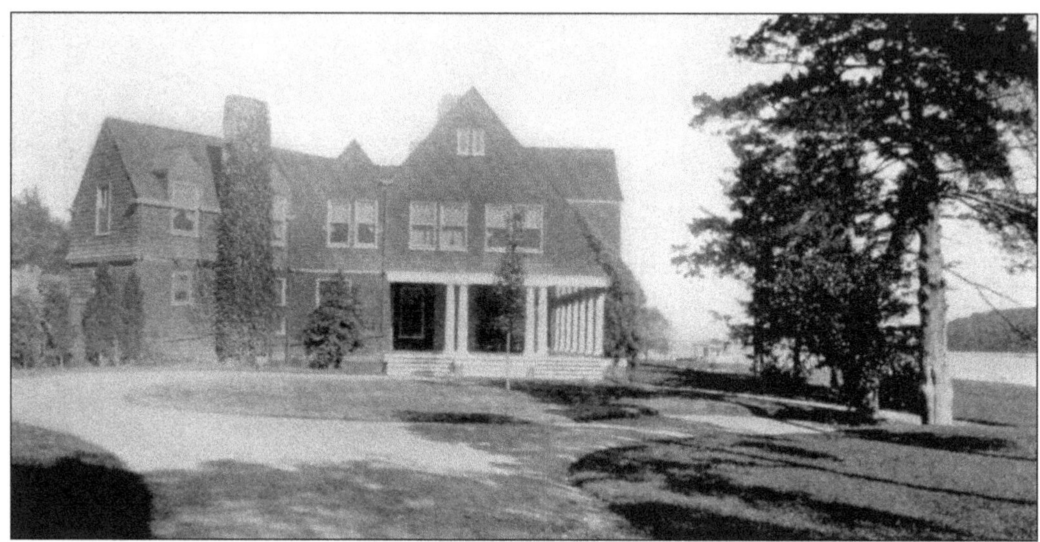

Morse had nearly completed a major renovation of the house when it was destroyed by fire in March 1902. Work on a new structure began immediately, and this handsome mansion was soon completed. The mansion was later purchased by the Centerport Harbor Yacht Club.

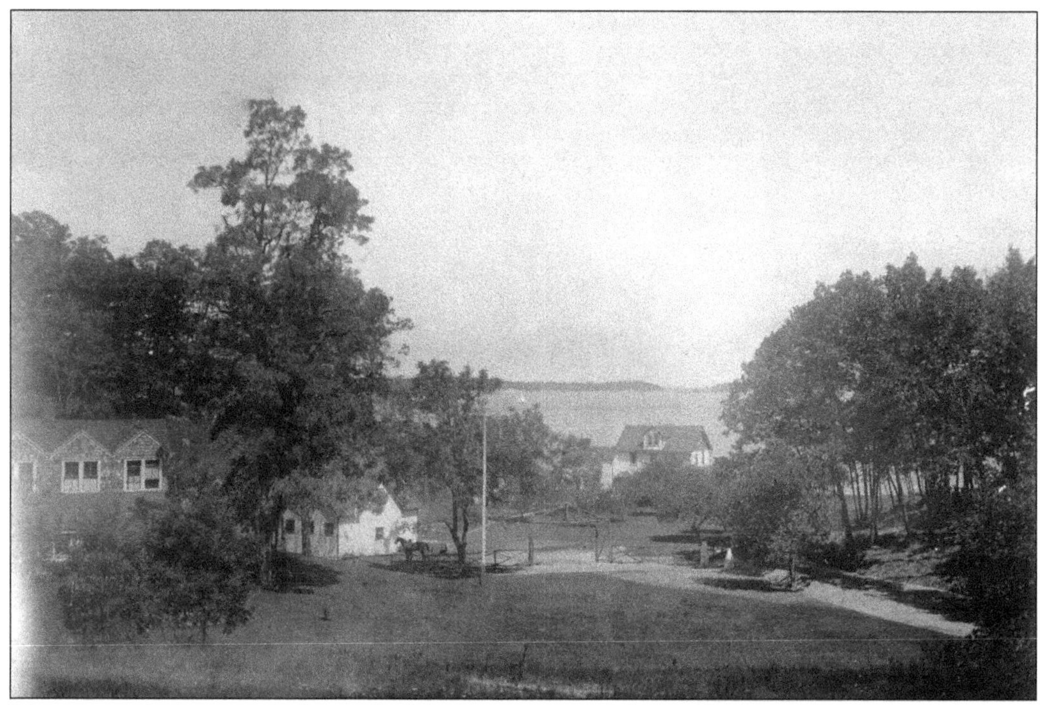

This unusual photograph shows the Morse estate around 1910. It shows the driveway close to the shore, the large garage and the back (servants') wing of the house. The angle from which this photograph was taken gives the impression that the Morrell mansion in the background is closer to Northport Harbor than the Morse estate, which is not the case. (Huntington Historical Society.)

Maude Morse (left) is holding baby Lawrence; Kate Morse is with Howard and Henry around 1910. This picture was taken on the side lawn of the house. (Greenlawn-Centerport Historical Association.)

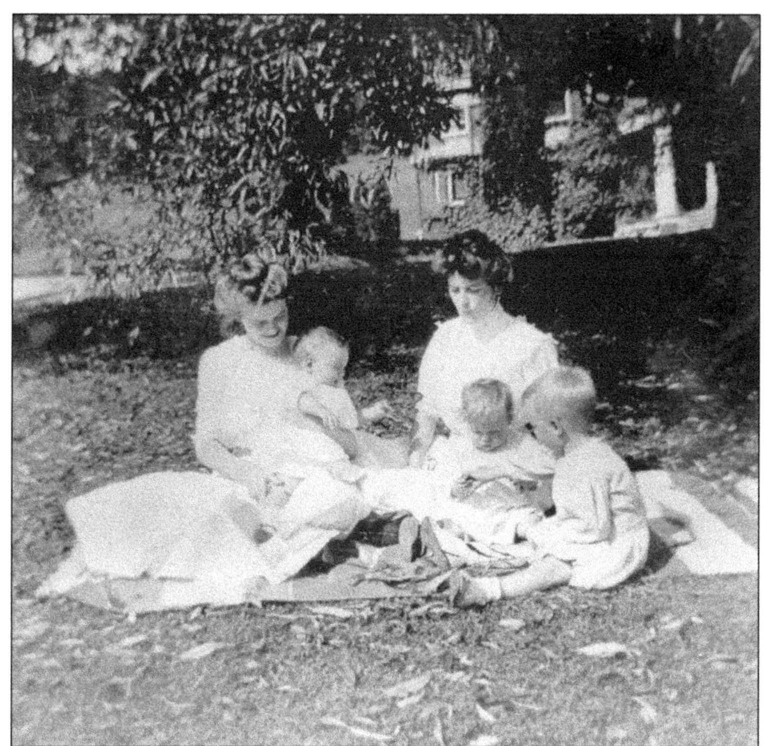

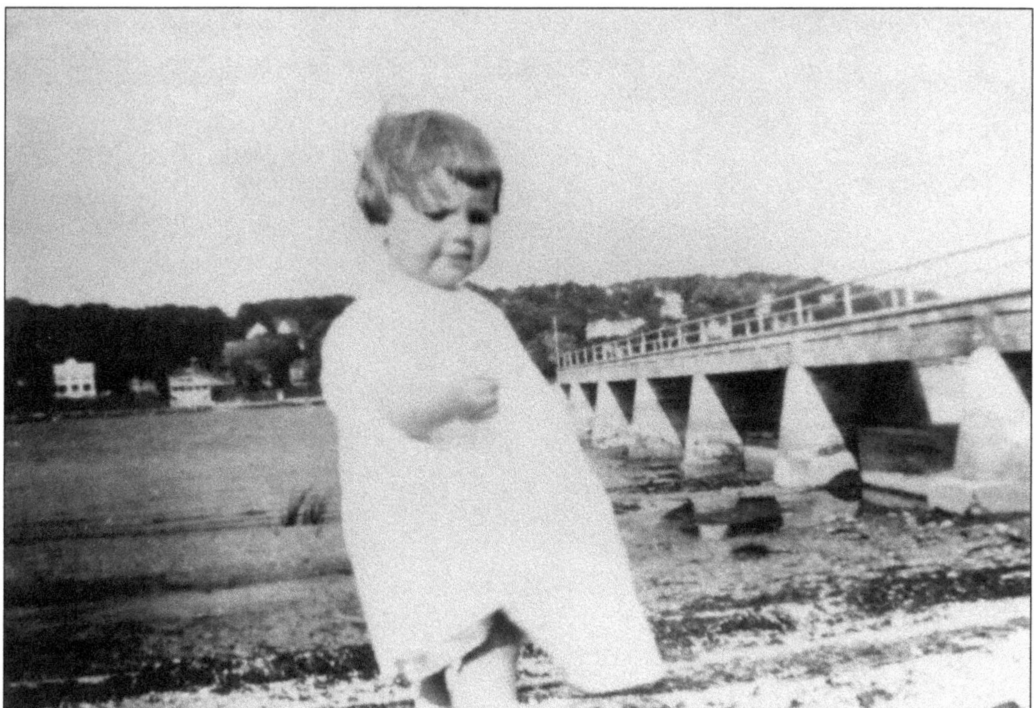

Janet Morse Johnson is seen here in front of the new concrete pier around 1919. The Centerport Harbor Yacht Club used the pier for years after purchasing the property. (Greenlawn-Centerport Historical Association.)

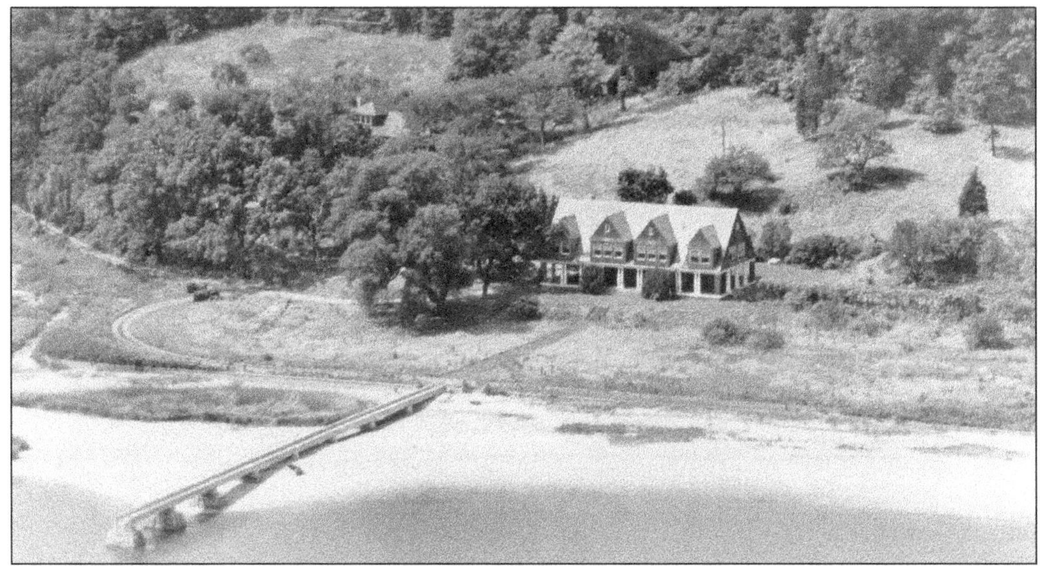

The Morse family sold the estate to Joseph Wunsch, who subdivided the property for residential development. The Centerport Harbor Yacht Club, which had been incorporated in 1947, purchased the Morse house and two-and-a-half acres from Wunsch in 1950. The new yacht club changed its name to the Centerport Yacht Club in 1951, but there is no connection between the current club and the earlier one, which was located on the millpond. (Greenlawn-Centerport Historical Association.)

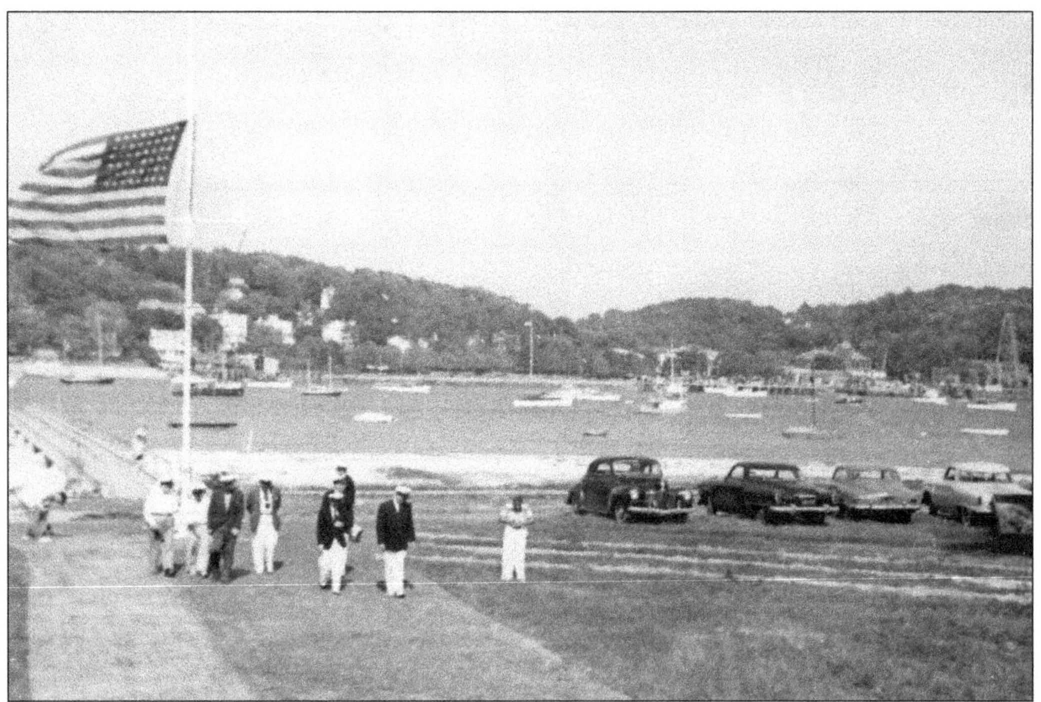

These men are going into Commissioning Day at the Centerport Yacht Club in its new and permanent home. The wide, flat lawn and the panoramic view of Northport make a wonderful backdrop for the ceremony. (Greenlawn-Centerport Historical Association.)

Looking south from the northeast corner of Centerport harbor is this view of the dock on the H.H. Koch property with a boy and the boathouse of Dr. Adam Schauf.

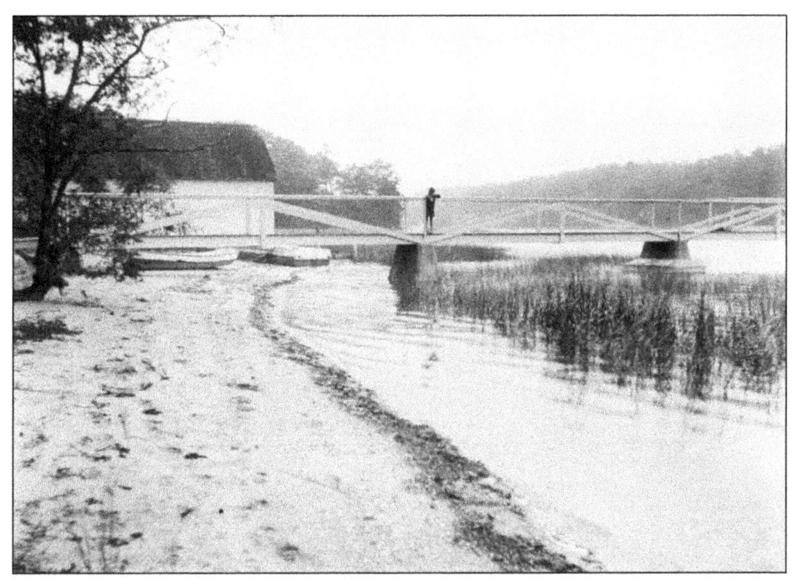

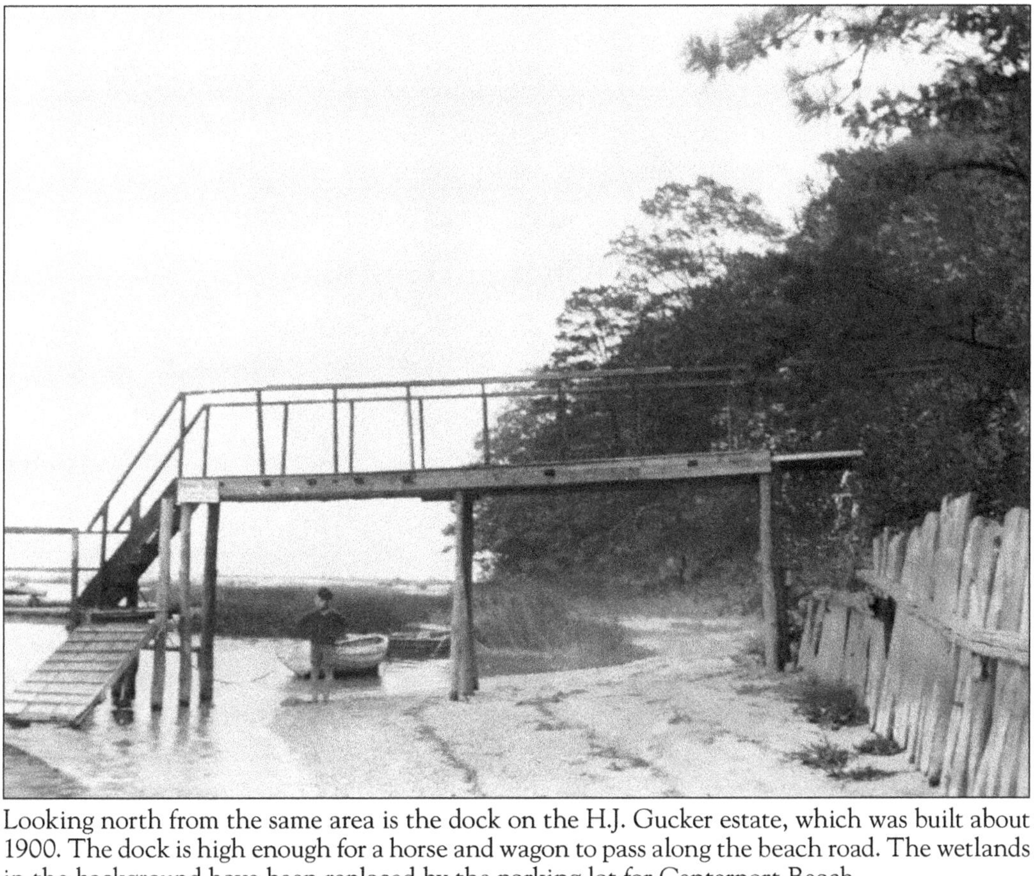

Looking north from the same area is the dock on the H.J. Gucker estate, which was built about 1900. The dock is high enough for a horse and wagon to pass along the beach road. The wetlands in the background have been replaced by the parking lot for Centerport Beach.

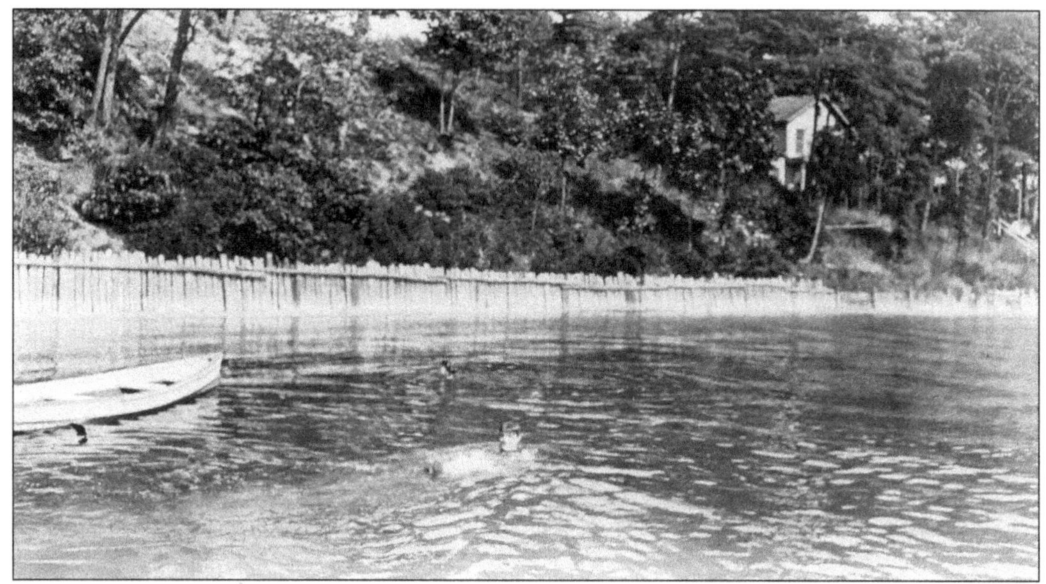

This photograph of a swimmer was taken by H.J. Gucker from his dock in 1909. The Sammis-Bunce house is in the background on the right.

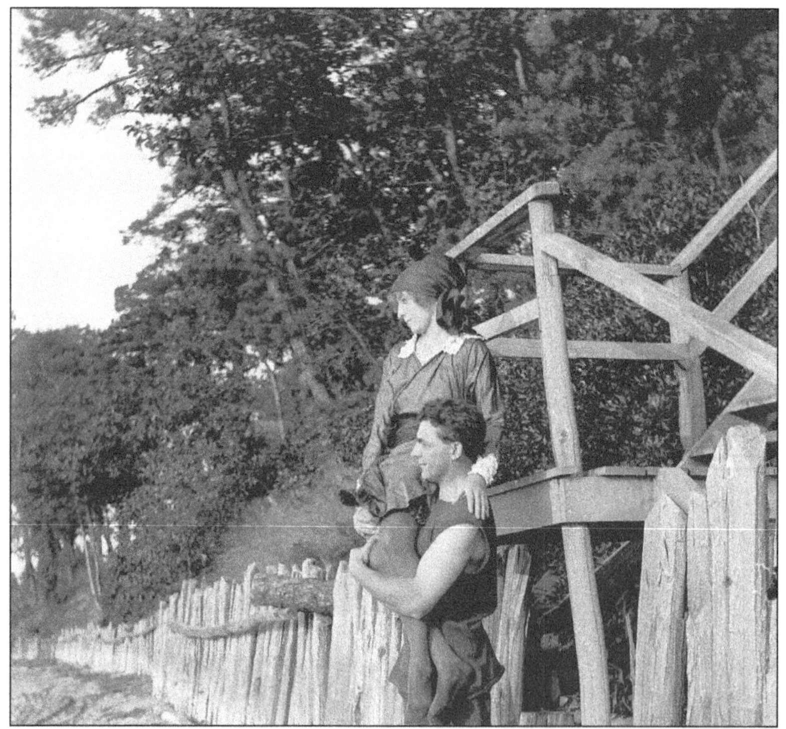

A couple relaxes on the beach in front of the Gucker summerhouse. Many of the original bulkheads in Centerport were composed of vertical locust posts.

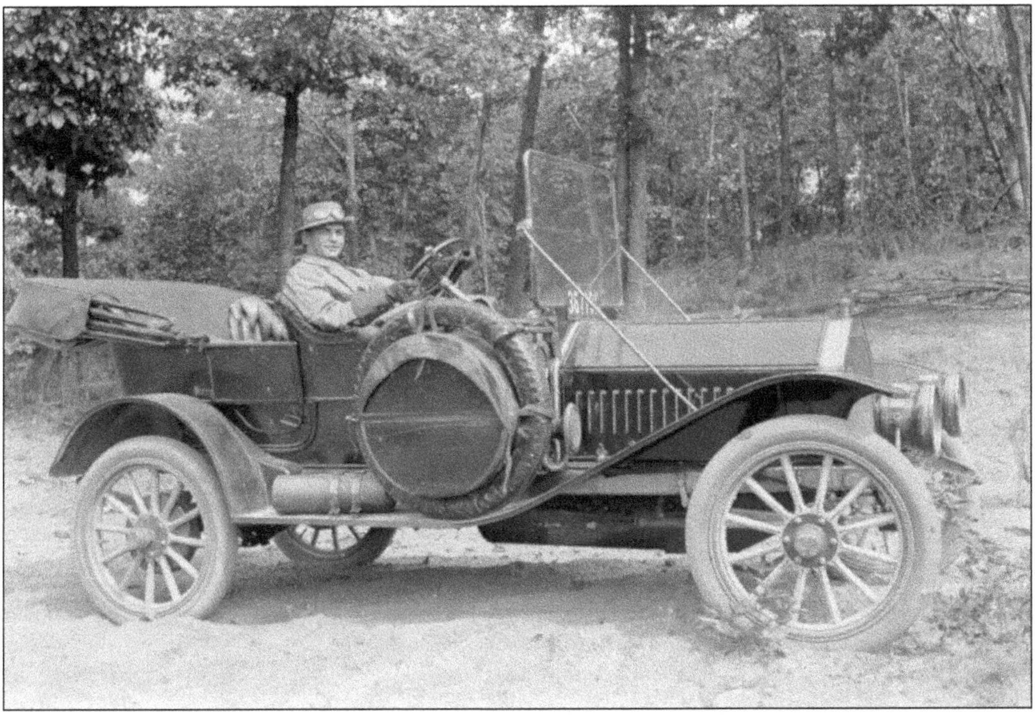

Gucker is seen here in his driveway, ready for a day of driving in a top-of-the-line Buick Model 39 five passenger touring car.

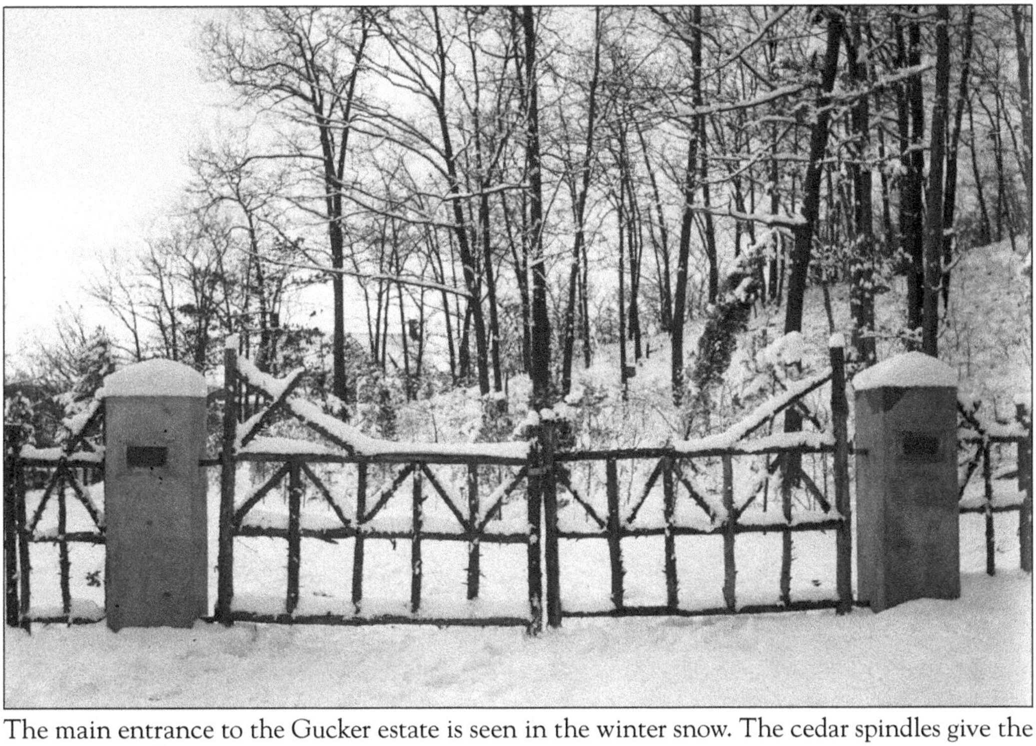

The main entrance to the Gucker estate is seen in the winter snow. The cedar spindles give the gates a rustic flavor.

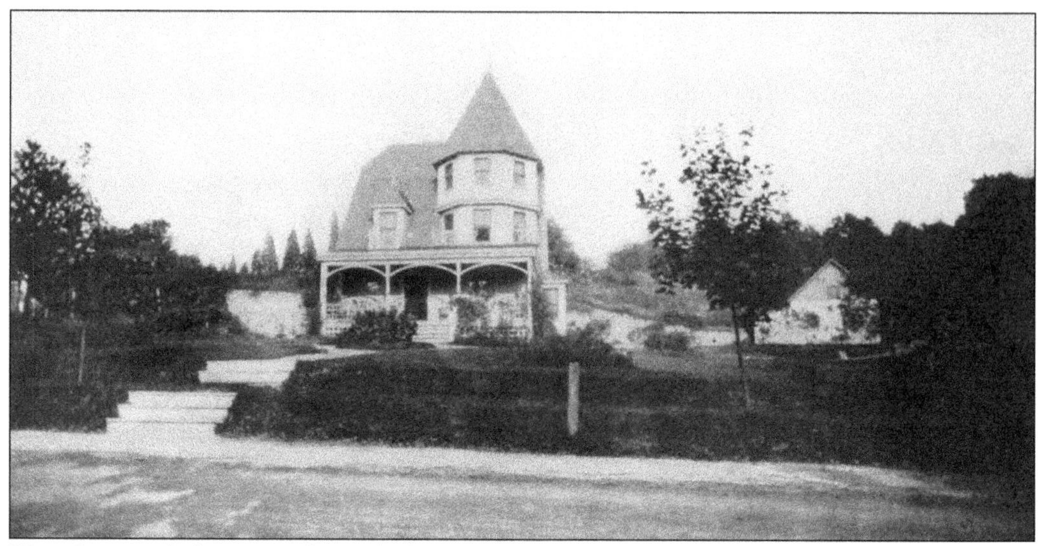

This photograph from 1909 shows the home of George "Rice" Swope on the east side of Little Neck Road. Brothers George and Charles "Barton" Swope were popular comedians of the vaudeville era. Their stage names were Rice & Barton. They were born in Three Springs, Huntingdon County, Pennsylvania, and came to Centerport in 1882. George was married to Anna Frances Seay, whose stage name was Frankie Haines. She later married August Hoddick of Buffalo, an architect. George died in 1909, and Charles died in 1917. Two more brothers, John and Erastus, also lived and died in Centerport. All four brothers and Haines are buried in the Northport Rural Cemetery with a substantial monument.

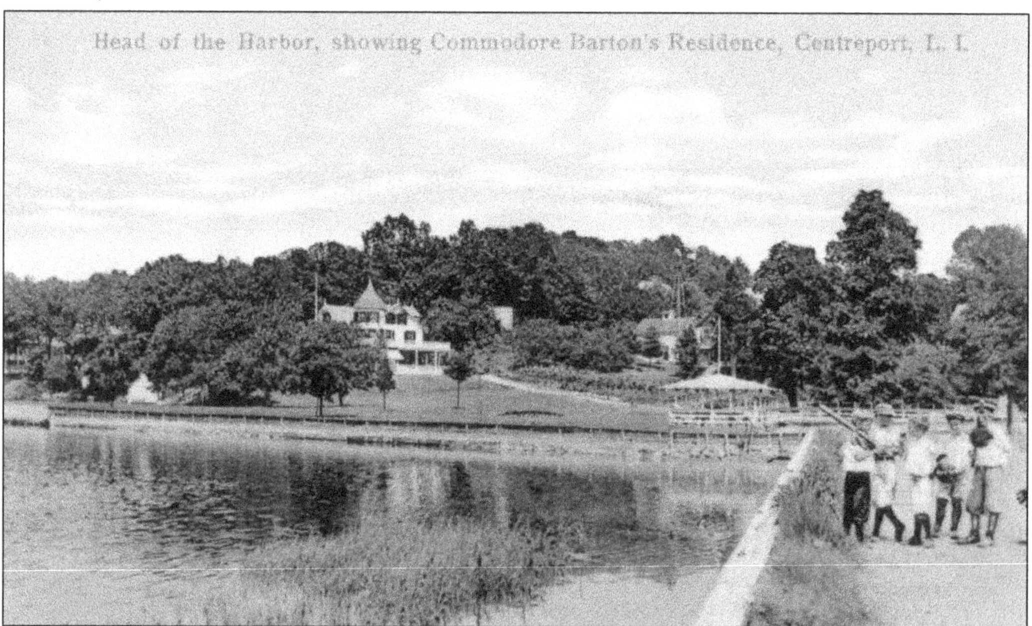

Perhaps this group of boys with baseball gear on the mill dam are on their way to the playing fields at the Centerport School, a short walk up the hill on the east side of the causeway. The buildings on the estate of Charles Barton in the background long dominated the inner harbor. Barton, who was commodore of the Centerport Yacht Club in 1913, loved the title and used it for the rest of his life. The property is now the location of Our Lady Queen of Martyrs Church.

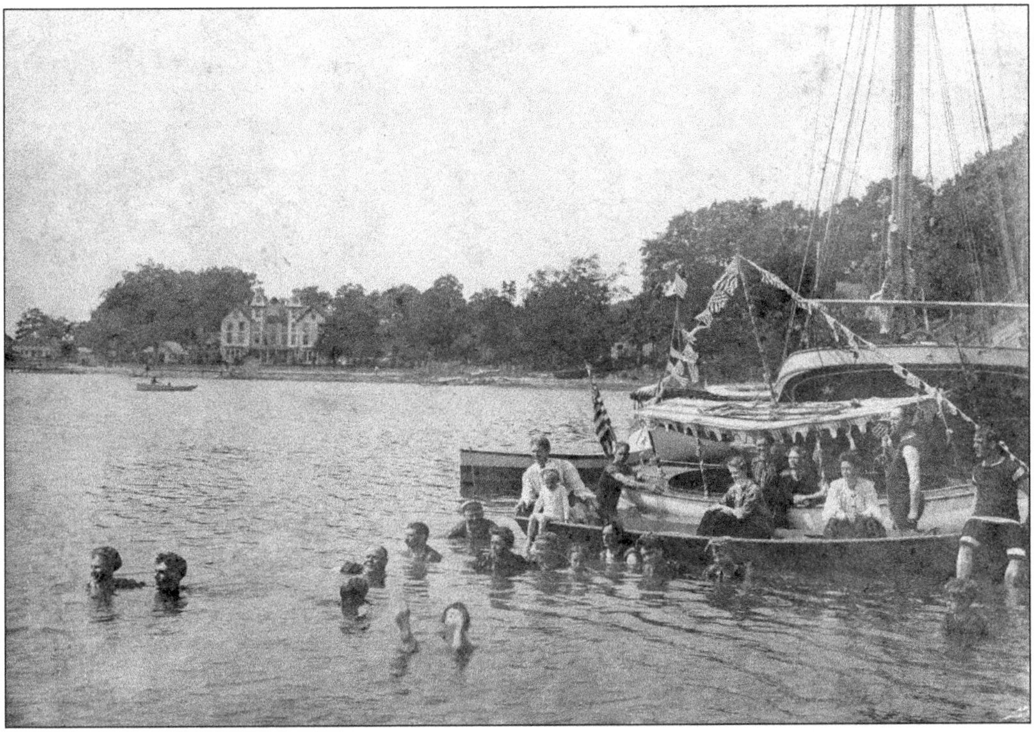

These swimmers in front of Commodore Barton's home during Regatta Day at the Centerport Yacht Club included Charles and his brother George. Other guests included George's wife Frankie Haines, Adelia Brown, and Charles Mack. (Greenlawn-Centerport Historical Association.)

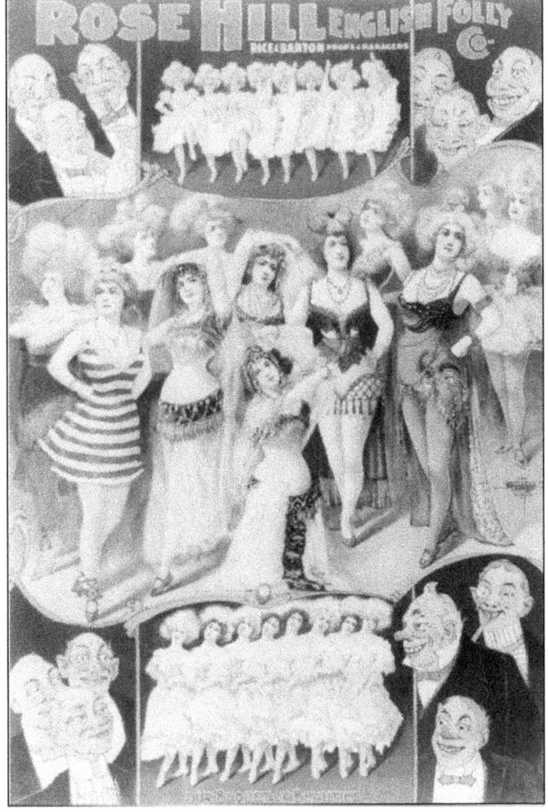

Rice & Barton managed and performed in the Rose Hill English Folly Company. Their show was also known as Rice & Barton's Big Gaiety Spectacular Extravaganza. They performed at the Columbia Opera House in Greenlawn and the Union Opera House in Northport. They sometimes used the former Methodist Episcopal church on the west side of the mill dam for rehearsals. (Library of Congress.)

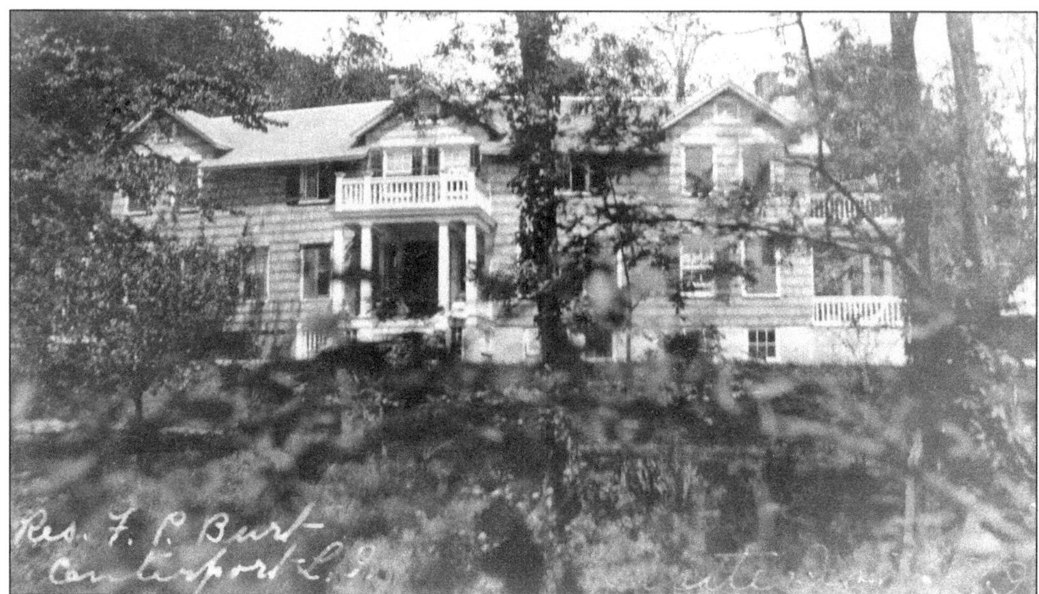

The Frederick P. Burt home, completed in December 1907 on Mill Dam Road, was up the hill behind the Dickinson house. Burt was the editor of the *Machinist News* as well as a member of the Centerport Improvement Society in 1907. He owned a yacht and was known to have power boated to Stamford, Connecticut. In 1909, the local newspaper reported, "Mrs. Cotton built a bungalow on the highest elevation of the Burt property." Idalene Cotton was a vaudeville actress with Rice & Barton. Her husband was the dancer Nick Long Sr. (William Townsend Perks.)

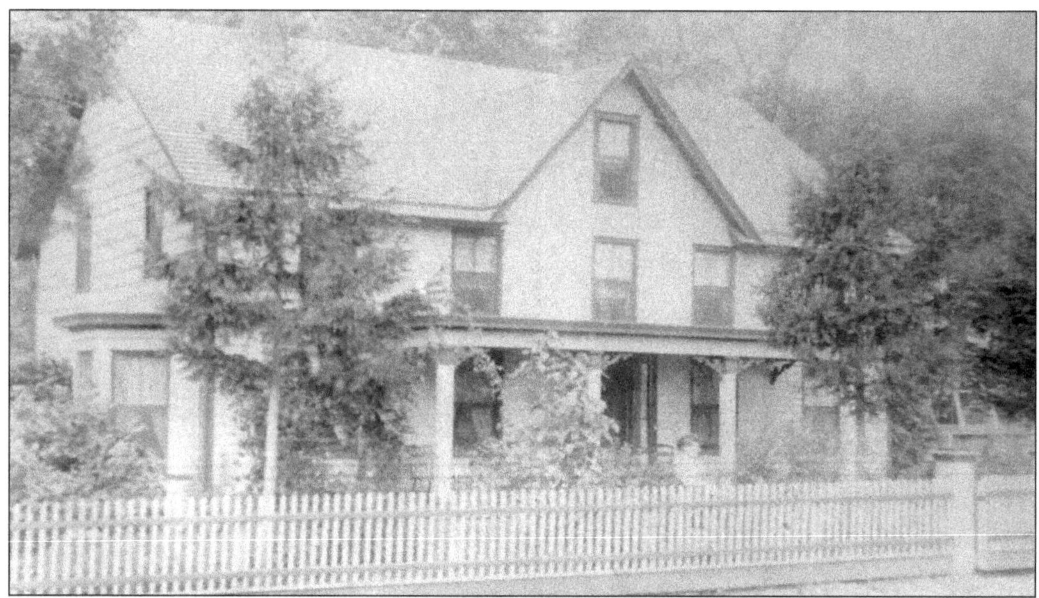

This house on Little Neck Road was built by Charles Higbie and purchased in 1888 by Miles E. Burling. This photograph is from around 1892. Miles E. Burling was a local farmer who took in summer boarders. He called it Locust Grove Cottage. An opportunity to go fishing was offered to his guests. Burling owned property on both sides of Little Neck Road. He died in 1922 at the age of 92. His wife had died 17 years earlier. (Greenlawn-Centerport Historical Association.)

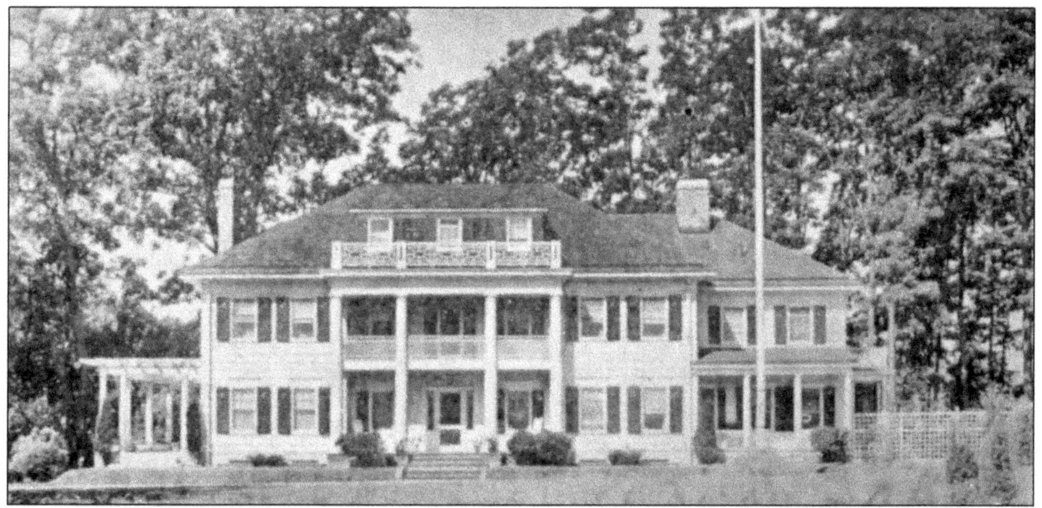

Miles Burling's son Charles E. Burling graduated from Huntington High School and was very successful in the wool trade. He tore down the old house in 1920 and replaced it with this more impressive house and gardens. He called his new mansion Nunna Koma, an Indian phrase for "On the Shore."

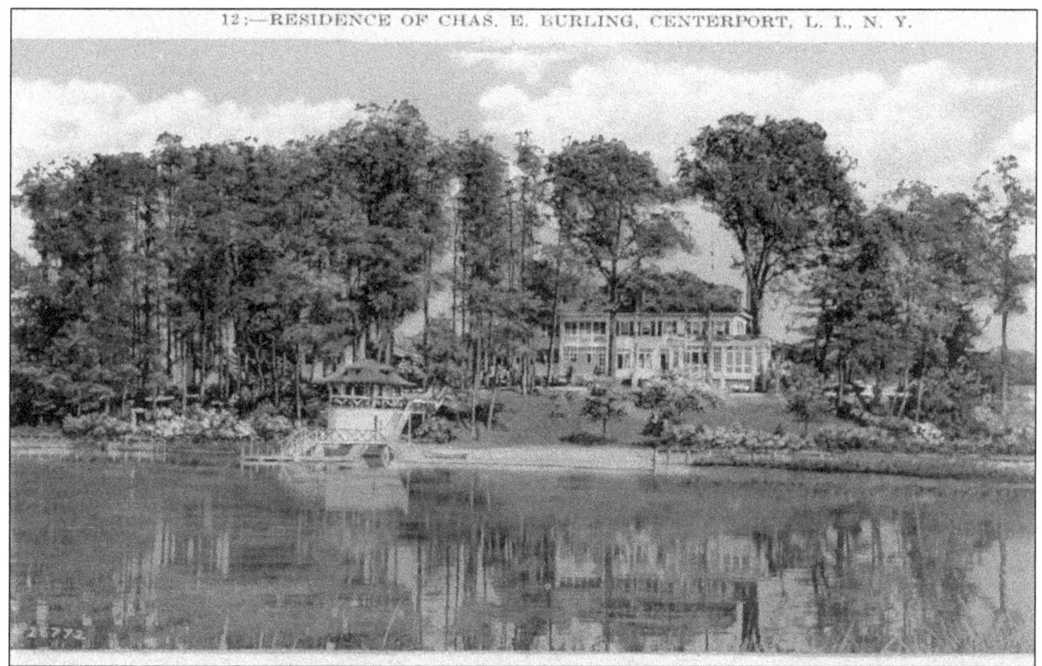

Charles E. Burling was superintendent of the Janes Methodist Episcopal Sunday school in Brooklyn, director of the Methodist Home for the Aged, and trustee of the Methodist Episcopal Hospital. He was a strong supporter of the Centerport Methodist Episcopal Church. His shorefront on the millpond featured a dock and a gazebo on an island.

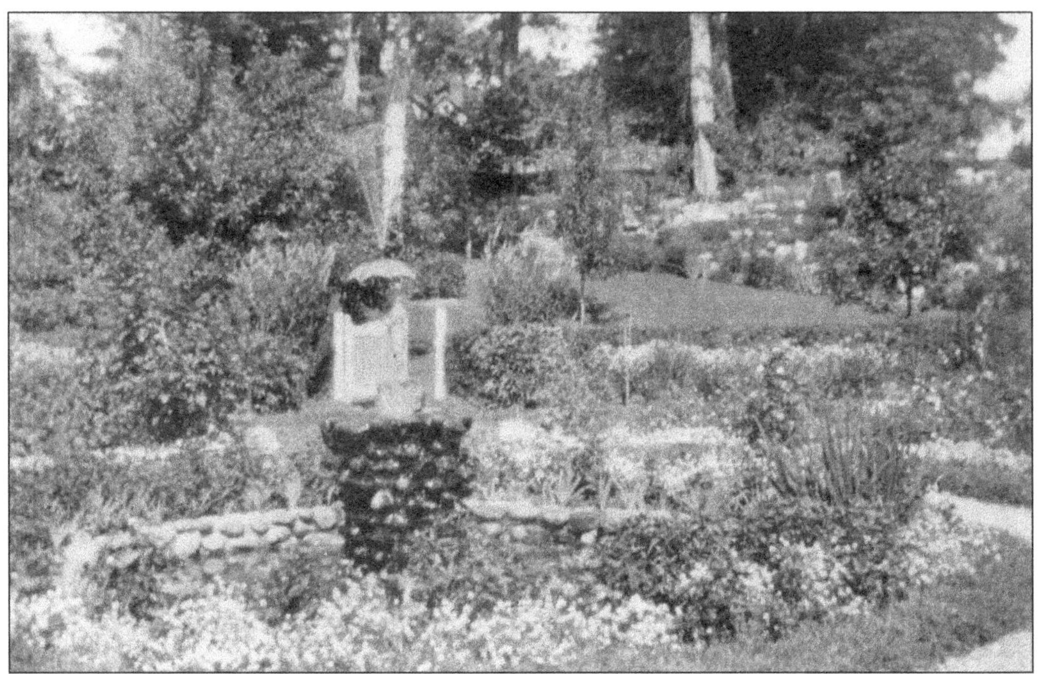

The sunken gardens at the Burling estate on the south side of the home are shown here around 1925–1927. Clara Burling would open her home and gardens to the public as a benefit for the Centerport Methodist Church. (Greenlawn-Centerport Historical Association.)

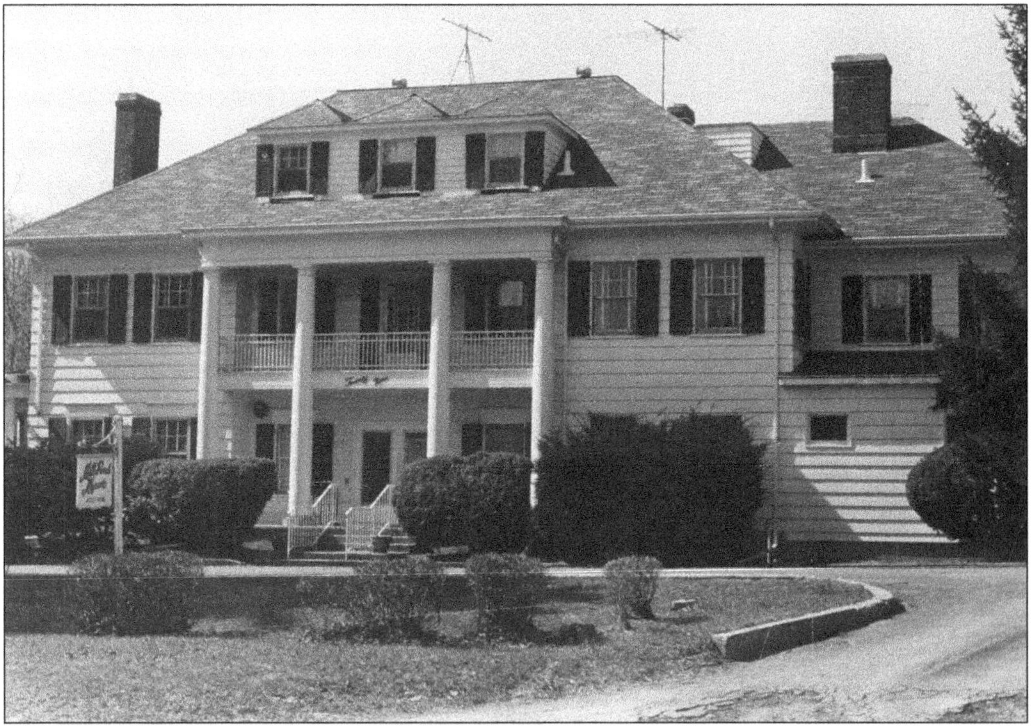

The Burling country house later became the Mill Pond Manor Rest Home. It was torn down in 2016 and replaced by two condominium buildings. (Greenlawn-Centerport Historical Association.)

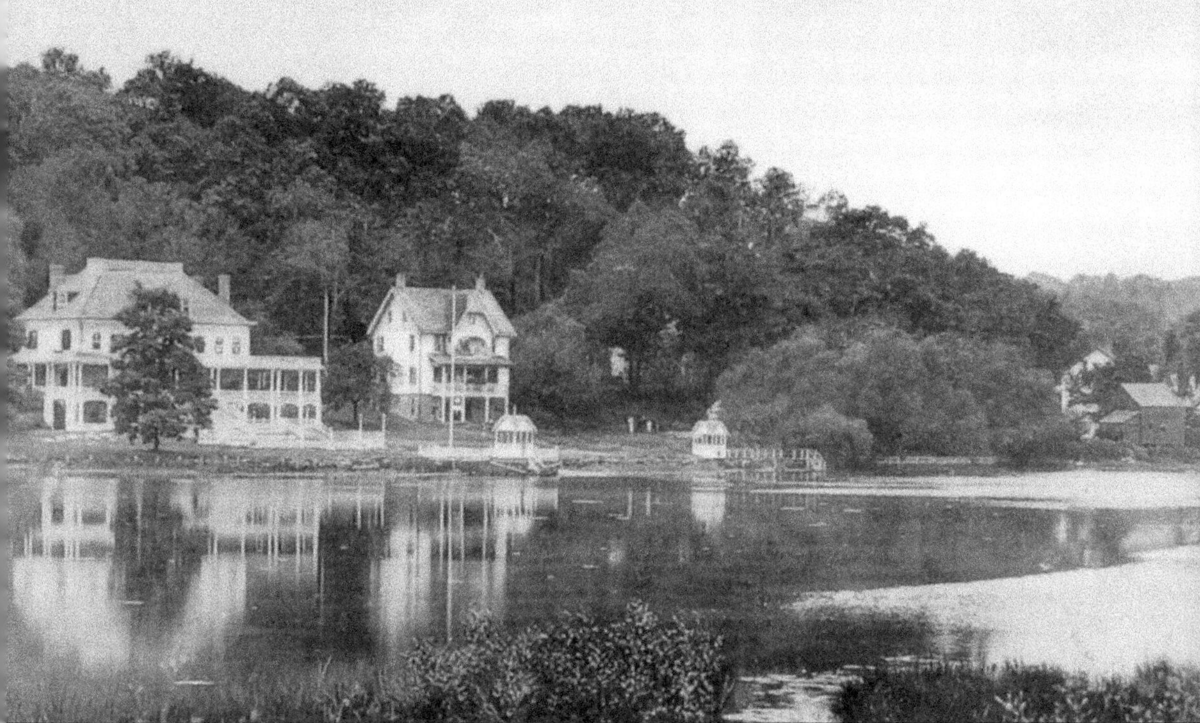

This postcard titled "Head of the Millpond" shows the residence of Charles Morse Whitney, called Castle Wigmore, on the left and the servants' quarters on the right. Whitney was a prominent Manhattan attorney as well as a talented musician. With other members of his family, he formed the Mozart Sextet, a classical music group that toured throughout the country. Whitney's daughter Estelle died in June 1920 and is buried in Northport Rural Cemetery. Charles himself died in December of that year and his wife, Emma, died a year later. The mansion house and the servants' quarters stand very close to the road from Huntington to Northport and have been used as restaurants for many years.

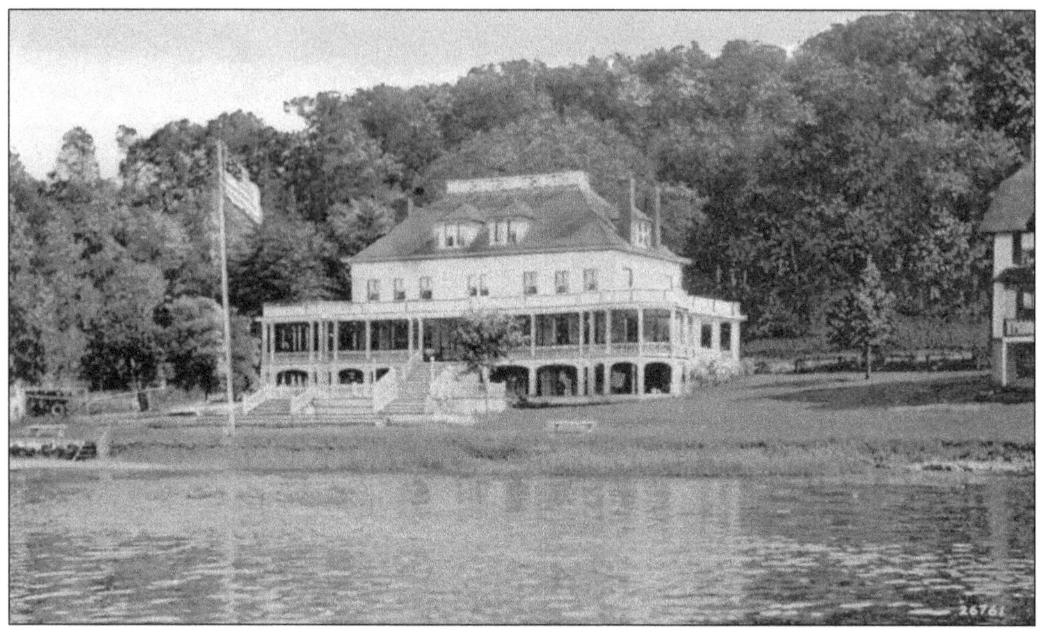

The Charles M. Whitney mansion, with its waterfront stairways and terraces, became a boardinghouse before World War I, and soon after, LaTorre's Restaurant. Taking advantage of its accessible shoreline and picture-perfect views, it has been a restaurant ever since.

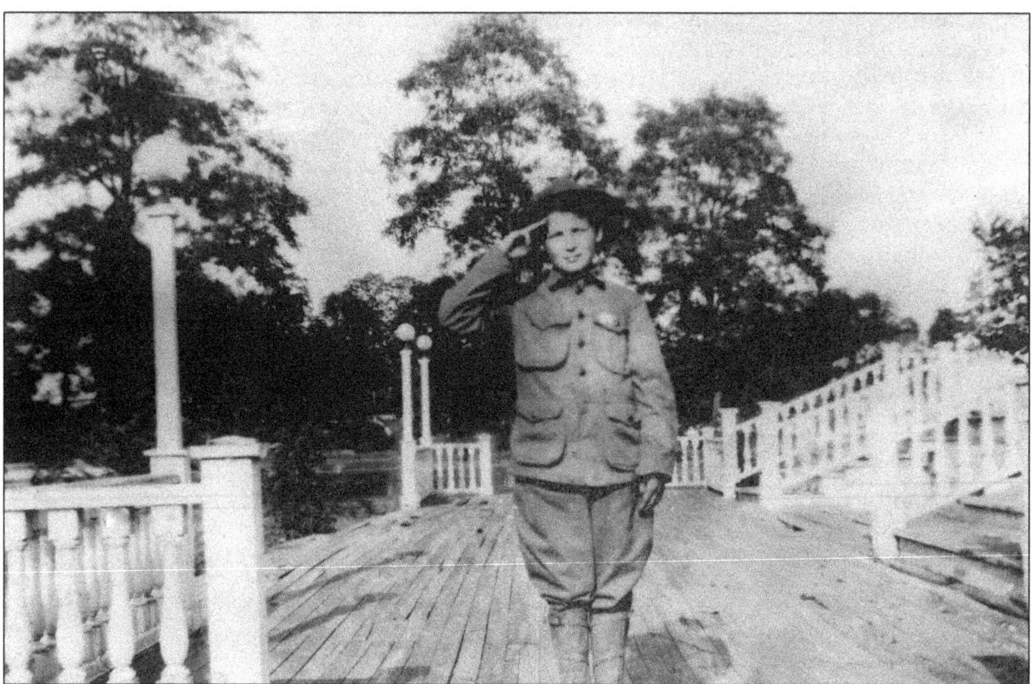

The Whitney mansion had a series of stairways and terraces leading down to the shore of the Mill Pond. This unidentified Boy Scout is standing on the steps of the mansion in the 1920s. (Greenlawn-Centerport Historical Association.)

Six

Drawing Diners

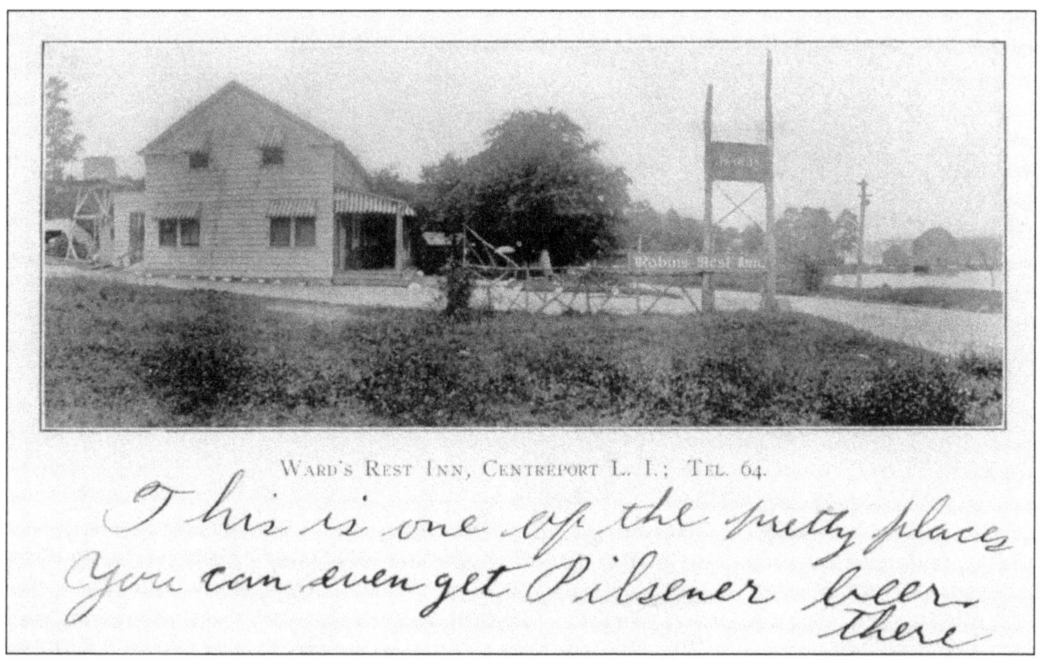

The popular Ward's Rest Inn had rooms for 10 guests but was better known as a restaurant serving "duck and shore dinners" and, apparently, pilsner beer. It was located "on the shore."

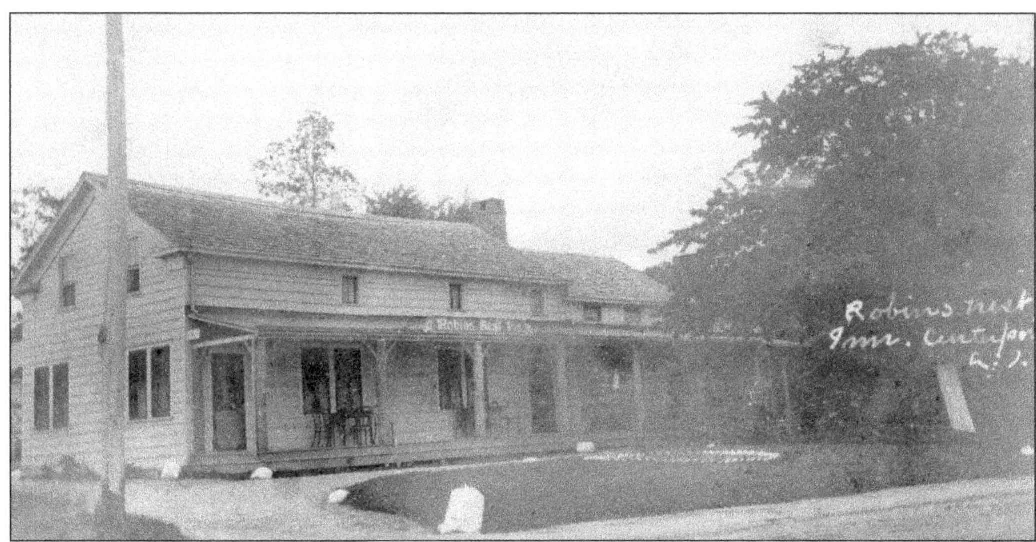

This building was first a grocery store run by Joseph Irwin, and later the post office was located here during the years 1889–1893, when John Hagglund was postmaster. Then Edward Robins established the Robins Nest Inn, which was popular at the turn of the 20th century but went out of business in 1906. George Ward opened the Ward's Rest Inn in 1908 advertising in the *Brooklyn Daily Eagle* that his inn was located "on Centerport harbor between Huntington and Northport; excellent for boating and bathing." (Greenlawn-Centerport Historical Association.)

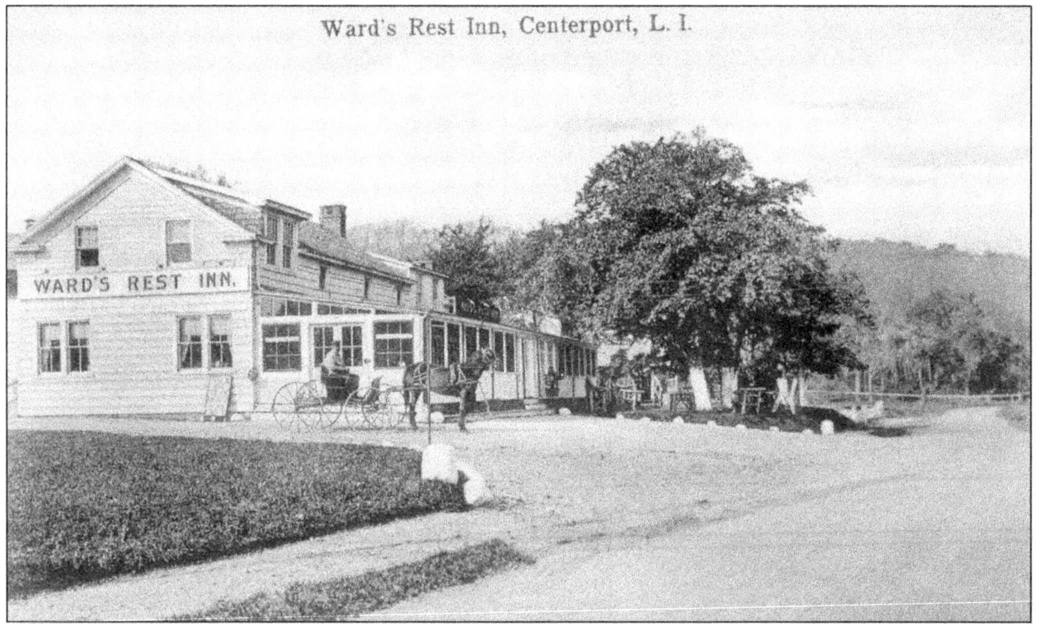

Ward's became famous for its shore, chicken, and duck dinners for $2.50. Albert L. Oppikofer was the proprietor, and when he died in 1926 his wife, Katherine, took over. She was replaced by Dan Cassidy. During the Great Depression, shore, chicken, and duck dinners were still served, and the inn offered dining and dancing nightly. The inn closed in the late 1930s, and the building was demolished in September 1940 following a fire. During the demolition, sparks from a fire on the property set fire to the adjoining former Methodist church. The fire department responded, but the building was heavily damaged and had to be torn down.

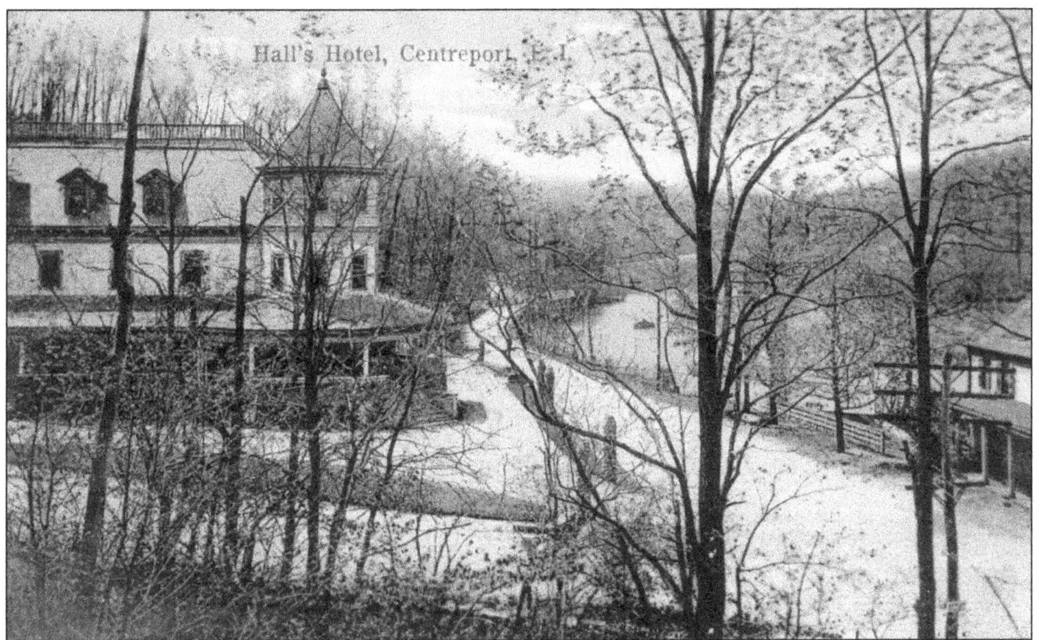

Archie Hall was the last manager of Doty's Hotel, which closed in 1902. He then built Hall's Hotel across the road on the south side of Route 25A. The new restaurant opened in June 1906. A corner of the old hotel is visible on the right through the trees.

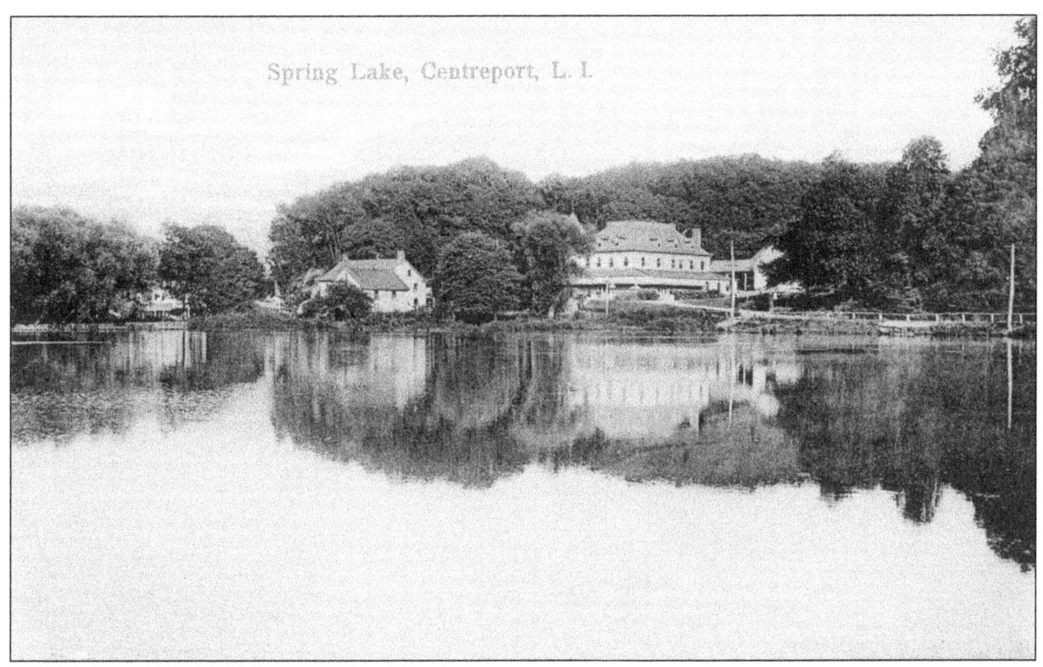

This scenic view of Spring Lake was published by James Bunce about 1910. The Cahill house, Doty's Hotel, and Hall's Restaurant are reflected in the calm waters of the lake.

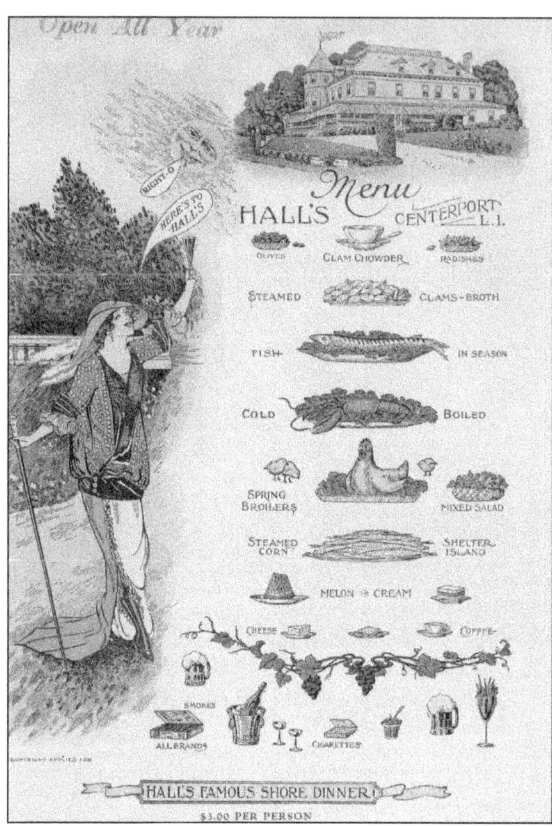

The "famous for seafood" shore dinner at Hall's on this menu from the 1920s was served for many years. On the back of the menu is a map of Long Island, with the main routes to Centerport highlighted in red.

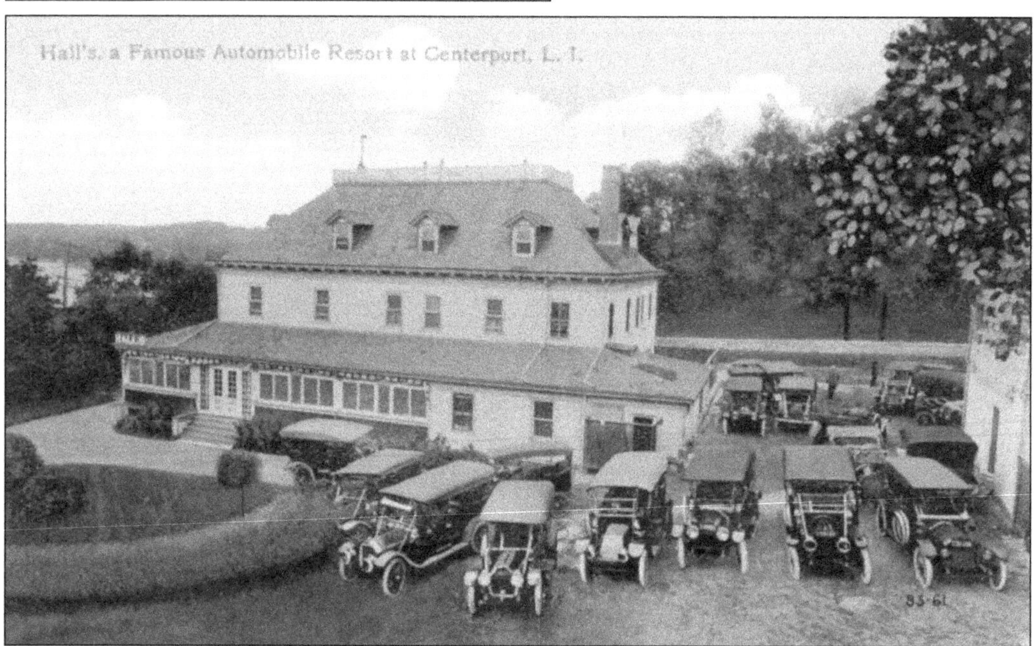

In its early days, celebrities, society people, and the political elite from all over Long Island and New York City traveled to Hall's in expensive cars. In response, Hall's marketed itself as a "famous automobile resort." This image is from around 1910.

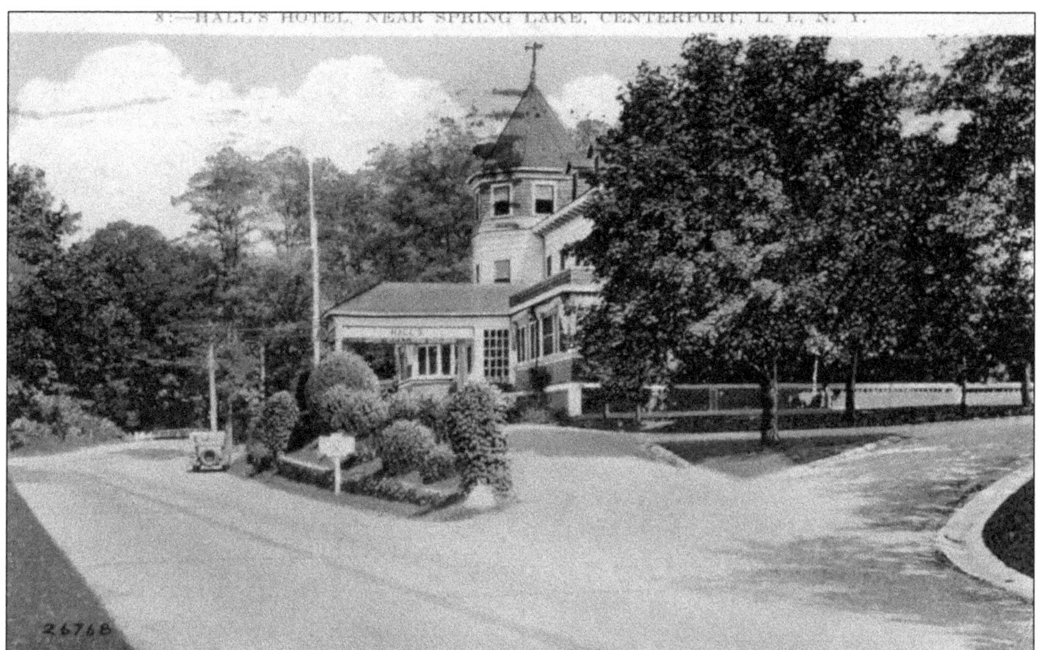

Archie Hall made sure that the entrance to his restaurant was an easy turn from Route 25A when approached from the west. Note that automobiles could discharge passengers under a portico or turn conveniently into the parking lot.

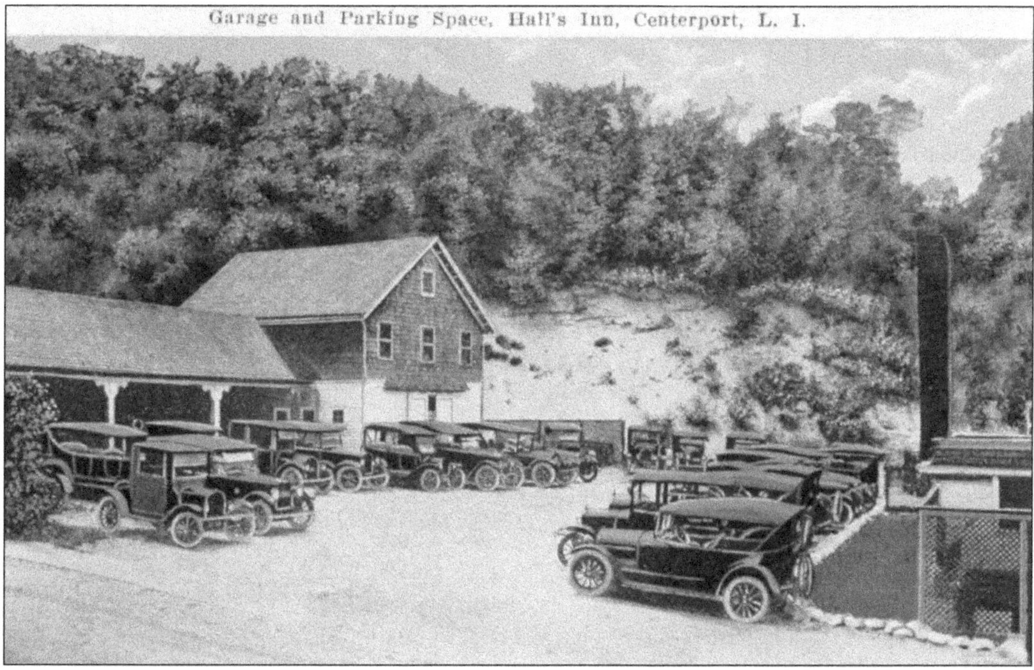

In the 1920s, more and more families owned automobiles, and Sunday excursions became a popular activity. Signs along the major roads directed people to Hall's, and the good food at reasonable prices insured their return. This is a view of the parking lot at Hall's around 1924.

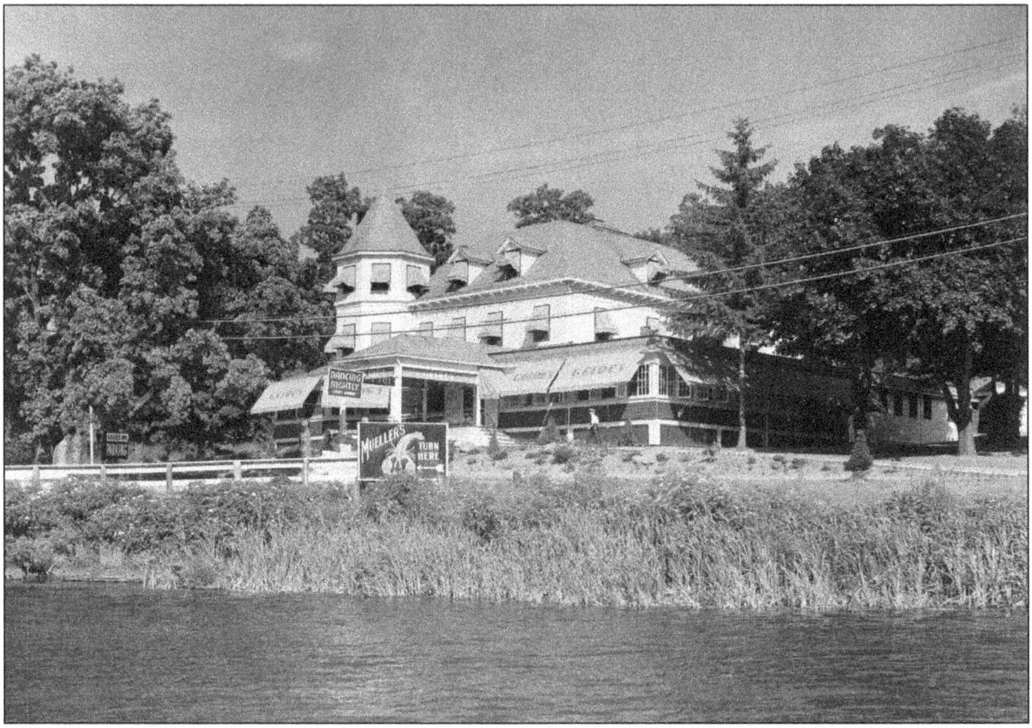

Hall's became Geide's Inn in May 1941, and more than 1,200 people came to the reopening. It operated as a restaurant and catering hall until it was destroyed by fire in January 1966. (Huntington Historical Society.)

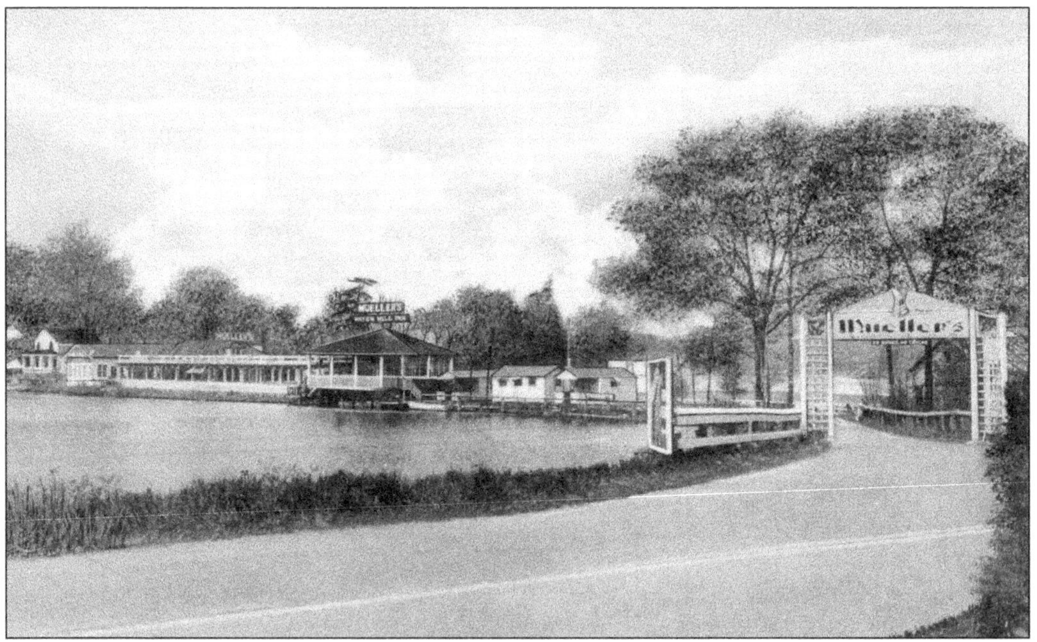

Fred Mueller created a working water wheel with the outflow from Spring Lake. He named his restaurant Mueller's Water Mill Inn. He advertised dining, dancing, fishing, and boating, rather a unique combination for a restaurant.

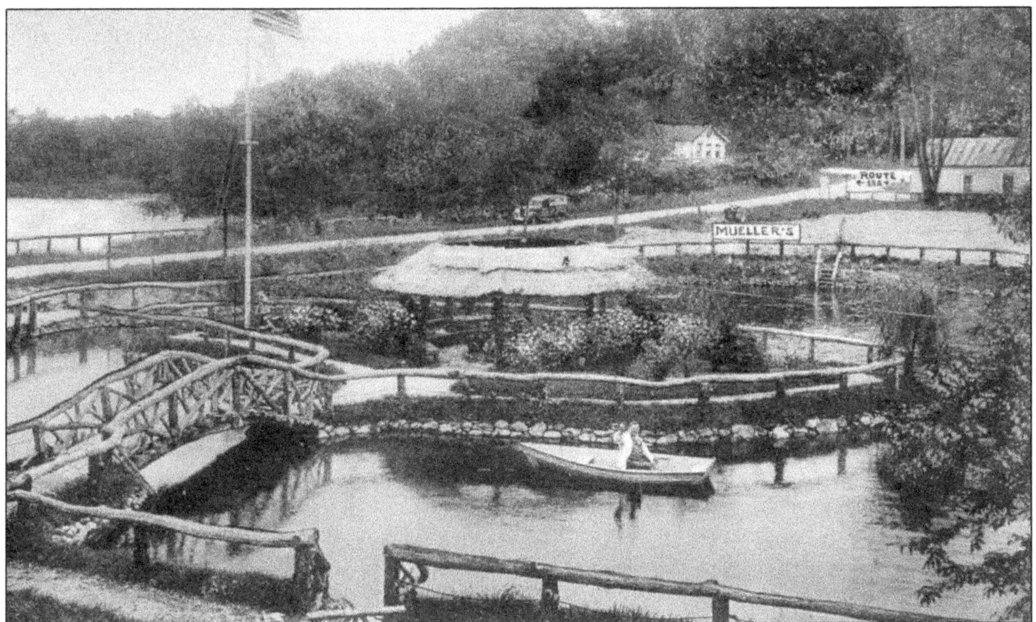

Mueller enhanced his property with a series of ponds and waterways by channeling water from Spring Lake, which ran through the property on its way to the millpond. The roadside novelty drew in a lot of customers.

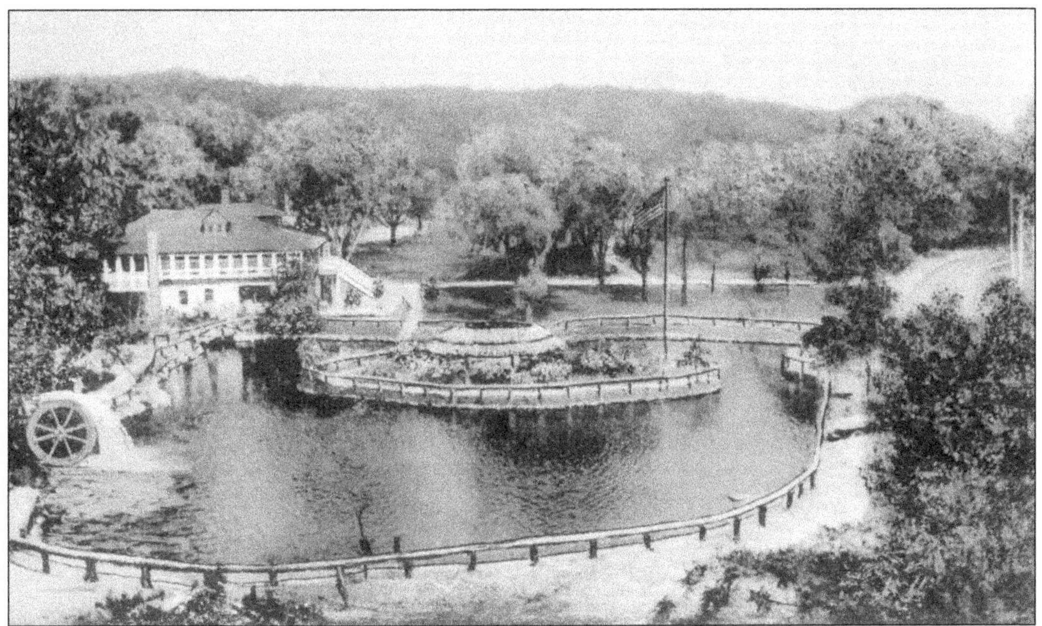

This was a favorite dining spot of the artists Arthur Dove and Helen Torr, who lived nearby from 1938 to 1946. It may have been the inspiration for Dove's 1942 paintings *The Inn* and *Muellers*. Mueller's closed during World War II, but Lazar's Restaurant took over the buildings "right on the picturesque lake." It later became Lazar's Lakeside Motel and restaurant, then the Lago Motor Lodge. By the 1990s, the motel was the Chalet Motor Inn and the original Mueller's restaurant building had become a Chinese restaurant called Tung Ting. Tung Ting closed and the building was demolished. Today, the property is the Chalet Inn and Suites.

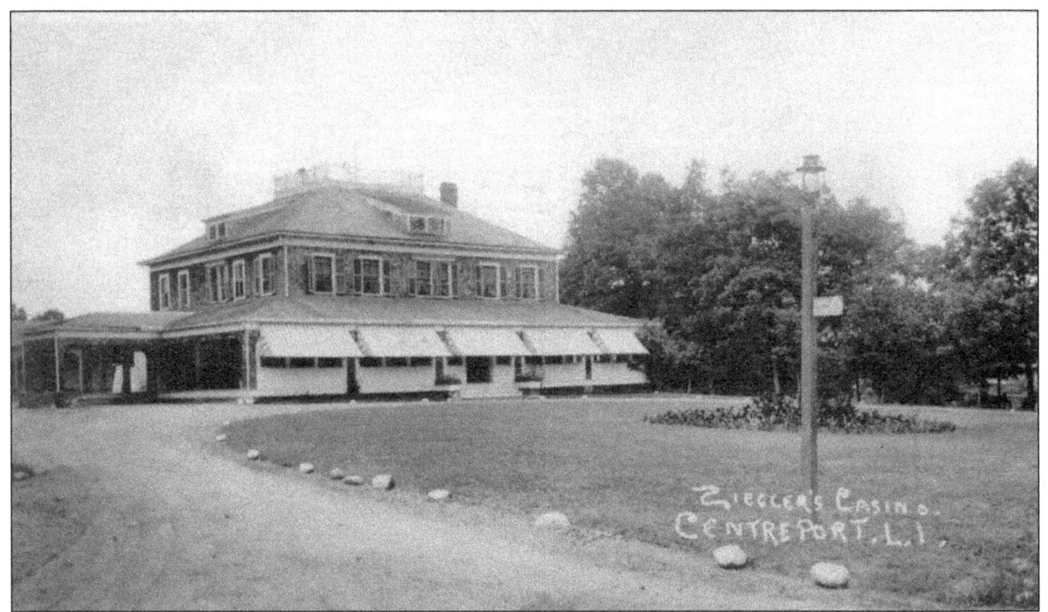

In 1906, C. Hallock of Huntington, who owned the popular Suffolk Hotel, offered this building for lease at a rate of $1,200 per month. The three-acre property was on the north side of Route 25A just west of Spring Lake, and the building had 26 rooms including 17 bedrooms. Ziegler's Casino advertised for just one year, 1911, and then disappeared.

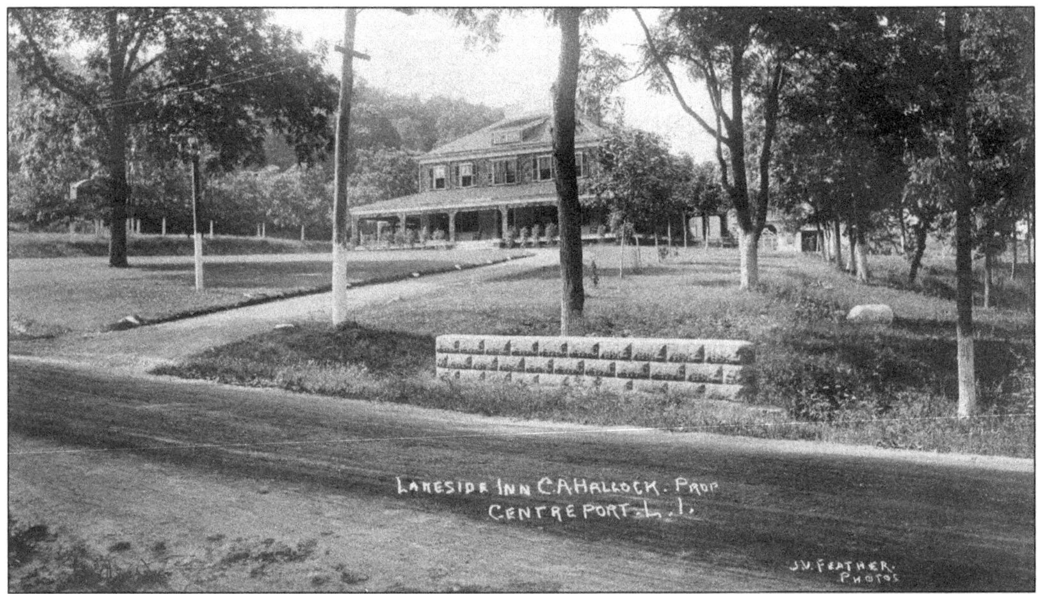

This later photograph by J.V. Feather is marked "Lakeside Inn C.A. Hallock, prop." At least five fire departments responded to a fire in the building in January 1925, but the building was a total loss.

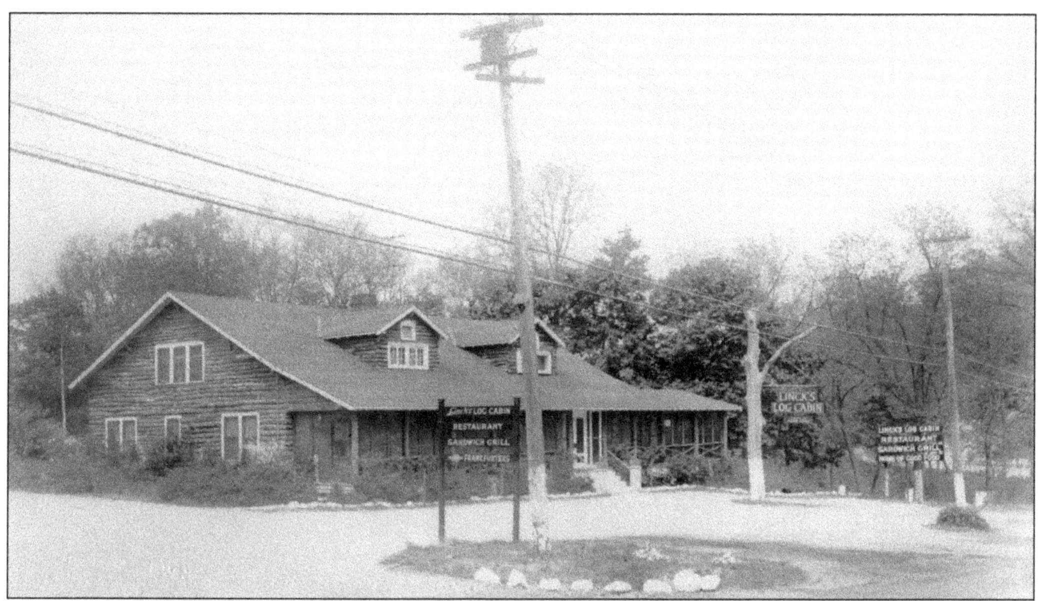

Linck's Log Cabin was built on the south part of the Lakeside Inn property in 1927 by Billy and Anna Linck of Astoria. It was a popular spot for informal dining until it closed in 1943. Ed Myers and Ted McCarthy purchased the property in 1944, and Lincks reopened in 1946. This photograph was taken in the 1930s. (Huntington Historical Society.)

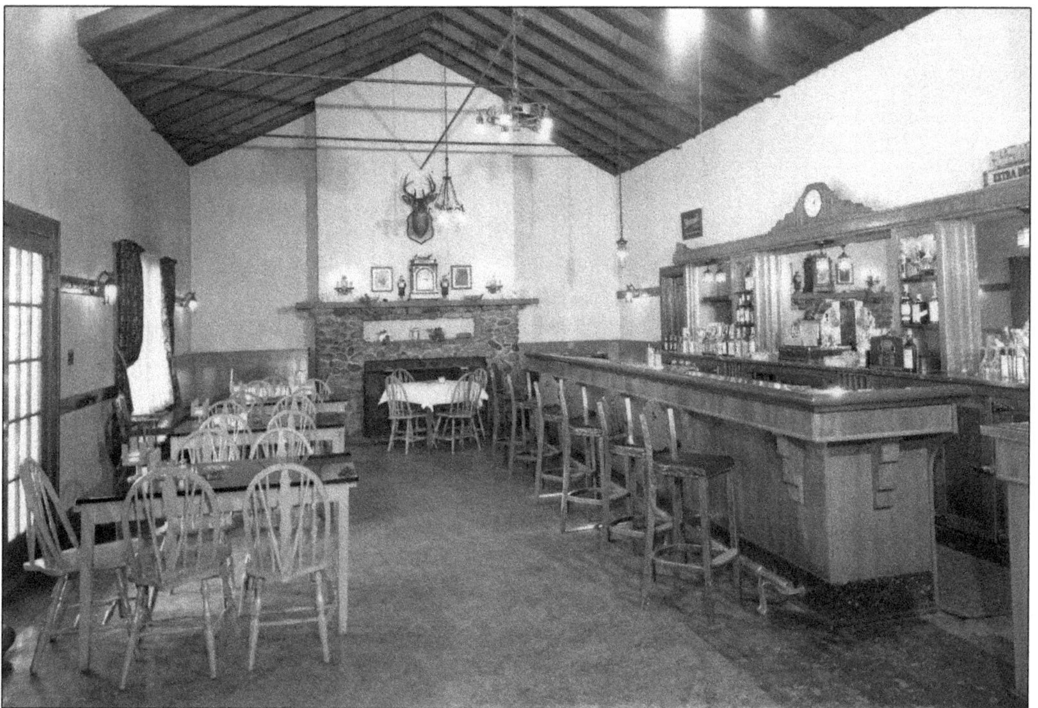

The bar area of Lincks Log Cabin is seen here in March 1941. The building suffered a fire in 1959 but was rebuilt. Lincks was a very popular restaurant through the 1960s and early 1970s. Unfortunately, it suffered another fire in 1981 and was replaced by a condominium complex. (Huntington Historical Society.)

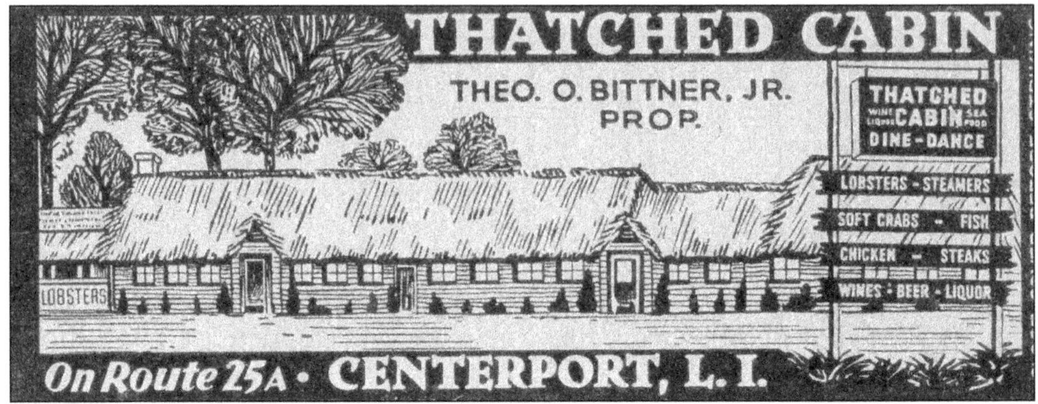

The Thatched Cabin was started by Ted Bittner as a gas station and seasonal hot dog stand. It is said that the building had an authentic thatched roof. It soon expanded into a restaurant and catering hall, changing its name to the Thatched Cottage and the roof to sculpted shingles that resembled thatch.

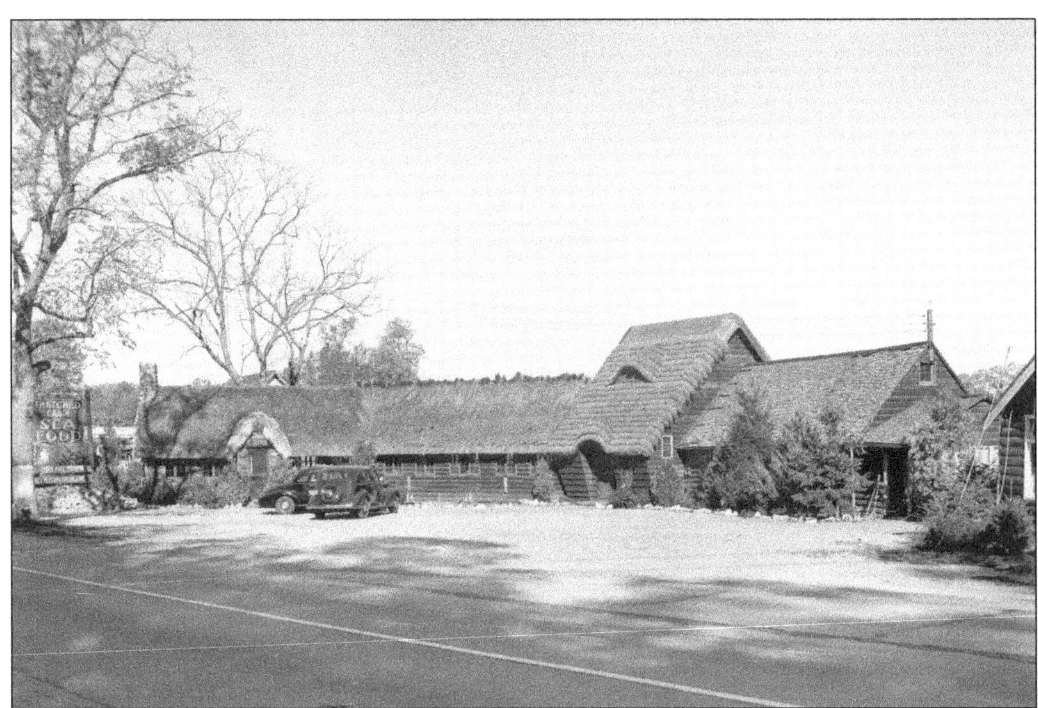
Ted Bittner's son Warren expanded the catering business but eventually sold the Thatched Cottage. This October 1941 photograph shows the extent of the expansion from the hot dog stand. The new owner went bankrupt and sold the building, and it was reopened but went bankrupt again. The building was damaged by Hurricane Sandy in October 2012. It was torn down in 2019 to be replaced with another catering hall. (Huntington Historical Society.)

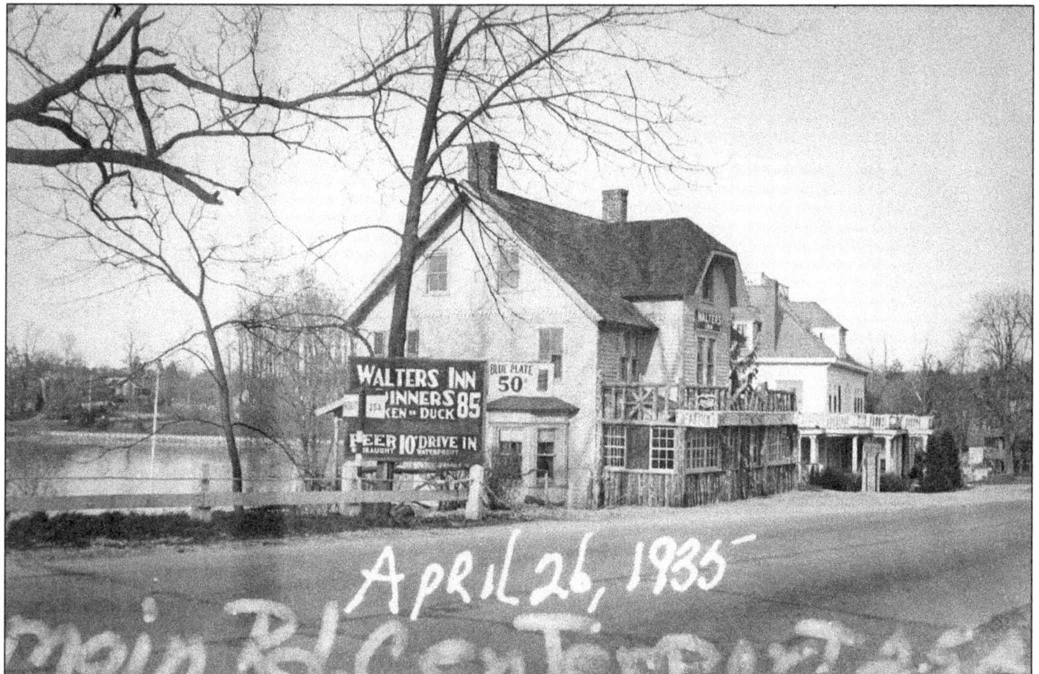

This view shows the proximity of the Whitney mansion to its former servants' quarters to the east, later the Walters Inn; both were built about 1900. The Whitney mansion has been a restaurant for about 100 years. A few of the incarnations of the mansion have been the Bella Vista, the Original Schooner, Brooks, and most recently, Viva Juan and the Jellyfish. A new owner plans to demolish the mansion and replace it with an apartment building. (Huntington Historical Society.)

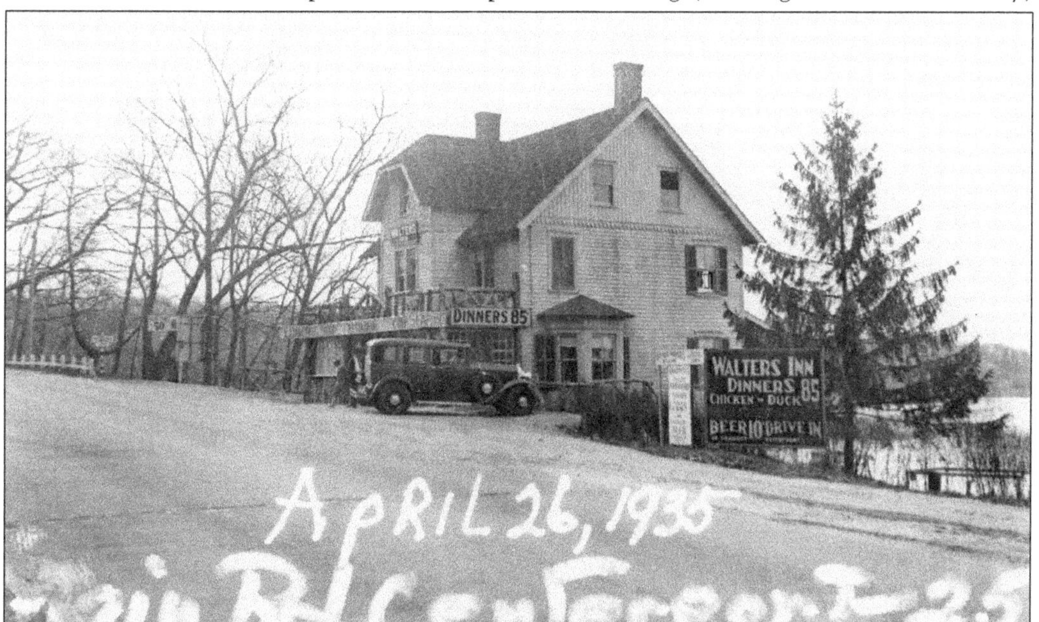

The Walters Inn Bar and Grill (previously the servants' house for the Whitney estate) is seen here in April 1935. The sign advertises draft beer for 10¢ and chicken or duck dinners for 85¢. The building is now the Mill Pond Inn/House. (Huntington Historical Society.)

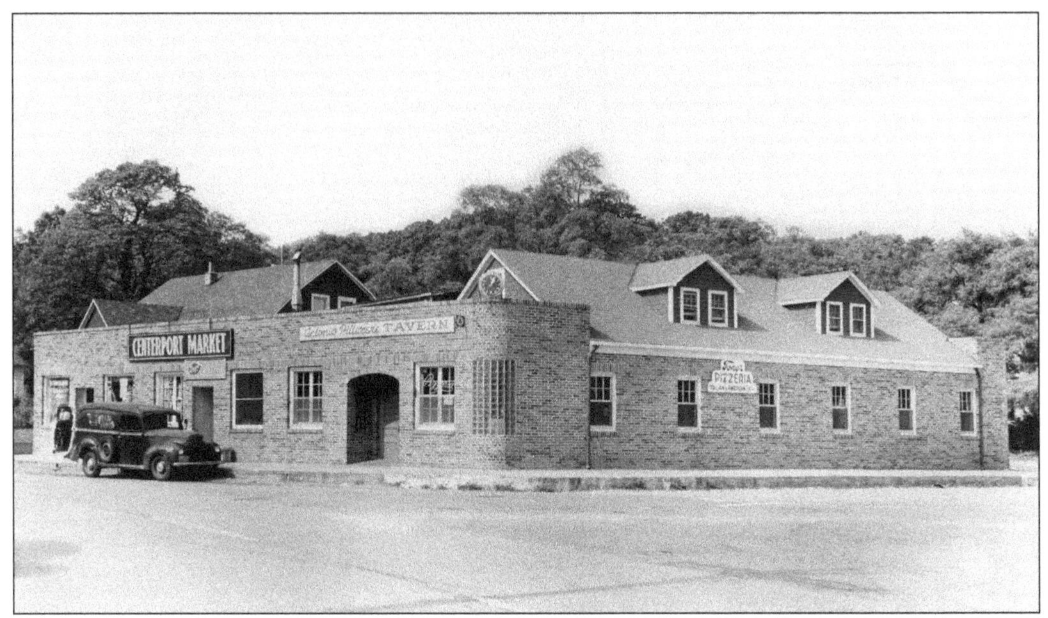

On the west side of the causeway was a commercial block that included several establishments popular with local residents including Centerport Market, Tony's Pizzeria, and the Anthony Pillucere Tavern. In more recent times, it has been home to Tony's Tavern, the Drifter's Reef, and Rock Hopper's Pub. This block was badly damaged by fire in 1993. Due to the efforts of the Centerport Harbor Civic Association, the land became a town park. One of the original millstones from the Townsend mill was installed at the site. (Greenlawn-Centerport Historical Association.)

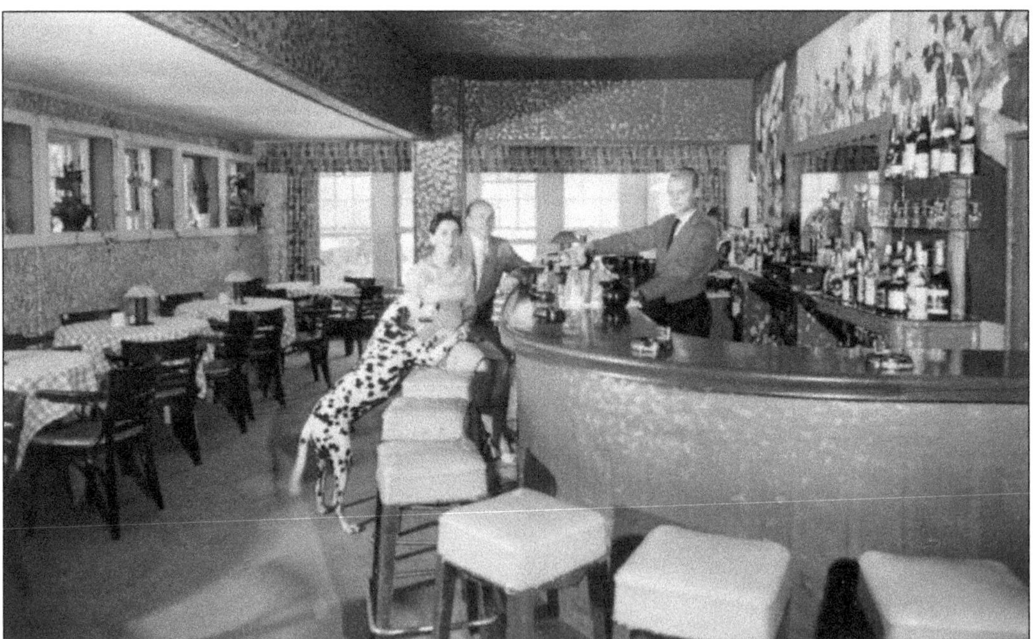

The sender of this card asked, "Where will you be on June 9th, 1956?" This interesting scene at Lazar's Restaurant (which was Mueller's Inn previously) demonstrates the ever-evolving nature of the restaurant business in Centerport.

Seven

NEIGHBORS

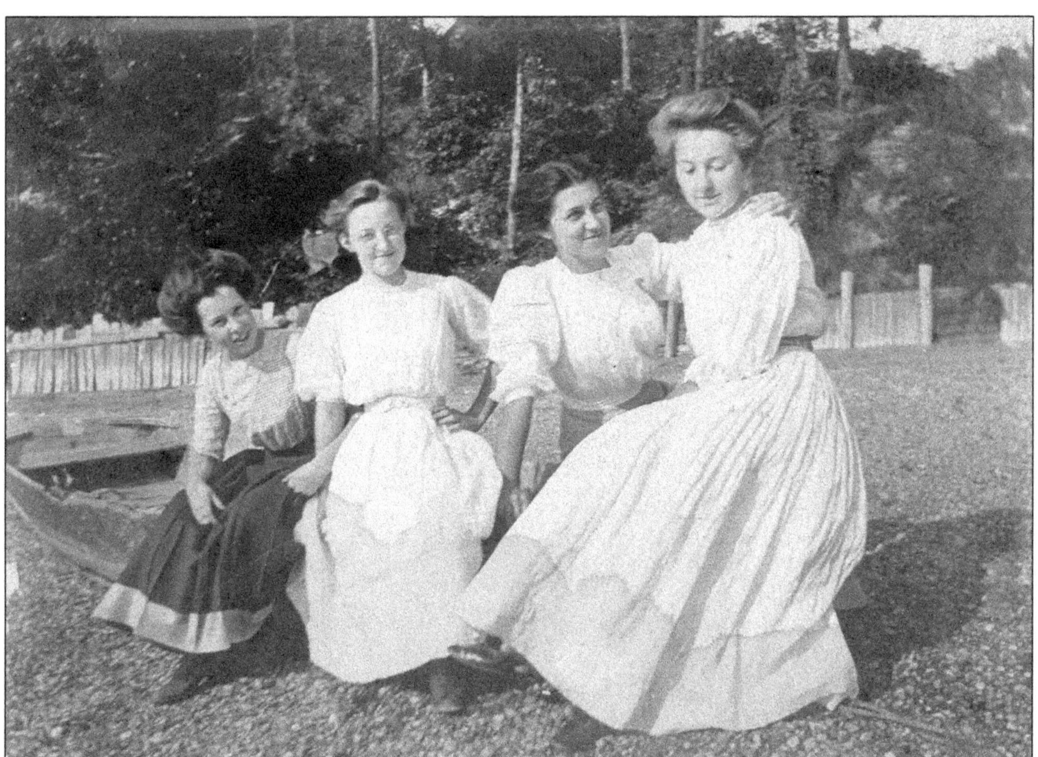

Sisters Lulu (second from left) and Mary Emma Bunce (far right) enjoy a day at the beach with friends. It looks like the two of them ventured into the water, marking their skirts. Centerport has always been a place for family, friends, and neighbors.

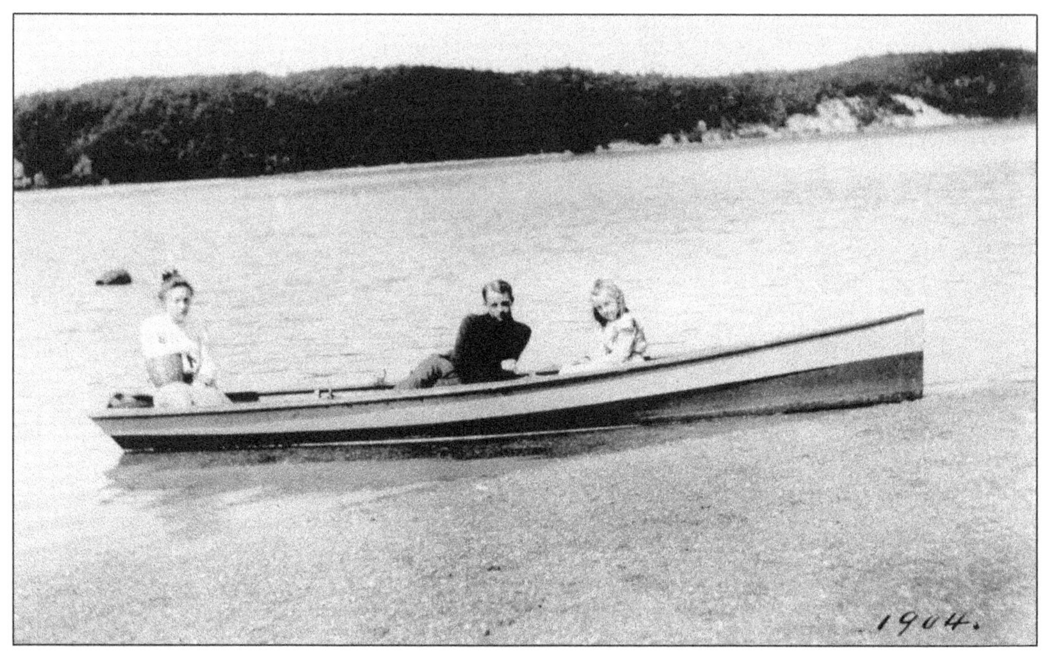

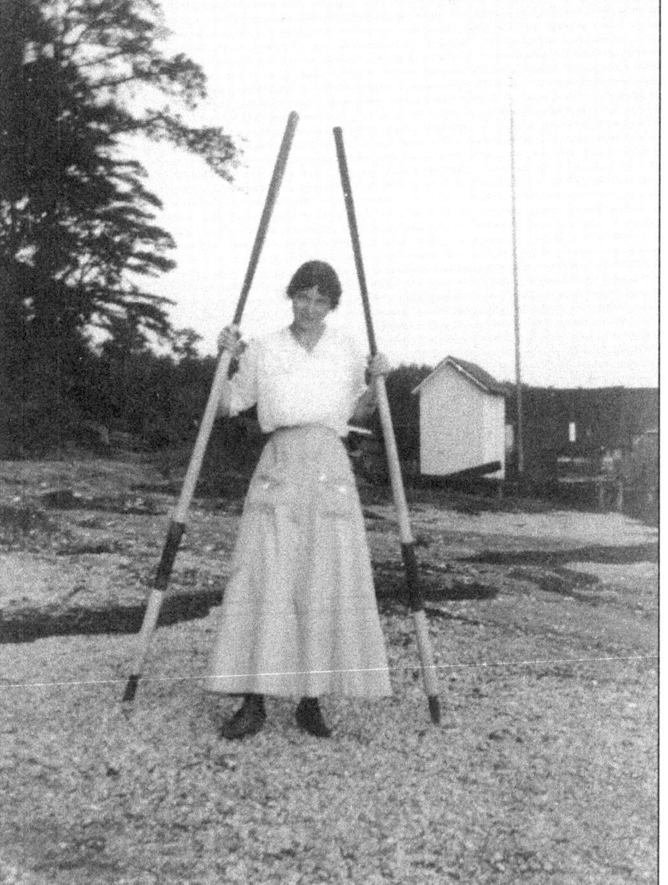

Mary Emma, Lulu, and their brother Arthur Chalmers Bunce, children of J. Ellsworth Bunce, relax in a boat on the harbor. They lived in Bayonne, New Jersey, but always spent their summers in Centerport with their grandparents.

Elizabeth Sticht, a boarder from Brooklyn, is getting ready for a row. She would later meet and marry Arthur Bunce of Centerport.

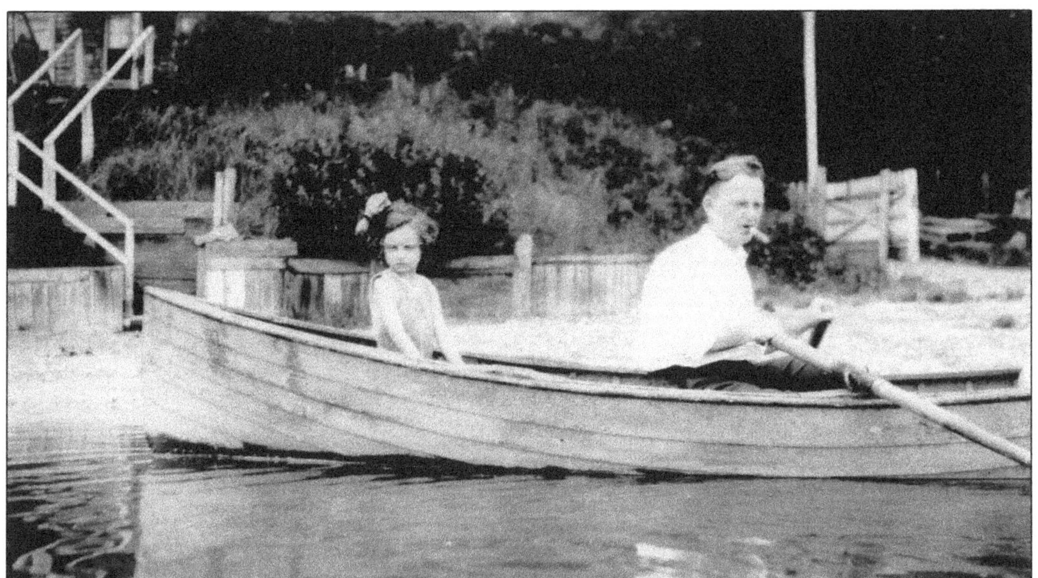

Arthur Chalmers Bunce and his daughter Shirley enjoy a ride in a round-bottomed rowboat in 1925. This photograph was taken in front of the N.S. Sammis house on the east side of the harbor.

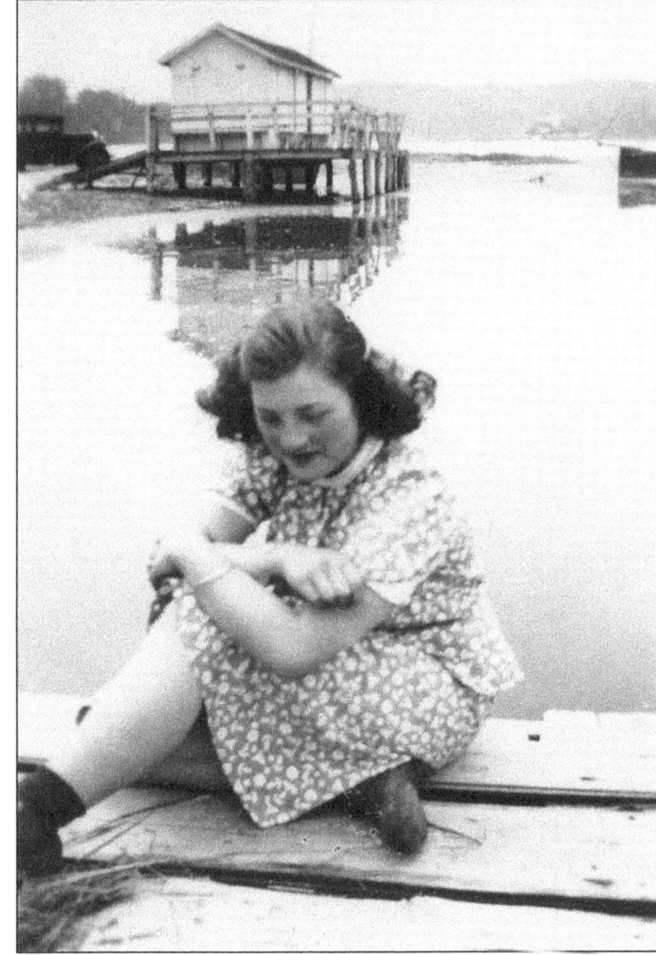

Bernice Townsend grew up on the Townsend (former Barton) estate. She is shown here around 1930 enjoying the harbor on a float. (William Townsend Perks.)

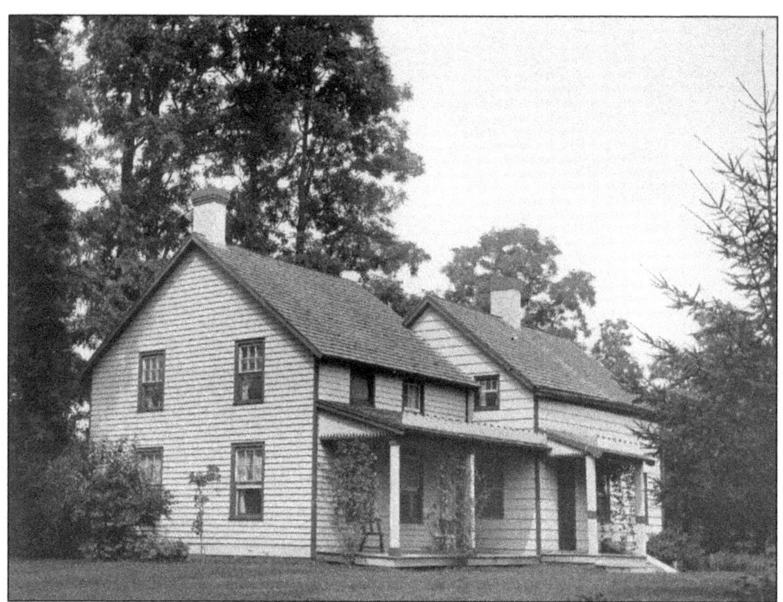

The Augustus Ackerly–Harned house at 26 Little Neck Road is a vernacular frame residence built around 1850. It also retains its late-19th-century barn and has been sensitively preserved. (Greenlawn-Centerport Historical Association.)

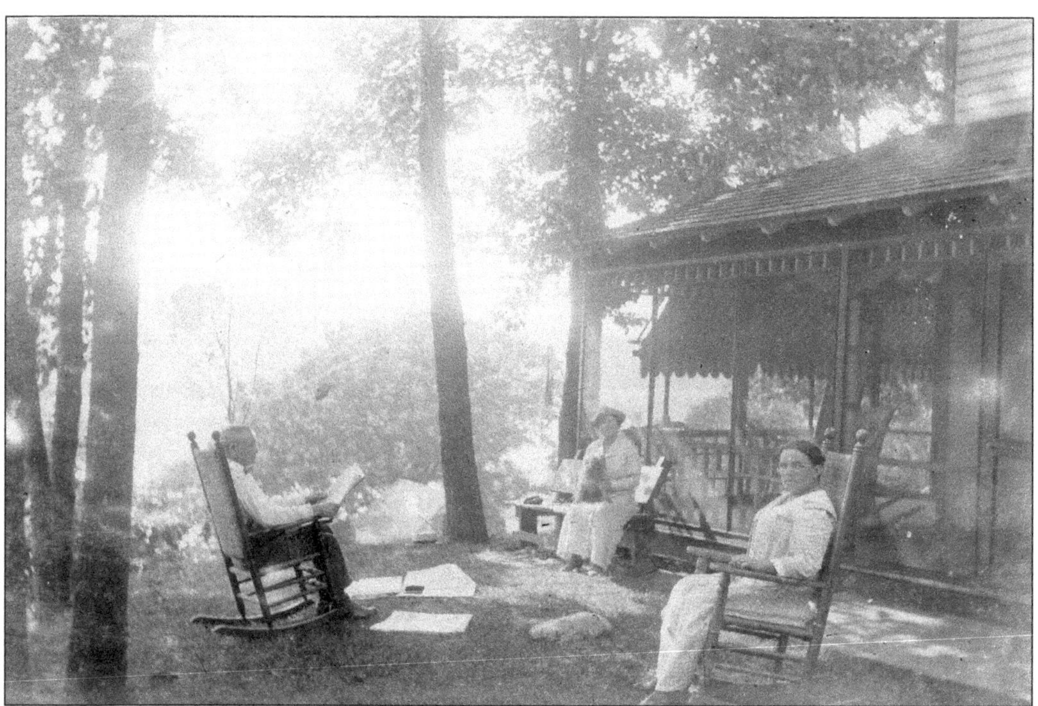

Three Morbach family members relax in rocking chairs in front of the Morbach house on Prospect Road. Edward Morbach was a musician. One of his neighbors, Bill Dillon, stayed in the Kaestner house across the road. Dillon wrote the lyrics to the song "I Want a Girl (Just Like the Girl that Married Dear Old Dad)," a popular song from 1911. With music by Harry Von Tilzer, it was second in popularity only to Irving Berlin's "Alexander's Ragtime Band," selling over five million copies of its score sheets and recordings. (Greenlawn-Centerport Historical Association.)

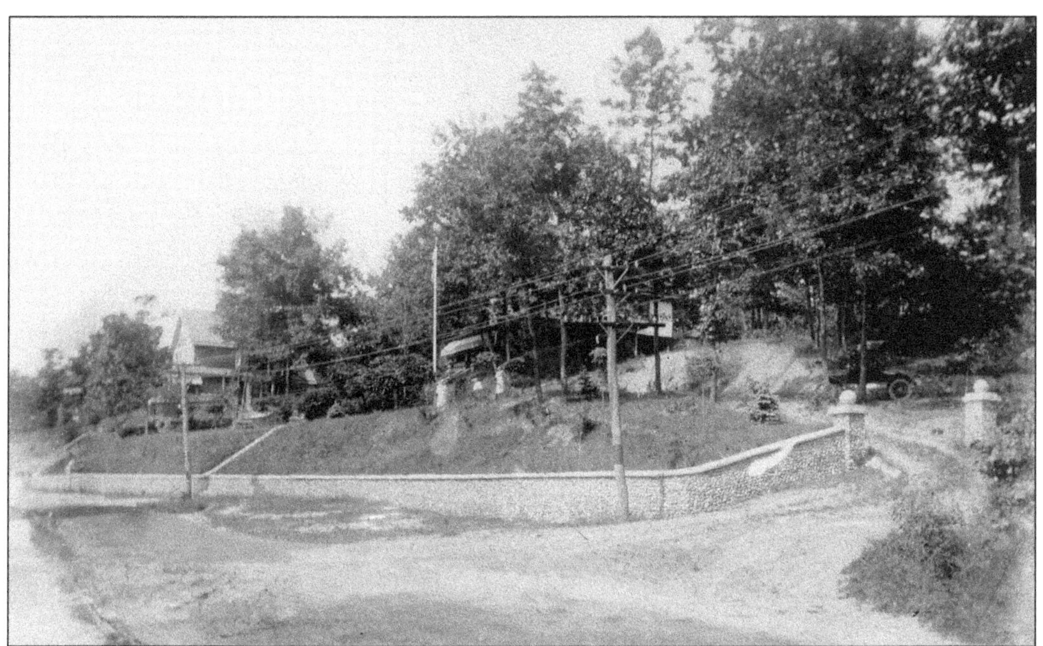

The stone walls on the Morbach property, seen in this c. 1905 photograph, are still quite visible from Prospect Road. (Greenlawn-Centerport Historical Association.)

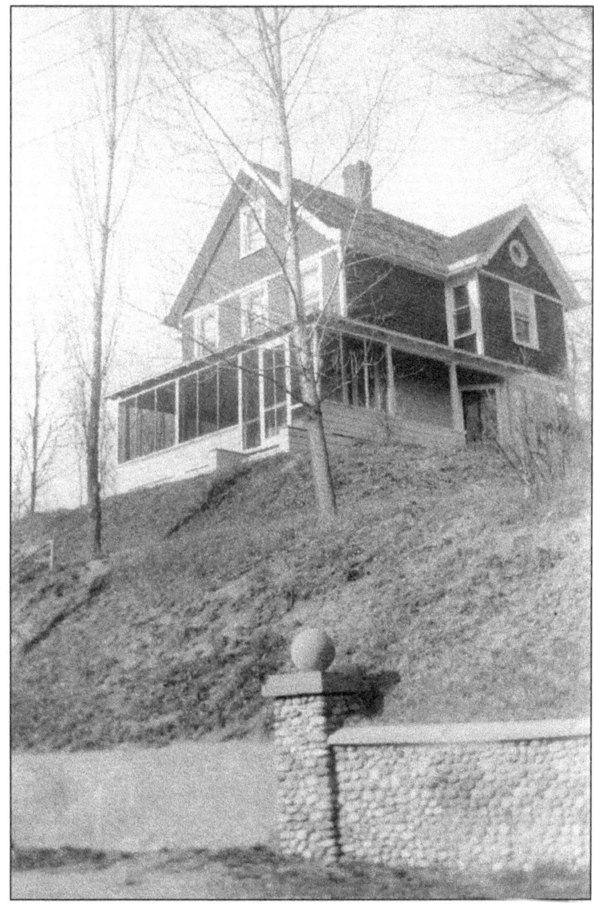

Next door to the Morbach house is the George Bunce house on Prospect Road. George Bunce was the nephew of Elkanah Bunce and was in the Centerport Fire Department for 53 years. (Greenlawn-Centerport Historical Association.)

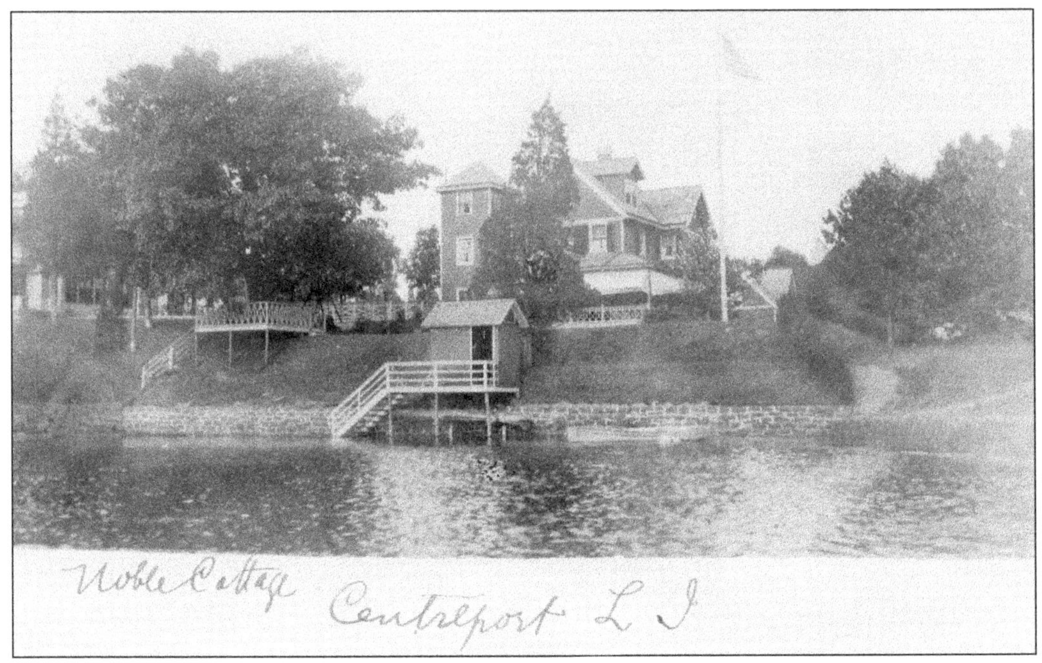

The Noble cottage on Prospect Road is a former guest house with a mysterious history. The house was built in 1892 by Theodore B. Sammis. In 1989, crematorial remains of Marilla Easterbrook were found under the floorboards during a renovation. Easterbrook lived in New York and bought the property in 1918 from Mary Noble and lived there with her younger sister and brother until her death at age 78 in 1930.

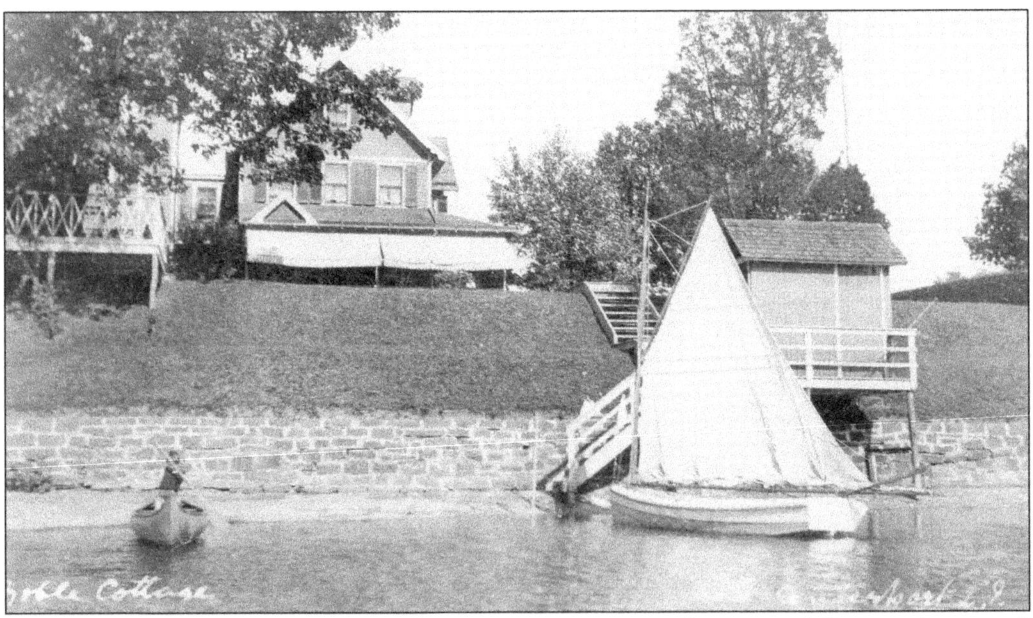

In this view of Noble cottage with a sailboat, someone wrote on the postcard, "I am in the canoe." The Noble House took in summer boarders and offered swimming, canoeing, and sailing.

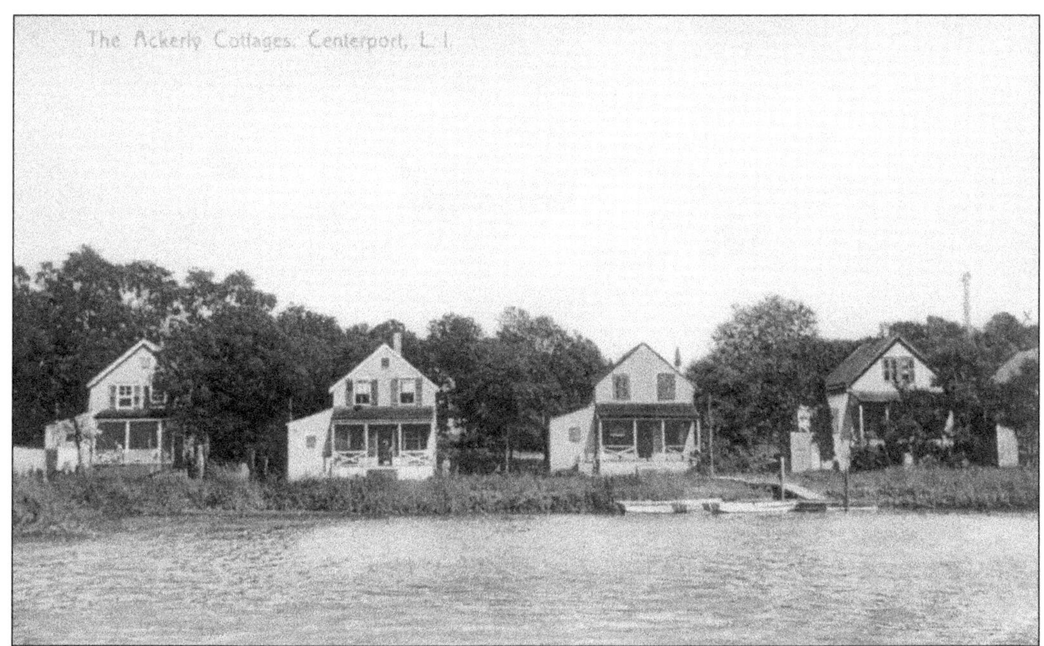

Hiram Ackerly, who owned a carpentry shop in New York City, built a summer home for his family on the east side of Prospect Road in 1873. In the early 1900s, he built these four summer cottages on the east shore of the mill pond, which he rented to summer visitors. Although expanded and renovated, all four of these houses remain in their original locations.

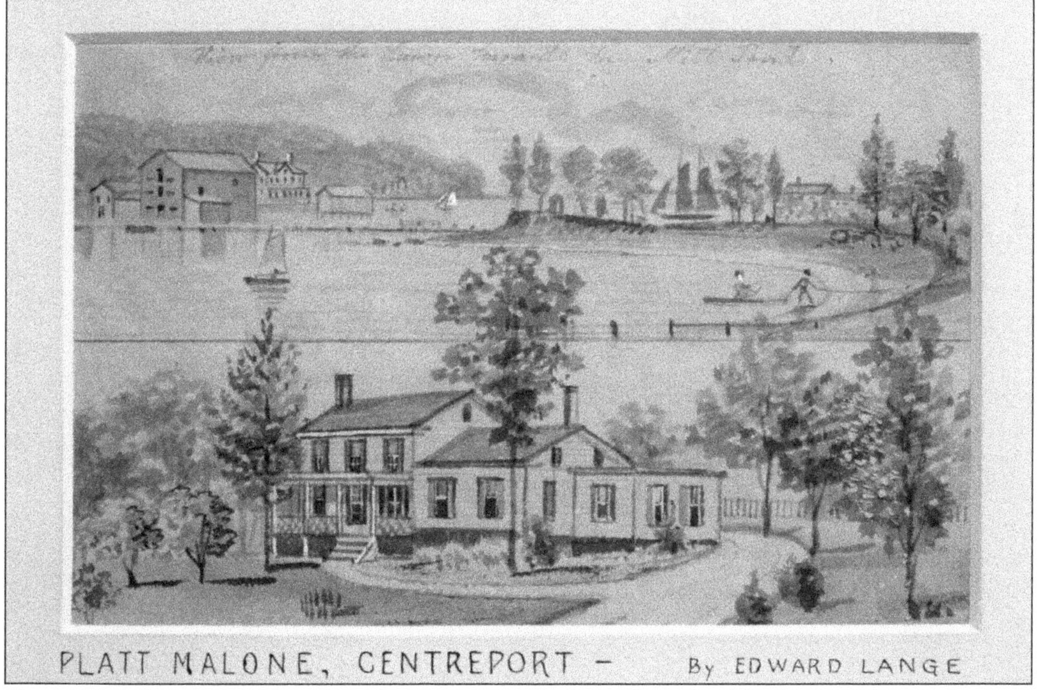

This undated painting, *View from the Lawn towards the Mill Pond*, of the Platt Malone home, was made by Edward Lange. The home was located on the east shore of the millpond on Prospect Road and appears on the 1909 Belcher Hyde map. (Preservation Long Island.)

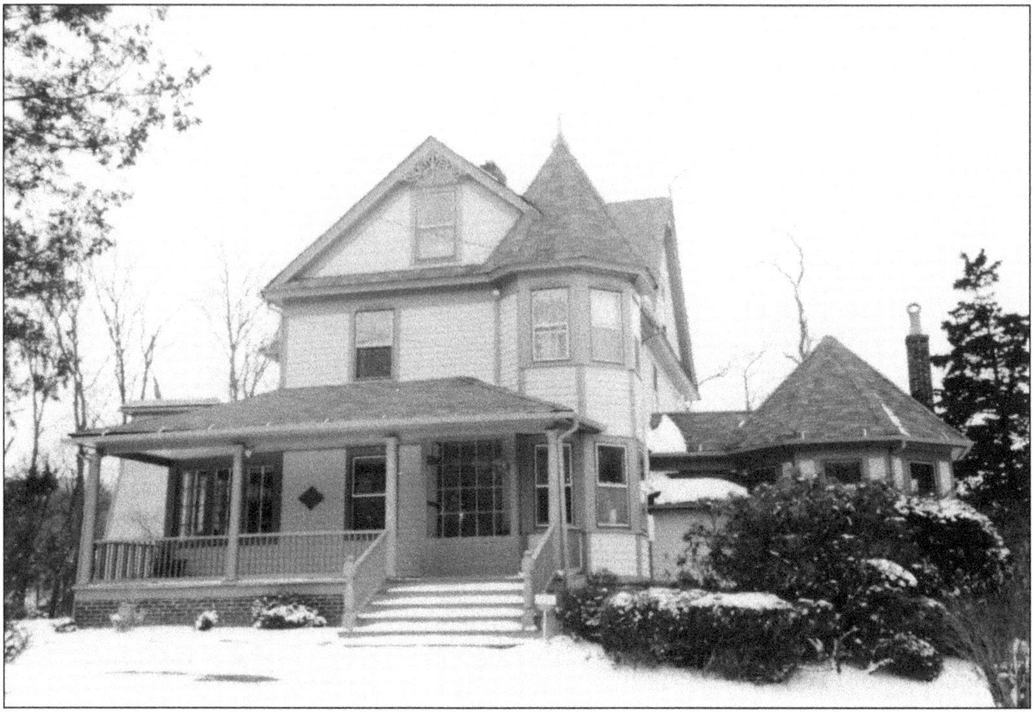

The Lyle Andrews house was a distinctive residence on the pond. In the 1915 census, Andrews is listed as a theatrical manager. His Scottish gardener and his family lived with him. (Greenlawn-Centerport Historical Association.)

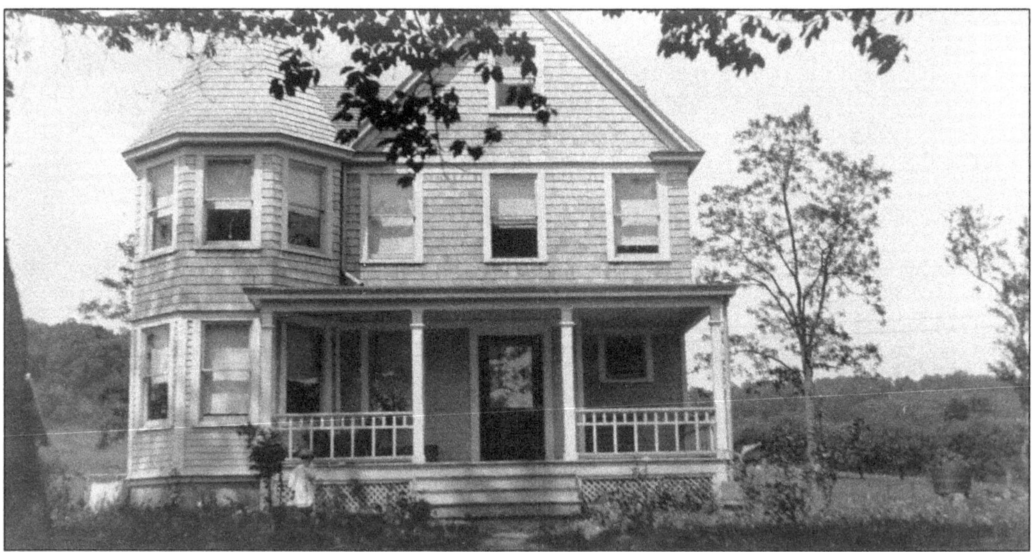

The Thomas Bunce house was on Centershore Road. It was converted into a nursing home for a time and is now again a private house. When the two Methodist churches were combined in 1901, Bunce was elected a trustee.

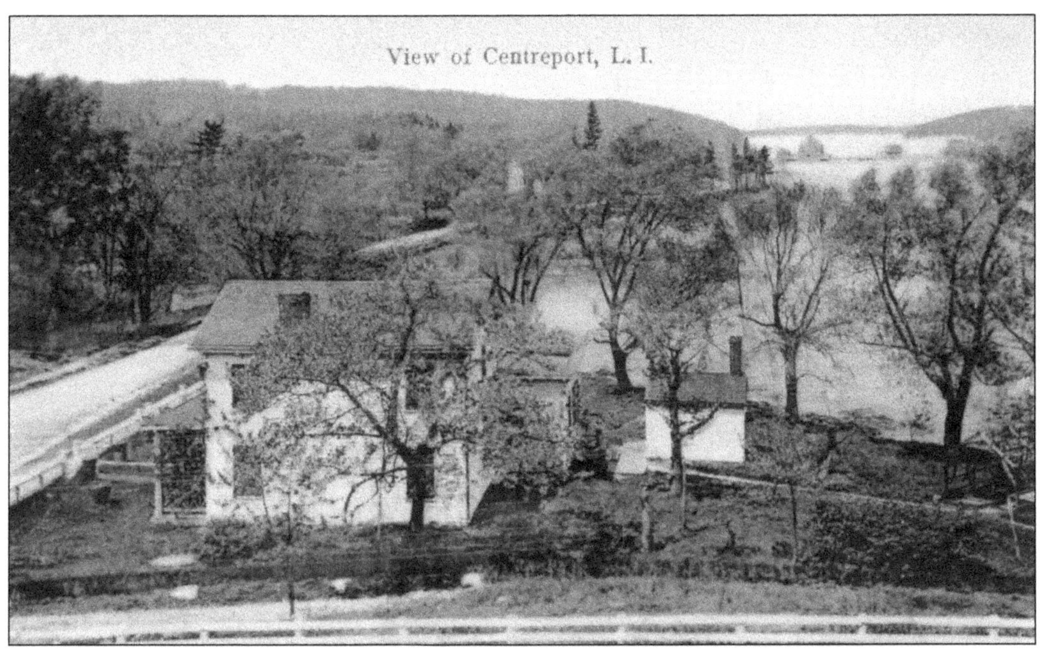

Here are two views of the Richard Cahill home. In the photograph below, by J.V. Feather, the western front of the Cahill house is seen. He also took the photograph "A Glimpse of Centerport" seen on page 9 from behind the Cahill house. The area behind Cahill's was used for loading cargo such as fish. This location is now a town park at Route 25A and Centershore Road.

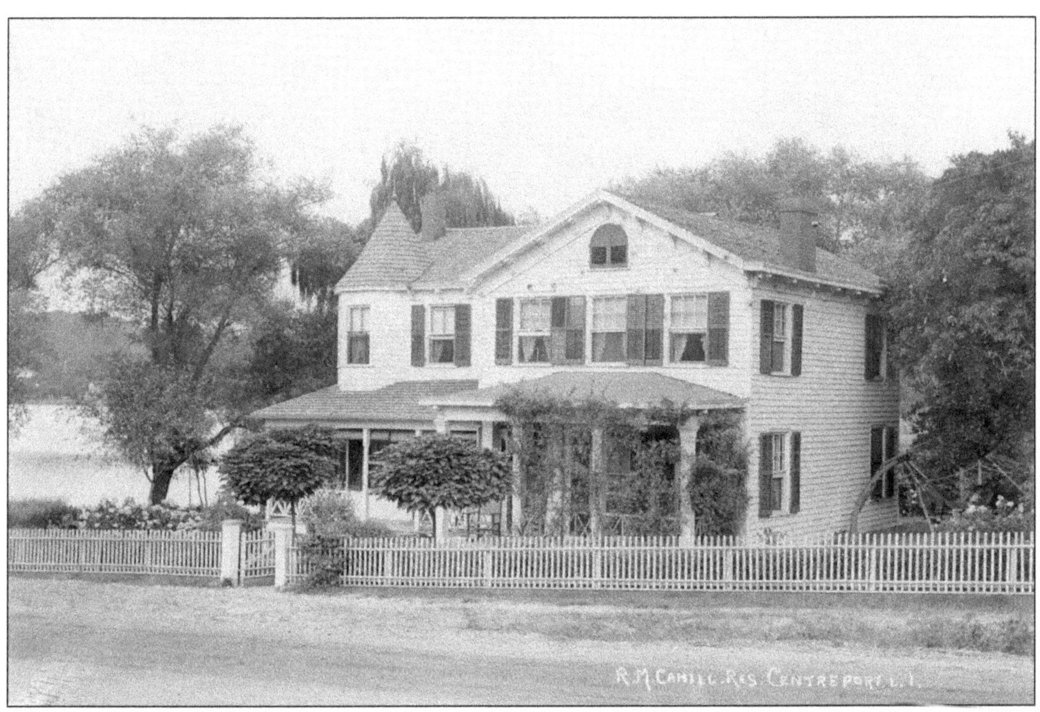

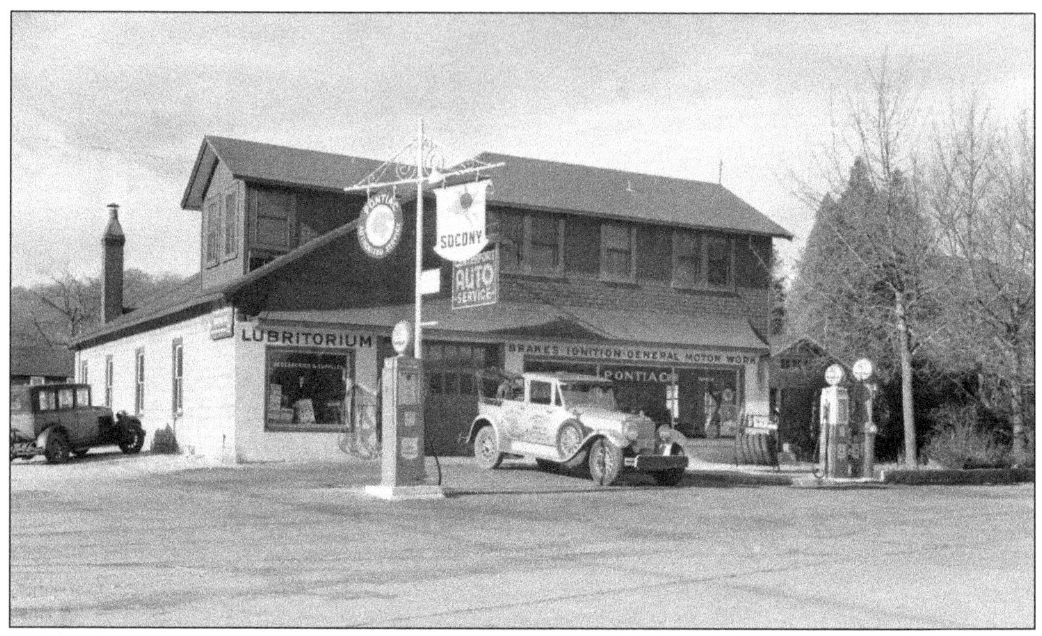

The best garage in Huntington was Centerport Auto Service, owned and operated by Bob Bohaty. A talented mechanic and machinist, Bohaty restored early automobiles, and at one time owned 12 of them including a Stanley Steamer. The garage is now Align Automotive. This photograph by Robert Stone was "taken for Christmas card" in November or December 1939. (Huntington Historical Society.)

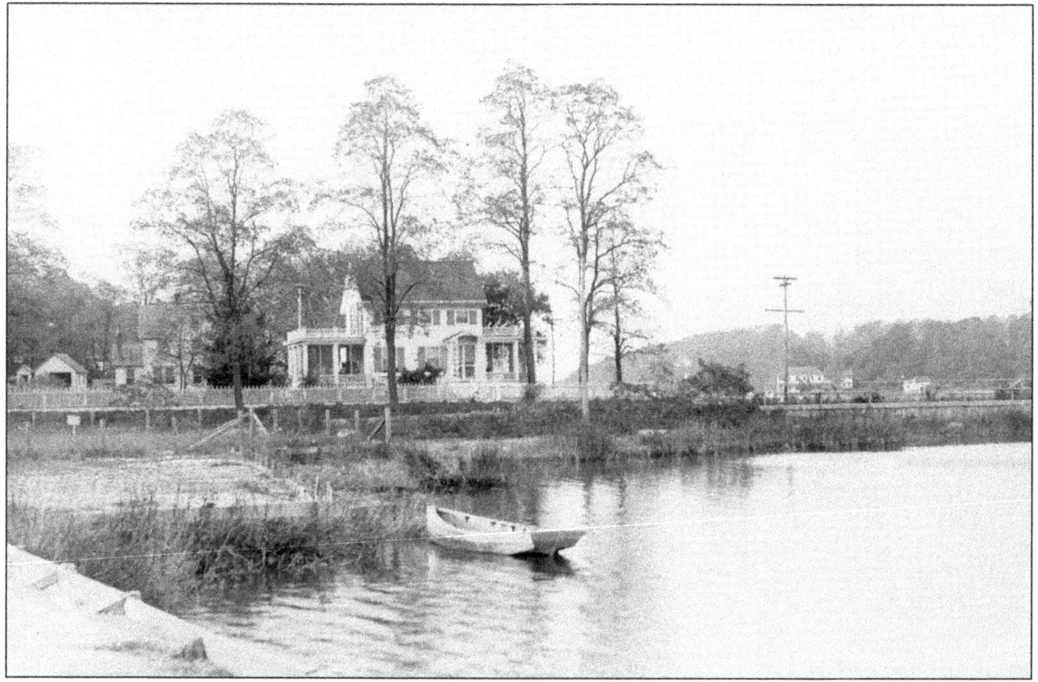

The Andrus L. Titus family residence, home to two generations of millers, is pictured here. His father, William, took over the Townsend Mill. This house was later the site of Tony's Tavern. The area is now a town park where one of the millstones is preserved.

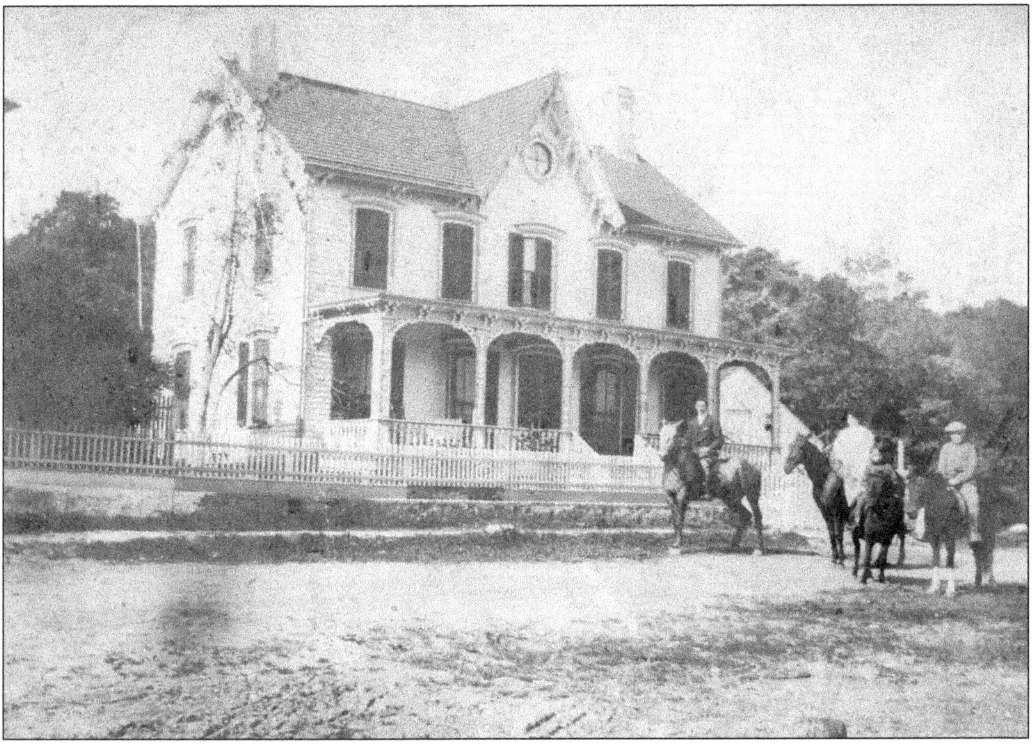

George Beatty (left) and friends May, Arthur, and Eddie enjoy a ride on horseback in front of his house on the west side of the harbor in 1909. This home is still a strong presence on Centershore Road on the west shorefront. (Greenlawn-Centerport Historical Association.)

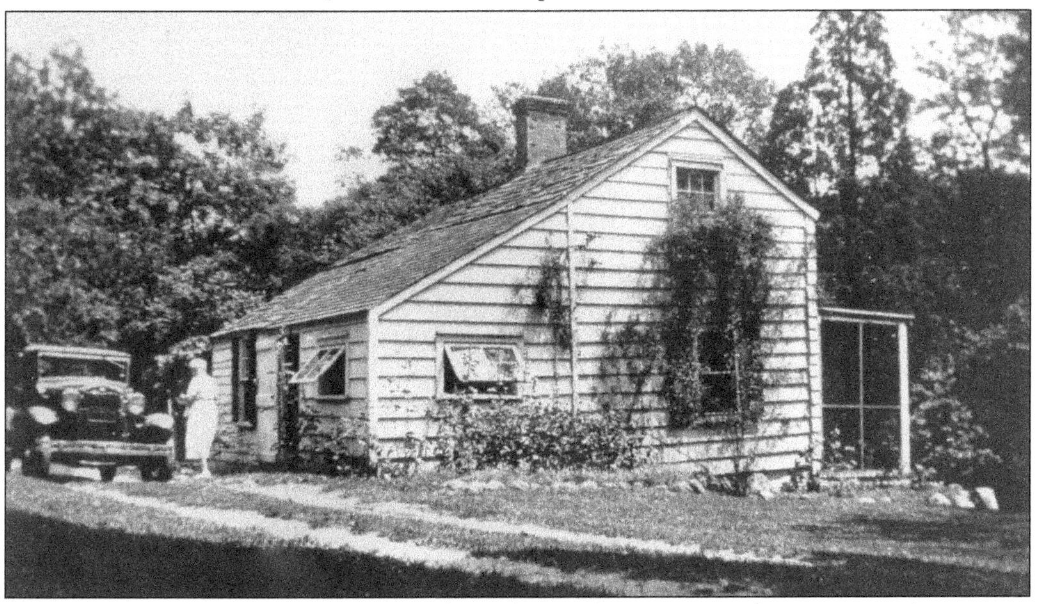

Isabella Barto, who was an executive with Lord & Taylor in New York City, is seen here in a c. 1930 photograph in front of her home, referred to as "the Nutshell." She purchased the home in 1923. The current homeowner received an award for restoring the house in 2016 from Preservation Long Island. (Greenlawn-Centerport Historical Association.)

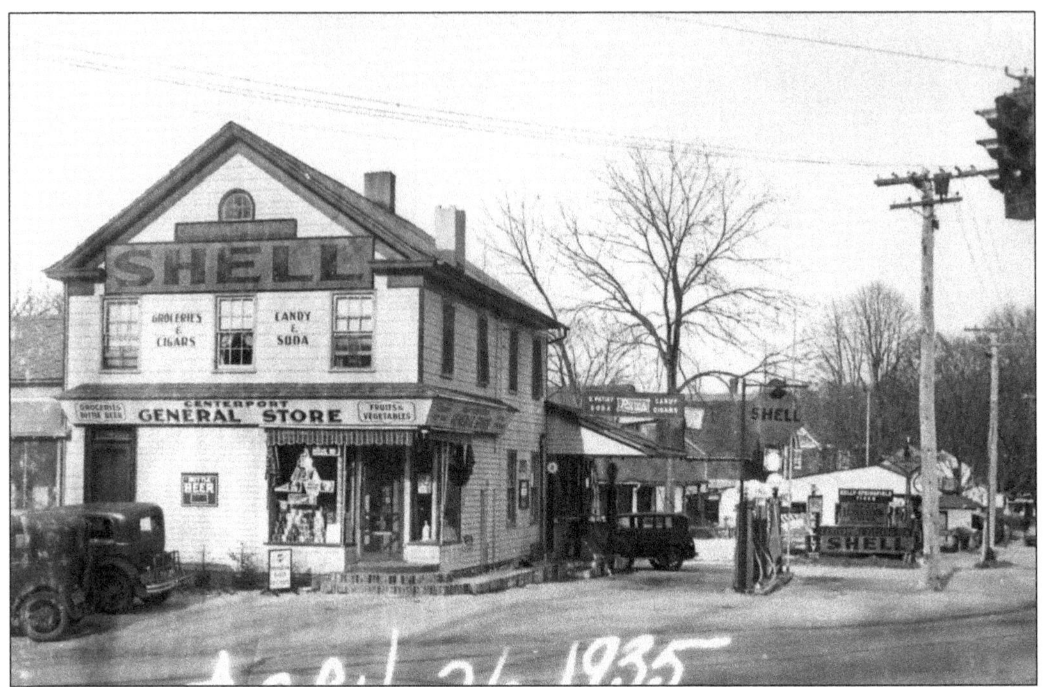

This photograph of Patiky's Centerport General store on Little Neck Road and Route 25A in April 1935 shows what a busy place it was. (Huntington Historical Society.)

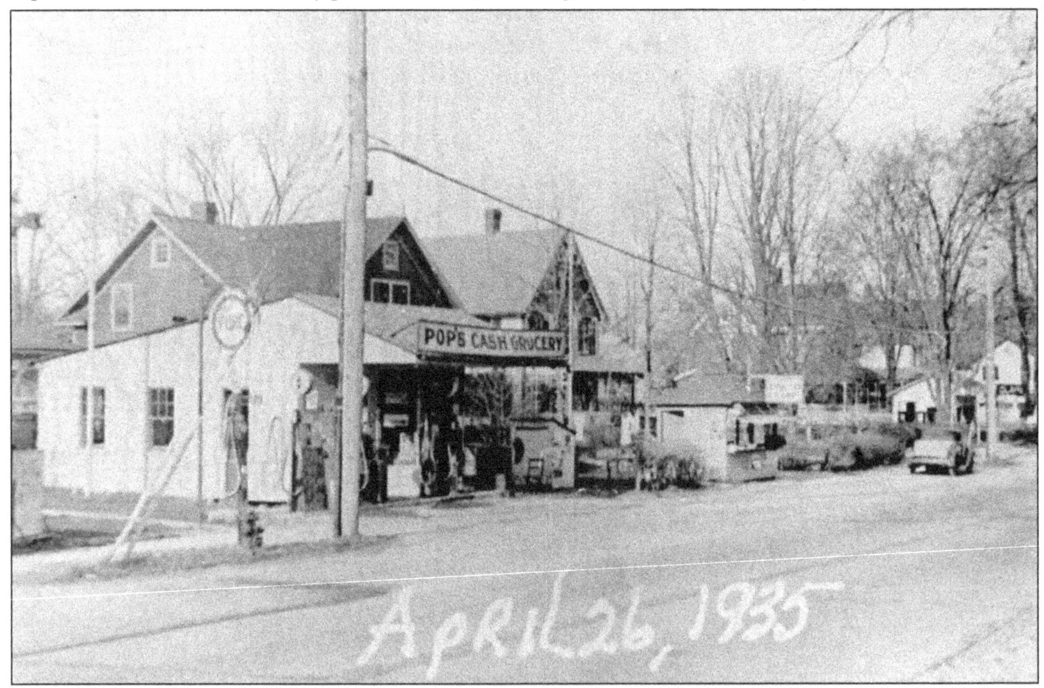

This photograph, also taken in April 1935, shows the stores east of Patiky's on Route 25A, including Pop's Cash Grocery and the "Tomato Lady" farm stand, which has been in continual operation since 1929. It is the last remaining small farmstand in the Huntington area. (Huntington Historical Society.)

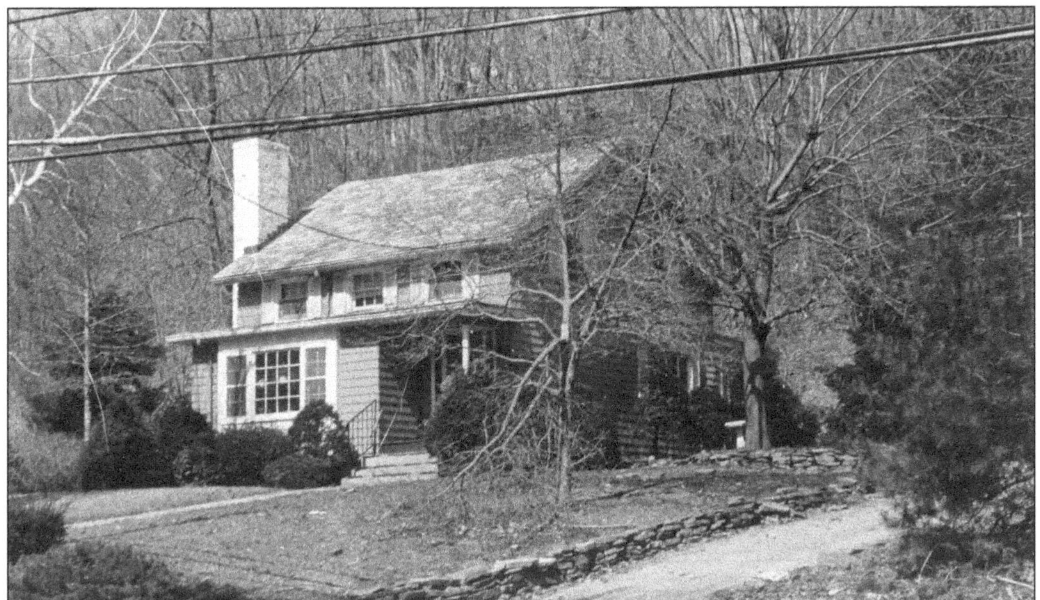

Henry H. Denton was one of the organizers of the Centerport Fire Department in 1899. This house was built around 1830, and he purchased it in 1888. He was a highway commissioner for the Town of Huntington. The house is on the south side of Route 25A with the Denton Hills housing development behind it. (Greenlawn-Centerport Historical Association.)

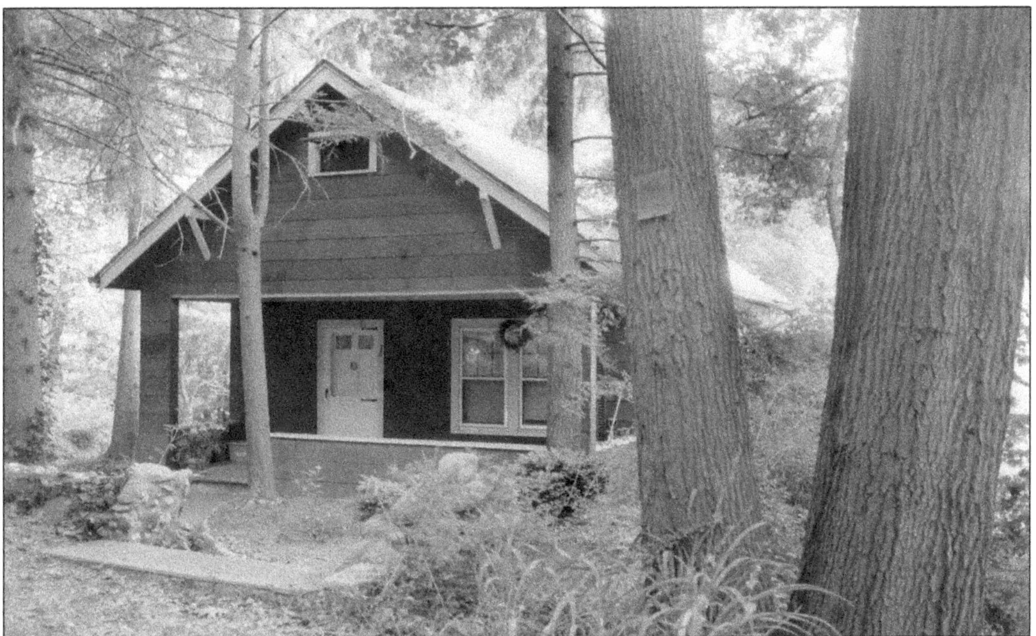

This Centerport bungalow, known as "the Spy Cottage," was apparently where the FBI operated a shortwave radio station to Germany during World War II. The German intelligence service in Hamburg thought it was actually being operated by their spy, William Sebold, a German-born American citizen, who was later found to be a double agent. More than 300 messages were sent from the house until it was discovered in September 1941. (Greenlawn-Centerport Historical Association.)

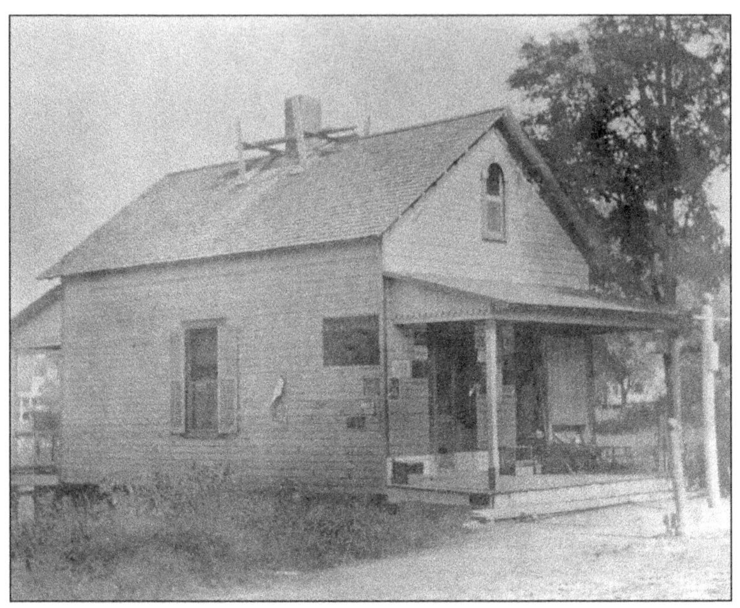

Artist Arthur Dove (1880–1946) has been called the first Modernist painter, as he was one of a group of abstractionists associated with noted photographer and art dealer Alfred Stieglitz. Dove and his partner, artist Helen Torr, spent eight years from 1938 to 1946 living in this small cottage on the edge of Centerport Harbor. The cottage had been Benham's store (1880–1899), and later the Centerport Post Office. (Huntington Historical Society.)

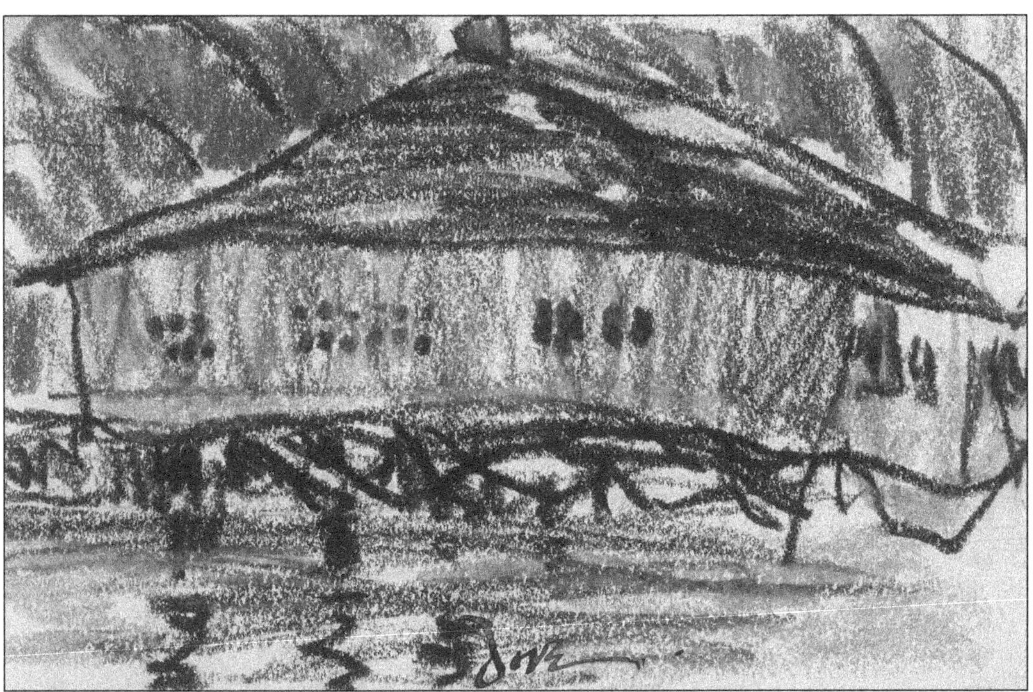

This painting, *Old Post Office, Centerport*, is by Arthur Dove. He and Helen Torr moved back to the north shore of Long Island after spending five years in Dove's hometown of Geneva, New York. Arthur Dove paid $980 for the cottage, which was one room of 400 square feet. Dove could see the old 1908 post office across the harbor from his home. The scenery and natural surroundings of Centerport inspired some of his best work. Previously, they had lived on a yawl in Northport Harbor and spent time living at the Northport Yacht Club. (Heckscher Museum of Art.)

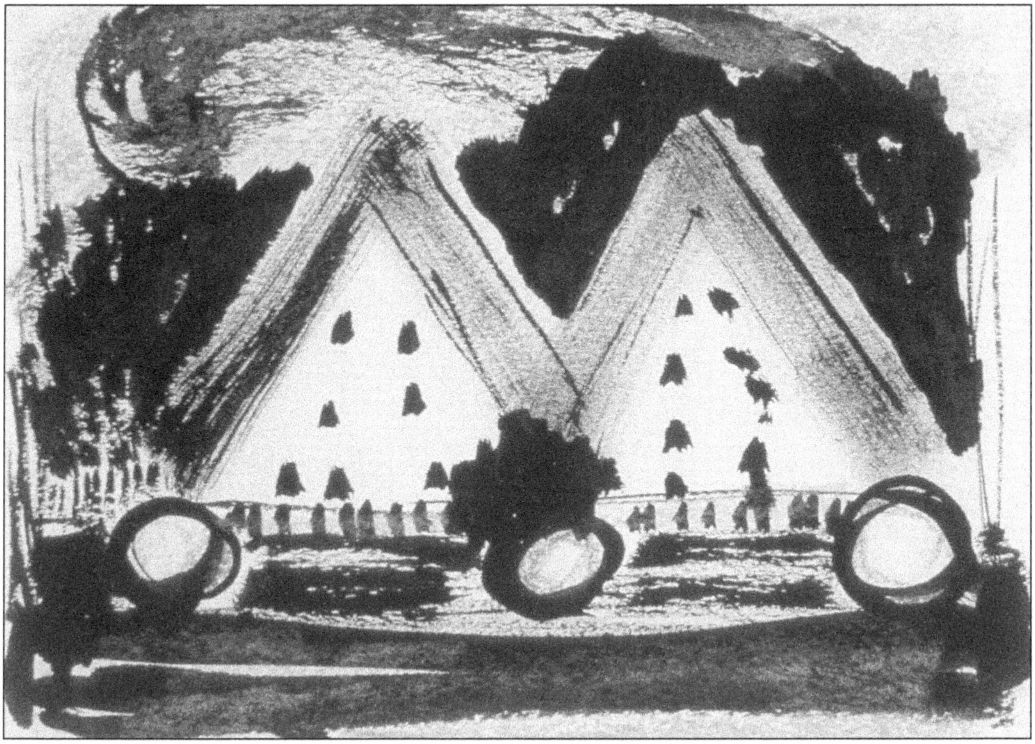

Seen here is *Study for The Brothers*, from 1939. One of the features of the Dove/Torr exhibit at the Heckscher Museum in 1989 was a group of 10 small watercolors, three by four inches, focused on his 1942 painting *The Brothers*. Local residents always referred to Alvernia as "the Brothers," perhaps for the Franciscan Brothers or the twin towers of the monastery. The series showed the evolution of the artwork from a realistic sketch to its final abstract forms. (Collection of the McNay Art Museum, gift of Robert L.B. Tobin through the Friends of the McNay.)

This is the final painting of *The Brothers*, which Dove created in 1942. Dove wrote in his diary that just staring at the pond from his small house was contentment enough, a view he likened to Paris. In a 1989 interview in *The New York Times*, Dove's son William said, "They loved the looks of the area, especially the feel of the place." (Collection of the McNay Art Museum, gift of Robert L.B. Tobin through the Friends of the McNay.)

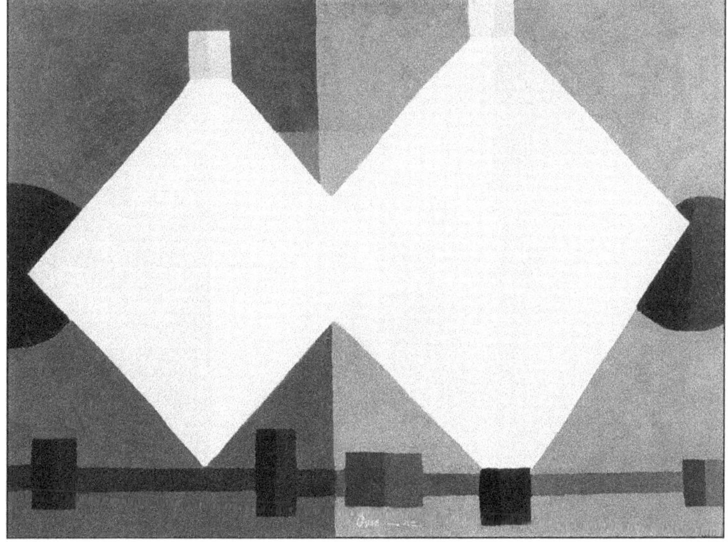

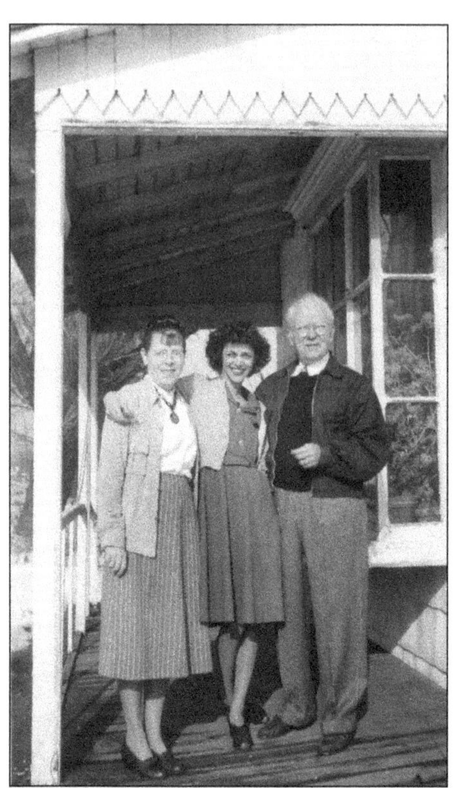

Helen Torr and Arthur Dove are shown here at the cottage with Dove's daughter-in-law Aline Dove in 1942. The building is listed in the National Register of Historic Places and is now owned by the Heckscher Museum of Art in Huntington. (Heckscher Museum of Art.)

Arthur Dove's health declined following pneumonia and a heart attack. Helen Torr continued to live in the house for more than 20 years following Dove's death in 1946. She did not sell any of her own artworks during her lifetime. Her sister Mary Rehm was instructed to destroy her artworks after her death in 1967, but fortunately, she did not. They are now in the collection of the Heckscher Museum, including this painting titled *Oyster Stakes* from 1929. (Heckscher Museum of Art.)

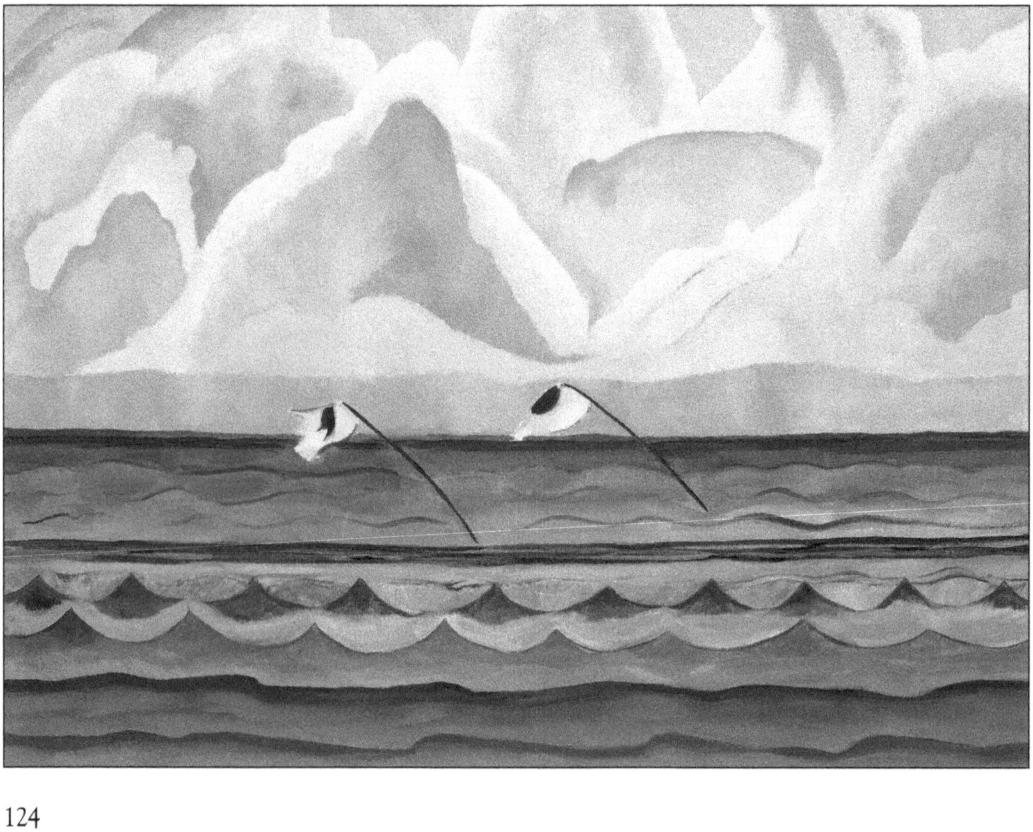

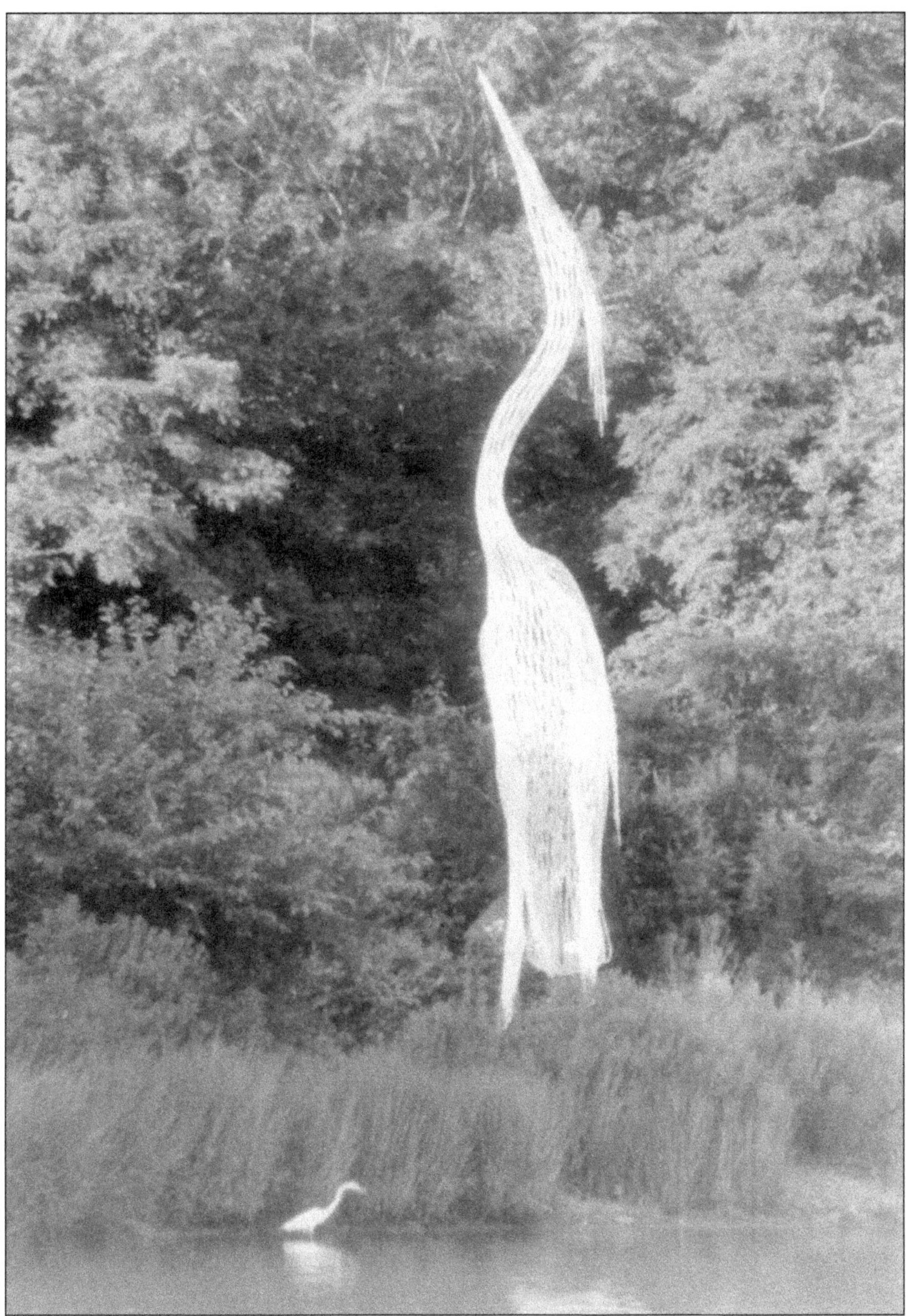

The Venezuelan-born artist Roberto Julio Bessin created sculptures of shorebirds in Centerport for over 10 years until relocating to Newport, Rhode Island, in 1992. For this nearly two-ton, 40-foot-high sculpture, he was inspired by the great blue herons and egrets of the mill dam area. It was on display in various locations in New York and Long Island. When complete, it was dedicated to the protection of Long Island wildlife. Through the efforts of the Centerport Civic Association, Bessin created a second sculpture, which watches over the millpond and harbor from the Town of Huntington's Heron Park. (Photograph by Harvey Weber.)

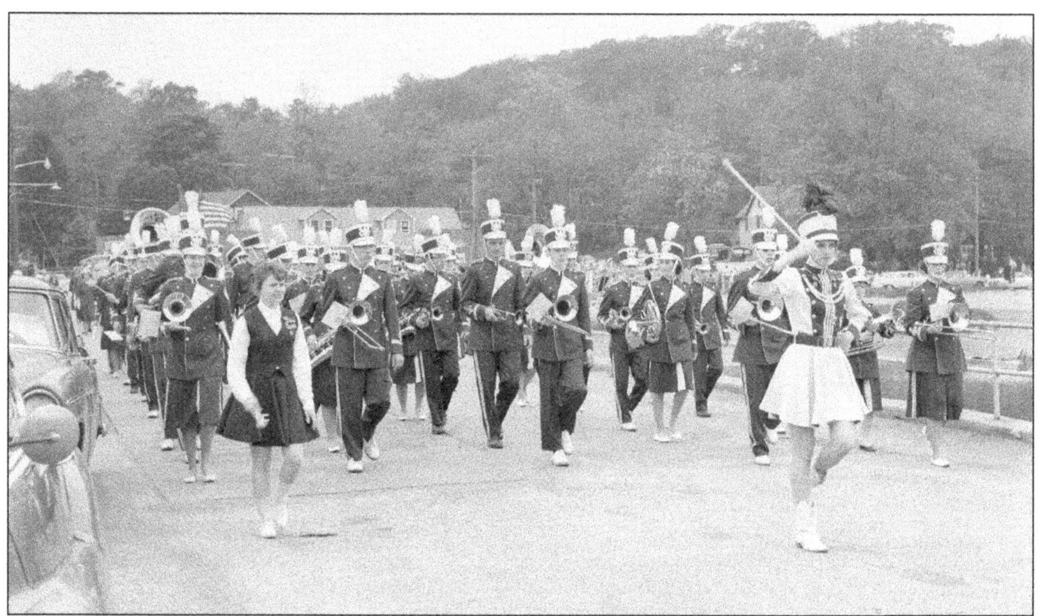

The Harborfields High School band is shown here marching across the mill dam bridge in the Centerport Fire Department's annual Memorial Day parade sometime in the 1960s. The Centerport Fire Department sponsors this annual event as well as the Holiday Tree Lighting in December. These two traditions remind residents and visitors of the value of living in the historic community of Centerport. (Photograph by Harvey Weber.)

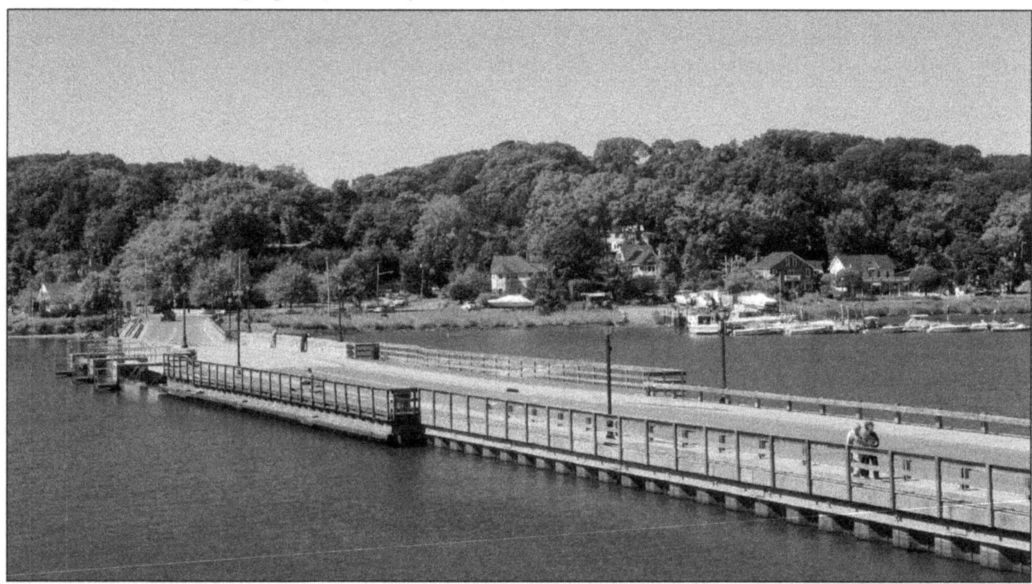

This contemporary photograph of the mill dam bridge was taken from the same place as William Deming's view on the top of page 21. Although 135 years have passed, this scene is instantly recognizable. Centerport has changed since it was settled 350 years ago, but, like the view of the bridge, some things have not changed. The harbor and millpond remain the center of the community and retain much of their scenic beauty. Centerport residents appreciate their history, and continue to support each other in times of need and to cooperate to protect and improve the community. Centerport is truly a hidden jewel. (Photograph by James Clemens.)

Bibliography

Brosky, Kerriann Flanagan. *Huntington's Hidden Past*. Northport, NY: Maple Hill Press, 1995.
Bunce, Mary Emma. "Memories of Centerport by an Old Timer." Written for the Centerport Sea Fair, 1959.
Centerport Fire Department, 1898–1998. Centerport, NY: The Centerport Fire Department, 1999.
Depietro, Anne Cohen. *Arthur Dove and Helen Torr: the Huntington years*. Huntington, NY: The Heckscher Museum of Art, 1989.
Dougher, Louise, and Carol Bloomgarden. *Greenlawn: A Long Island Hamlet*. Charleston, SC: Arcadia Publishing, 2000.
Greenlawn-Centerport Historical Association. *The History of Centerport and Greenlawn: A Brief Outline*. Greenlawn, NY: Greenlawn-Centerport Historical Association, 1975.
Gress, Stephanie. *Eagle's Nest: The William K. Vanderbilt II Estate*. Charleston, SC: Arcadia Publishing, 2015.
Haskell, Barbara. *Arthur Dove*. Boston, MA: New York Graphic Society, 1974.
Holmes, Brother Edmund, OSF. *Alvernia, a history: the Franciscan Brothers of Brooklyn at Centerport*. Centerport, NY: Alvernia Bookworks, 2007.
Huntington, Northport, Centreport, Cold Spring Harbor, Long Island. Illustrated America Series. New York, NY: American Photograph Company, 1909.
Pane, Julia and Bob Teufel. *Music over the Sound: Rachmaninoff in Centerport*. Greenlawn, NY: Greenlawn-Centerport Historical Association, 1982.
Weber, Harvey A. *Centerport*. Centerport, NY: self-published, 1990.

Visit us at
arcadiapublishing.com

www.ingramcontent.com/pod-product-compliance
Lightning Source LLC
LaVergne TN
LVHW060624110826
845147LV00015B/932
* 9 7 8 1 4 6 7 1 0 3 9 1 6 *